Speeches of Deception

Speeches of Deception

◆

Selected Speeches of Saddam Hussein.
A Story of Propaganda which began in
Kuwait 10 Years ago today is not over.

Compiled by Salomon Ruysdael

Writers Club Press
New York Lincoln Shanghai

Speeches of Deception

Selected Speeches of Saddam Hussein. A Story of Propaganda which began in Kuwait 10 Years ago today is not over.

Writers Club Press
an imprint of iUniverse, Inc.

For information address:
iUniverse, Inc.
2021 Pine Lake Road, Suite 100
Lincoln, NE 68512
www.iuniverse.com

ISBN: 0-595-27039-5

Printed in the United States of America

I dedicate this book to Sabine Zarda with my best regards

"Oh sons of Arabs and the Arab Gulf, rebel against the foreigner...
Take revenge for your dignity, holy places, security, interests and
exalted values."

—Saddam Hussein, January 5, 1999

Contents

Saddam Hussein's Iraq

Foreword

The oppressive and totalitarian nature of Saddam Hussein's regime enables his deception and deceit. This regime, which became expert at obfuscation during the 1991 Persian Gulf War, has now had more than a decade to perfect these practices.

Propaganda is central to Regime of Saddam Hussein. This book is a collection of English translations of Saddam Husseins Speeches for the period 1988–2003. The goal is to help people understand the great totalitarian systems of our century by giving them access to primary material

Acknowledgements

In the process of compiling this book, I have learned much about research from many people: fellow teachers, fellow thinkers, readers, students, and kin. I am grateful to Ahmet Cemal, Levent Cihangir and Ordinarius Selahattin Kozan for what a writer or editor needs, honest helpful reactions to parts of the book at various stages.

Deep thanks to my friends who helped sustain me in countless ways through many unmet deadlines. Also deep thanks to the contributors of each article of this book.

My greatest debt in editing this book is to my parents for the love and support that made it possible.

Salomon Ruysdael
Frankfurt am Main, Germany
06th Februar 2003

Introduction

The use of rhetoric to persuade the masses has long been a device used by figures great and small to achieve their goals of both triumph and destruction. Nowhere is this clearer than with Saddam Hussein. In particular, his use of rhetoric is important in understanding how he rose to power. There are two fundamentally different kinds of speakers: those who use reasoning, and those who speak from the heart. The speaker who uses reason implements the use of facts and statistics to create a strong and powerful speech, minimizing error. The speaker from the heart, on the other hand, directs his speech to the listeners' emotions, often igniting a plethora of responses from within the individual. Saddam Hussein is the latter kind of speaker, who indeed speaks to the masses on an emotional level, which creates a tight unity among the Iraqi people. His extraordinary ability to create spectacle, manipulate language, and reinvent ideas allows him to control the masses and to rise to power despite the ugly truths that are masked behind his rhetoric.

One example of why Saddam Hussein's rhetoric is so successful is his use of spectacle. Saddam's Baath Party uses various forms of spectacle to make their rhetoric stand out. In studying these points, it can be seen how Saddam Hussein manipulates language to achieve his ultimate goal of purity and perfection. The concept of inborn dignity centers on the idea that all human beings have a basic dignity that they are born with and which should be respected by others. Saddam Hussein perverts this doctrine so that only the Arab race has inborn dignity. Thus the Arab's inborn dignity is a superiority rather than a commonality and everyone else is inferior. After the defeat of Iraq in the Gulf

War, there are especially strong emotional needs that this compensatory doctrine of an inborn superiority attempts to gratify.

Another aspect of Saddam Hussein's unification rhetoric is his use of projection devices. This term, related to psychoanalysis, involves the projection of the problem onto another group or individual. On a social level, this term is known as scapegoating. The Iraqi economy, a seemingly domestic problem, is blamed on the international Jew. Saddam Hussein's use of rhetoric here is an attempt to displace the issue at hand with something irrelevant. This is especially appealing to the middle class, who is encouraged to feel that they could conduct their businesses without any basic change whatever once the businessmen of a different "religion" were eliminated.

Next in this rhetorical process is a means of symbolic rebirth. Once the problem is blamed on the Jews, Saddam Hussein has to advocate their elimination and promise the Iraqi people a better life. He offers his people a positive vision of the future in order to unite them against this common enemy. The projective device of the scapegoat, coupled with Saddam Hussein's doctrine of inborn national superiority, provides his followers with a "positive" view of life. They can again have the feeling of moving forward towards a goal.

The idea of commercial use can be seen in Saddam Hussein's attempt to offer a non-economic interpretation of the economic ills in Iraq. He is able to sell his rhetoric to Iraqis without even addressing issues pertaining to the economy. As such, it serves with maximum efficiency in deflecting attention from the economic factors involved in modern conflict; hence by attacking "Jewish" finance instead of finance, it can stimulate an enthusiastic movement that leave "Arab" finance in control. All of these features lead to a unifying voice for the entire nation and give Saddam Hussein seemingly immeasurable power over his people.

The use of Unification Rhetoric (U.R.) contributed to making Saddam Hussein a powerful speaker. Under U.R. there are three points that explain how this is done. The first is a geographical materialization of Saddam Hussein's ideology. Saddam Hussein points to Jerusalem. Jerusalem symbolizes a geographical Arab aspiration. Saddam Hussein's interpretation of "all roads lead to Jerusalem" is an attempt to unify the Arab people. This give his people a physical location in an effort to understand what it means to be an Arab nationalist.

Another principal under U.R. is the idea of "the common enemy," otherwise known as the international Jew or Zionist. Saddam Hussein labels the enemy as an "ultimate evil" in order to unite the masses against a common evil. Having this common enemy is a great tool for Saddam Hussein to use to appeal to the emotions of the Iraqi people. It is the role of the leader to create the rhetoric that unifies his people against a common enemy. Saddam Hussein's rhetoric is not only powerful in manipulating his people, but it is also a powerful tool against those who reject his ideas. His "conspiracy theory" turns his listeners against anyone who does not see reality the way he does. It is simple yet effective; anyone who opposes him is part of the conspiracy and therefore against the Iraqi cause.

For Saddam Hussein there are only two possibilities: either he remains ruler of Iraq and the Arab nations or he comes under the thumb of the Jews. Thus he delivers two options, and two options only, to the Arab people: Either you are Iraqi and Arab or you are controlled by the Jews. Through this example, it is clear that the Arabs could be under the control of the Jews and, as a result, have to band together to make their nation strong. This type of rhetoric makes his listeners' decision easy, with a clear and concise end result.

The third section under U.R. is the parliamentary attacks that Saddam Hussein leads through speeches and rallies, which make him a more powerful and respected leader. Saddam Hussein believes his people need to speak with one voice and they all need to be on the same page. In these attacks, it can be seen that Saddam Hussein is taking the attacks on capitalism and transposing the problems onto the Jews.

Saddam Hussein's rhetoric also becomes successful due to the totality of his vision. He proposes an all-encompassing plan that appears to offer a solution to all of Iraq's problems. His ideology is a complete worldview, meant to explain anything that is encountered. Saddam Hussein's ability to convince the masses of the totality of his vision brings unity to the Iraqi people and is largely based on the eradication of what he calls "the ultimate evil," i.e. the Jews who are the Iraqi nation's true enemy. Saddam Hussein's all encompassing worldview is meant to be the answer to any possible question. All fingers are pointed at the Jews for Iraq's problems, and their extermination is part of Saddam Hussein's totalitarian vision for a pure Arab nation.

In addition to his use of spectacle and totality of vision, Saddam Hussein uses the power of religion to make his rhetoric successful. Saddam's Baath Party is officially secular, but in 1993 he launched "the grand faith campaign," in what is seen as a bid to win the loyalty of Iraqis who had turned to religion after losing loved ones in war and as their economy suffered under sanctions. The Iraqi leader's words often mix the historical with the religious. Saddam refers often to the eight-year war with Iran, which claimed one million lives on both sides, as al-Qadisiya—the name of the decisive battle in which the Arab Muslim army inflicted a huge defeat on Persia in 637. He depicts the Gulf War as the victorious Um Al Maarek, or "mother of all battles."

A deconstruction of religion proved to be a key influence in making his rhetoric stand out. In this sense, Saddam Hussein turns religion on its head. He overturns the power of religion and uses it for secular goals. He make the sacred profane and the holy impure. His control of religious power and religious rhetoric proves to be a key ingredient for his success as a speaker. Saddam himself is sometimes calls "Rasul al-Arab" or "prophet of the Arabs" and "Seif al-Arab" or "sword of the Arabs."

The art of propaganda lies in understanding the emotional ideas of the great masses and finding, through a psychologically correct form, the way to the attention and hence to the heart of the masses. Saddam Hussein's ability to use rhetoric gives him the ability to execute his totalitarian vision, mastering the art of manipulation and persuasion. Appealing to a person's emotions is crucial in order to convince or persuade them towards certain ideas or to initiate a certain response. Saddam Hussein's ability to create spectacle, manipulate language, and reinvent ideas are key factors to his success as a speaker and have ultimately aided him in his rise to power.

It has been said that Saddam Hussein held an almost hypnotic force over the Iraqi people when he spoke. Without a doubt, this volume reveals that Saddam is an amazing orator who uses his special talent to obilize a nation to do his bidding. This book is a window into the present where we can witness the power Saddam Hussein's words had over the masses. The consequences of a nation…of a world…rested upon this unique blend of propaganda and emotion. No one should forget the devastation brought about by President Saddam Hussein and this collection of 27 Speeches by the dictator is a unique opportunity to experience how words can be used to incite a nation.

Speeches and Letters of
Saddam Hussein

President Saddam Hussein's Address on the 10th Anniversary of the Day of Days, 8 August 1988

In the name of God, the Most Compassionate, the Most Merciful.

"If you prayed for victory and judgment, now has judgment come to you, if you desist (from wrong), it will be best for you."

Holy Quran, VIII, 19

Great people!

Valiant members of our armed forces!

Arab men of struggle and jihad, sons of our glorious Nation!

God's peace, mercy and blessing be upon you!

Ten years ago, on 8 August 1988, a great event in the life of our Nation and our people took place with the announcement of that great and decisive communique. It was in the evening of that glorious day, the day of all days, that the communique of communiques, the seal of all communiques announced throughout the war between Iraq and Iran, was declared.

As a ripe fruit, and as a merit proportionate with their levels, the Iraqis picked the reward of eight years of fighting, patience and endurance.

Ever since that day of crowning glory and of outright victory, the Iraqis, together with the noble sons of our glorious nation, recall with an appreciation of special taste that great day.

Others may recall that day politically, or as a mere historical record of the event, when we remind them of it, or when they browse their diaries, but not as a recall of a lesson learned or a moral drawn.

Why do we then celebrate this day in Iraq? And why do the honourable Arabs react with it with rejoice?

In the life and history of nations, events of special meanings happen. The more positive the effect of the event is on the life of other nations, apart from the nation concerned, the wider the focus of attention becomes and the more dignified the very event is held.

Judging from what you have come to know of our conceptions which draw a line between sheer force, in the material, professional or technical sense, and power, in its comprehensive meaning and profundity: Is it force or power that triumphed on that day, the day of all days!?

On that day, power turned out victor over force, just as power stood fast, triumphed and is still scoring triumph over force throughout all phases of the confrontation in the eternal Um al-Ma'arek battle (Mother of All Battles). And just as those concerned in Iran failed to predict the limits of confrontation between force and power, having been blinded and intoxicated by their imagination that the course of events was already tilting in their favour, on the basis of a mere comparison between force and force, the Americans and their allies failed to estimate the effectiveness of Iraq's power in countering their brute force.

Thus, the failure of the opposite party was ensued on the starting line, just as our victory was achieved on the starting line too.

On this basis, the triumph of power, with its well-known factors, freed and will free those concerned in Iran from their brute view of force, with its well-known factors, including fanaticism as compared to an open and fair viewpoint.

Hence, the most important factor of Iran's weakness in that confrontation was that force, and the illusion of force prevailed in the minds of those who believed in it. Whereas power, which we firmly believe in, with its well-known factors, filled us with certainty and faith and rendered us more balanced and fair towards ourselves and towards our enemies.

Yet, some people, on that day, did not properly realize this truth, neither in Iran nor in the world.

Moreover, those involved in the aggression against Iraq, in the 30-state armies and in the unjust blockade, have also remained ignorant of this fact to the present day. They, in turn, committed and are still committing the same mistake, and their harvest will be, God willing, full of thorns, with its yield more bitter than colocynth in the mouths and souls of those nurtured with evil and aggression.

Hence, the day of all days is not a mere day of victory of an army over armies, nor a mere triumph of a will of determination, on its material basis, over a counter-will with shaken material basis, but rather, an official declaration for those with reason, heralding the birth of a new will, commensurate with the new call in Iraq, the country of challenge, faith, civilization and commitment.

Accordingly, when its main bases were complemented with suffering, forbearance and human, intellectual and psychological sacrifice, the will of power achieved victory over the basis of illusion, fanaticism and brute force, whose bases were shaken by the facts encountered in life in its broad sense, and by the former's attachment to the values of the Lord of Heavens and Earth, when the confrontation extended over eight years, and when all good-intentioned calls failed to curb or dissipate the illusion of those under its spell, to weaken their covetousness and to defuse their bigotry.

We confronted, at first, what was inside our souls, and we overcame what was negative and discouraging, before we were able to settle once and for all the situation on that memorable day by the use of power and its perspicacious and fair will.

For this reason, brothers, we celebrate this day every year, not only for our sake or for the sake of our coming generations, at present or in the future, but also for the sake of other generations, including Iran's, because that day has opened, for everyone with insight, a window on life and on goodwill values. In so doing, we hope that the illusion would dissipate gradually so that, instead of hatred, grudge and fanaticism, the elements of love, heartfelt and positive interaction and perception of truth, as it is, with the entire Nation, will prevail.

That is what we wish for Iran. We implore the All-Mighty and All-Powerful to help Iran to live up to it. We do so without having any premeditated purpose nor any construed intention of interference in its internal affairs.

Force held power captive in Iran, whereas power overwhelmed force in Iraq, and everyone knows what was the result.

At any time power finds itself free from force in Iran, Iran will be the victor. And at any time Iraq abandons power in pursuit of the brute force only, God forbid, its loss will be heavy.

Judging from this yardstick, we see that some Arabs have been infected with a new and serious disease. This disease does not fall within the terms of the illusion of force, but it falls within the illusion of weakness. Thus, they have begun to look for force rather than for power to cure their fatal sense of weakness and their hope-dispersing illusions.

They have felt fatigued and frustrated when faced with tables of quantities and figures on their part and on the part of their enemies, while comparing force with force.

Since force, in its primitive, brutal sense, does not originate inside the Arabs, except when afflicted with the fatal disease of fanaticism, and since the Arabs are not goaded to fanaticism, except under exceptional circumstances, the material calculations have overwhelmed their state of weakness and have driven some of them down to their pits.

Instead of disembarking on the safe shore, with their own power and the power of their Nation, which God has characterized the Nation with, they went looking for a safe shore by counting on the force of others.

And since others do not help them to any real safe shore, some of them have thrown themselves on their shore as corpselike bodies, or remained suspended, drifted by the whims and schemes of the enemies and the covetous.

Hence, brothers, when Iraq emerged victor on that day, it had, before that, defeated jugglery and imposture with certainty, loss with faith and the cause, disunity with unity, aversion with piousness, grudge with tolerance, hatred with love, egoism with altruism, loneliness of isolation with company and collective work, darkness with light, introversion with extroversion, feeling of weakness with invocation of factors of capability inside oneself, hesitation with decisive resolution, indifference with seriousness and clear stand, laziness with perseverance and work, arrogance with modesty, exaggeration withexactness, igwith knowledge, unbalanced haste with accuracy and patience, negligence with alertness and presence of mind, disruption with continuity, pessimism with optimism, slowness with speed, quantity with the faithful quality, lies with honesty, honesty, and honesty, vagary with truth, fear of foreigner with fear of God, obedience of foreigner with love of our people amidst the Nation and humanity, with full trust in the people and in oneself, after our trust in God.

Hence, the victory on the day of all days was not a traditional military victory according to the standards of victory of one army over other armies, when only the technical and professional preponderance is in favour of the victor party. By the same token, it was not a victory for Iraq only, but for all what is contrary to weakness and feebleness, which we have mentioned and which is well known to everyone. This victory, apart from being a victory for Iraq and the Nation, on the basis of these conceptions, is also a victory for those who believe in these conceptions in Iran. Indeed, it is a victory even for those who are still in need of someone to lift for them the veil and burden of illusion, darkness and aversion with these conceptions in Iran.

Therefore, the war ceased. It would not, otherwise, have stopped, without all that had happened, when the grand battles of liberation, having ripened on the battlefields, further intensified after the liberation of the dear city of Faw, as a fruit of all the generous sacrifices and great jihad throughout eight years.

Thus, when the Iraqis were freed from the weakness which afflicted some segments of the Nation, Faw was liberated, as was every part of Iraq usurped by the Iranians and on which calculations of their known illusion were built. On the basis of their well-known cover or covers of illusion and aversion, they formulated part of them in the shape of slogans for Iranian warriors, when they misled them into believing that (a pilgrimage to Kerbela' can only be made through the occupation of Baghdad and then Kerbela'), and not through establishing proper relations with Baghdad to reach Kerbela'. Against this background of the past, we see that some well-known quarters in Iran still hesitate to visit Baghdad and Kerbela', now that such a visit has been made possible to those who want to make it peacefully, as the people of Baghdad and Kerbela' have accepted that with their own free will.

Hence, Iran had been victorious twice throughout its history, despite its military defeat: once, when the Arab Moslem armies killed the leaders of war, arrogance and aversion in the first battle of Qadissiya, Nehawand and other battles, such as Hormuzan, Rustum and finally the King of the infidels Kisra Yazdejird. The second time was in the second Qadissiya. So, we shared with Iran two victories, over ourselves and our common enemy: viz., the two victories at the two battles of Qadissiya.

Then, just as the victory at the first Qadissiya was a victory for humanity and a victory for faith, so too the day of all days at the second Qadissiya was a great victory for humanity and faith.

Therefore, it is on this basis and for those great meanings that we recall, first of all, the sacrifices made by the noble martyrs and by the living, and celebrate this glorious day.

If some quarters in Iran abandon what is not praiseworthy of the past, they will see and find that the Arabs, including Iraq, have abandoned this and left it behind long time ago. They will also find every righteous, beneficial cooperation from the Arabs, first and foremost, Iraq.

The Arabs, notably Iraq, are not expecting the officials in Iran to break a chain for them, nor relieve a burden on them or to get involved in battles which are the responsibility of the Arabs, in the first place, though this does not fall beyond the responsibility of those who have pronounced faith and guided aright.

The Arabs, including Iraqis, hope and call upon the officials and peoples of Iran not to become a tool in the hands of the covetous foreigner to harm Arabs, primarily Iraq. The Shah of Iran Mohammed Riza Pehlevi did that in the past, and so did his father and others before him. Iraq and the Arabs were subjected to serious harm after 1979. The war broke out and continued for eight years, despite incessant attempts by all parties concerned, mainly by Iraq, to put an end to it.

The accelerated calls for the use of force, for harming Iraq and for launching aggression against it, until the war started on 4 September 1980, the persistent continuation of war, and the call for all that run counter to and contradict peace, are all matters that can hardly be interpreted except by saying that Iran had gone astray, taking a direction contrary to all that could help man achieve victory inside his soul and in his environment, over the elements of evil and over failure and weakness.

Has Iran, in whole or in part, recovered from this!? We pray to God, the Most Exalted, to help the peoples of Iran and its officials to attain this. Our laboratory, whose tests can never fail, will be the relationship between Iraq and Iran. This is because, while the factor of geography makes Iraq the most capable of observation and verification, other additional factors: historical, social and spiritual make it the most capable of understanding Iran and the reality there as it is, and not as projected every now and then.

Arab brothers! Moslem brother!

Throughout eight years, we were of the opinion, believed and worked on the basis that our objectives would be materialized in peace. Therefore, we called for it. Whereas the officials in Iran, until the last days or last months prior to the victory on the day of all days, were of the opinion that their objectives would be materialized in war and aggression. Our evidence, on our side, is all the legacy of the glorious Qadissiya, of what was said or done in public, day and night. On Iran's side, it is all their legacy of what was said or done in public, day and night, including the last official address by the highest-level official who accepted the ceasefire, which, once in effect, spared further bloodshed. He said: I wish I were dead before I announced or ordered a ceasefire…He also said in the same address that (his acceptance of Security Council resolution was for him more lethal than poison). On our part, the Iraqis, in the forefront of whom the officials, celebrated the end of the war and of the bloodshed on both sides, rejoicing that day and thanking God, the Most Mighty and Exalted, for his grace, from the farthest point in the north to the farthest point in the south in Iraq, for seven days and nights.

Greetings of appreciation, with the most profound meaning of glory and faith, to our noble martyrs, the martyrs of the glorious Qadissiya. May their souls dwell in heavens.

Greetings of appreciation to the day of all days, the day of victory and peace.

Greetings to the day we look forward to when the foundations of Arabs' relations, including Iraq's, with Iran are laid on their proper ground.

God is the greatest!

God is the greatest!

God is the greatest!

Long live Iraq!

Long live our glorious Nation!

Long live Palestine, free and Arab country!

President Saddam Hussein's Address on the 7th Anniversary of Mother of All Battles, January 17, 1998

In the name of God, the Most Compassionate, the Most Merciful

"Be sure we shall test you With something of fear And hunger, some loss In goods or lives or the fruits But give glad tidings to those Who patiently persevere."

"The Cow" Sura 155, The Glorious Koran

Our great people!

Valiant members of our brave armed forces!

Our glorious Arab Nation!

Good people and friends everywhere!

Peace be with you!

When our master Abraham, peace be upon him, the father of prophets, and the grand grandfather of our prophet Mohammed, peace be upon him, decided to leave Iraq, where he was born and lived together with his family, to roam other part of the Arab Homeland at the order of God, to preach his call for monotheism and faith which he had originally started in Iraq, In the name of the Compassionate, the Merciful, "And Abraham: behold, he said to his people, 'serve God and fear

Him: What will be best for you—if you understand!", he had nothing other than a stick in his hand at that time to confront the surprises of the road and to face up to the ill-intentioned who were opposed to his call. He had only a stick to scare away a wolf or a dog that tried to harm him. Thus was the case with Prophets, Messengers, and great reformers throughout eternity, since God created the Universe and its inhabitants and suggested the significance of monotheism and faith in the relationship between the Creator and the creature between the zeal that is generated by the soul along the drive in the vast land of God and in the creation of the new life and its prerequisites to confront the aspects of nature, wild creatures and the factors of elevating them and man to that which can maintain progress uninterrupted on a sound basis.

This is what we have learnt and known since we were pupils. This is what we have grown up to believe in our consciousness so much so that it has constituted, together with all the sublime meanings and the implications of well-seated faith, the basis of the background of our thinking and the core of the ingredients of our Ba'thist ideology in terms of the outlook to the creation of the new life and the confrontation of the challenges that obstruct the course of justice. This is the background of today which is burning with capability and influence in the Iraqis' mind and thinking or rather in the back of all Arabs' mind and conscience, each according to his faith, consciousness, and of faith that forms his psychological structure. Relying on such faith, we have confronted and resisted the terms of submission set by the despot of the last years of the twentieth century, and his call on Iraq to surrender under his oppression and arrogance. This despot imagined this could be achieved by the mere show of the brute force at his disposal after he had based his conclusions on concepts that are detrimental to a conscience and mode of thinking which are out-moded in terms of comparison based on materialistic consderations. This materialistic perspective blurs the ability of officials in that state which acts tyrannically in terms of brute force and deviation of justice to conjure up the backdrop of the thinking and attitudes and above all, the historical, spiritual and cultural formation of great Iraq, of our greater glorious Arab Nation and the legacy of the glorious 17–30 July Revolution.

One aspect of this is the fact that God has made the enemies underestimate Iraq and the Arab Nation and made Iraq see his enemies numbered although they are too many. It is His will.

In the name of God, the Most Compassionate, the Most Merciful. "And remember when you met, He showed them to you as few in your eyes, and He made you appear as contemptible in their eyes: that God might accomplish a matter already enacted. For to God do all questions go back (for decision)." (The Glorious Koran)

Thus, there was the Iraqi rejection of the terms of submission and surrender, roaring across the horizons. The banner of Allah Akbar (God is the Greatest) is hoisted high at its mast. The showdown started at its two ends, with a stick we were waving or striking at any of the dogs of aggression, some with nuclear teeth, who approached our fortress.

So in appreciation of the meanings of our position, the great stance of the brave Iraqi army and people and recollection of all the meanings of martyrdom at the battlefield, we make this recollection so is the case with generations in the Arab Homeland and Iraq which will later make their recollections of these meanings, and will never forget them. They in fact live with so that momentum and action would be higher and greater whenever they are faced with injustice and a tyrant, tyranny and a despot, so that faith would remain unshaken in the bosoms and the consciences would remain capable of feeling the places, courses and aims of justice as opposed to injustice.

God is the Greatest.

Great people!

Valiant members of the armed forces!

Sons of our glorious Arab Nation!

Friends around the world!

Today is January 17 when, seven years ago at 2.30 early morning, the devil implicated America and others who were also involved (in the aggression) after their feet went astray from the true path of God. It was the day when 28 armies led by the American tyranny acting on behalf of more than 30 states that had allied themselves for aggression, unleashed the shells of malice, hatred, evil and whim at Baghdad, the city of virtue, great history, glory, and of distinctive mark in attitude, and characteristics in the entire Arab Nation of glory and virtue. It was God who chose for the entire Arab Nation and Iraq roles and messages in appreciation of the characteristics of Iraq to which it is the capital. It is a role to serve tortured humanity throughout ages against despots of successive eras and the ruthless devils on their way to hell.

Since the bombs and rockets of evil hit Baghdad and Iraq in its entirety, that day became a dawn of additional glory in the history of Baghdad, the capital of AL-Rasheed, AL-Mansour and the great Ba'th and throughout Iraq of jihad too from north to south. The dawn increased in magnificence and light when honourable Iraqi men and women held out, hoisting the great of banner of jihad, the banner of Allah Akbar (God in the Greatest) high over the corps of jihad and honour.

Eversince, that day has become another stain of shame and disgrace in the face of those who wanted it to be a day of shame for them. As time elapsed, and with the adherence of Iraqis to their principles, American officials have become witness to their shame and perfidy. Whenever they stood before the mirror, they found their faces covered with disgusting leprosy, not of a curable temporary type. It is the leprosy of mischief, designed to achieve a false objective. Leprosy has spread to other parts of the body as obstinacy, malice and the desire to hurt the heroic people of Iraq and the sincere army of the nation increased the verdict of God which has appeared on all parts of the body. Whenever a wind blew, it revealed the weakness of those who chose to insist on the same attitude, refusing to rectify it. In the forefront of the line of the despaired and the deceitful, stands America of the ominous evil against the peoples and nations of this age.

Brothers!

On this day, January 17, the world was preoccupied by the wedding ceremony of America, to be crowned at a place they termed a peak after so many stars had nose-dived and after America was able to tear apart the banners of its arch rivals who were not letting it ascend to or infiltrate into whatever it sought to reach.

While the American official was poised there to announce he had become the unrivaled and unopposed King of the World and that all must kneel obediently to him without having the right to reject his crowning or to oppose any stance by Washington, and while false witnesses and slaves were about to place on him the absolute crown on which the names of most world states were inscribed save two or three who tacitly grumbled with discontent, albeit with a faint voice and shaken rejection, and, when the tyrant viewed with contempt everything, a breeze carrying the scent of prophets who were born in dignified Iraq and who bore the meanings of message and the great revelation blew on dignified Iraq to reinforce faith in the chests of the men and women of Baghdad. They recalled the memory of our master Abraham. In the Name of God the Most Compassionate, the Most Merciful: "Ye, Fire be cool and save Abraham," "The Glorious Koran" he had only a stick in addition to his call, which he had, at the request of God to take to the land of the Pharaoh and its people. It was a call for monotheism, a true faith, not fearing the discrepancies in material capabilities.

They remembered too the stick of Moses, peace be upon him, which God turned into an evidence in the face of the Pharaoh of that age.

They remembered the stick of Jesus, peace be upon him, which he never raised against anybody. They remembered that who made the pledge and took the stance of the great Jihad, Mohammed Bin Abdullah, peace be upon him. They remembered how he faced up to the tyrants and despots of his time, how the armies of Moslems destroyed the edifices of these empires to establish justice after they had routed all forms of injustice.

The people of Iraq recalled all that when the two parties were face to face at the two ends of the battlefield. They mistakenly believed they could force Iraq to say "yes" with others to crown the evil American official as the unrivaled King of the four directions. Then, the hearts of those who were frightened gaped up their throats. In the name of God, the Most Compassionate, the Most Merciful: "Behold! they came on you from above you and from below you, and behold, the eyes became dim and the hearts gaped up the throats, and Ye imagined various (vain) thoughts about God." "The Glorious Koran" Here in Baghdad and in the battlefield, across Iraq, the fervor of faith and steadfastness intensified fearless of the confrontation of the despot.

All Iraqis said it in one voice: "No". With this Iraqi and Arab "No" the shells of evil roared. Their warships and frigates flocked (into the area) bringing in ominous snakes and ravens, their warplanes and missiles to hit every living thing and everything essential to life. The roar of the Iraqi and Arab "No" was louder, God willing, than all their weapons. The crown of the unrivaled King which they thought impregnable then rolled down as the echo (of the "No") swept across all parts of earth, after this crown had slipped from the hand of the helpless, there at the coronation stand. It was smeared with their shame and the kingdom remained God's alone. In the name of God, the Most Compassionate, the Most Merciful: "Blessed be He in whose hands is Dominion, and He over all things hath power." "The Glorious Koran"

The guests who were forced to attend the fallacious coronation then walked away. It was a coronation with a testimony made by false or forced or blindly docile signatures because it is God's will that despotism should not prevail in the world. He has never allowed this to happen throughout ages.

As the crown rolled, the chair of the king began to shake with every passing day, taking stances of arrogance and evil against Baghdad. Meanwhile, the attitude and the banner of Allah Akbar (God is the Greatest) has become visible in the remotest parts of the world, winning admiration, respect and love on the largest scale after God has blessed it with firmness, virtue and faith.

Dear brothers!

From the essence of these meanings, basic aspects and the reasons for the 30-state aggression against Iraq could be understood. The essence of these meanings underlines why and how Iraq said "No", stood firm, resisted and emerged victorious. Among these meanings is the message Iraq sent on the People's Day, November 11, 1997. It was the day in which previous days culminated to reveal to the whole world all that America tried to conceal, to uncover a considerable part of the disinformation process which America, its media and lackeys pursued before the representatives of states or before the people who remained astray from the truth or might have looked like this.

Hail, the People's Day, its vanguards and the great people who brought it about with patience, forbearance and challenge.

God is the greatest!

Arab brothers!

In our speech of last July 1997 and in the series of statements made by the leadership and senior officials in Iraq, there were successive calls on the importance of an Arab solidarity on the governmental level, which we believe inevitable for fulfilling the requirements of development and of countering foreign ambitions and hostility. Our noble call has been well-received by some Arabs (and appeared in their statements) who have a fair amount of knowledge about Iraq and its leadership. Yet, few of them still have a suspicion that our call has been originated from a feeling of weakness, fear and concern about the future of Iraq alone. To remove the veil which has blinkered their eyes we would like to say to them that our noble and responsible call was never mentioned so successively and clearly in the years 1991, 1992, 1993, 1994 and 1995 as the Leadership did not want to announce it then lest it should confuse some officials, Arab or foreign, as to its causes and effects. But now that nearly seven years have passed since the beginning of the aggression in which every well-known means, capabilities and weapons were used on the battlefield, it has become apparent that all these means have failed to discredit Iraq' s principled attitude or to damage its true patriotism and strict commitment to pan-Arabism. We have assumed, and perhaps rightly so, that there will be no more ill-judgment that may deceive the majority of the nation's rulers and their loyal subjects into believing that Iraq' s call to the nation to join forces on the path that safeguards its strength, dignity, power and wealth, could be interpreted in a way that might empty the call of its original and responsible content and hinder its progress for discharging its role with honour and responsibility. Should our call were a tactic for crossing a certain phase, it would have been better to be addressed to America and Zionism as some frustrated inferiors do. Our call, however, was aimed at the nation at a time when Iraq was fighting, with power and faith, America and its lackey the Zionists whenever there was a new aggression against Iraq. Such an attitude by Iraq is almost unique. It was the same, thirty years ago, when Iraq appealed to the nation and the circumstances at that time were congenial and the conditions surrounding it did not permit of any equivocation or ambiguity. It was on this account that our call was construed by prudent men who bear no malice, prejudice or covet of revenge in their bosoms and souls.

The motive which prompted our call, together with the calls made by our comrades in the Leadership, for a united stance that could further augment the nations's spiritual and temporal existence, has always been a concern over the entire Arab nation, its interests and riches, as has it a concern over the events taking place in practically every individual country. It was by no means a concern over Iraq alone. Iraq is protected by God. It is in trustworthy and powerful hands and in hearts full of faith and courage. It resides in the eyeballs of the revolutionaries who never have faint hearts or faltering courage.

Harm might be done to Iraq, and blood might be shed on its land in larger or smaller amount than before, and cases of martyrdom increase among those who will be bitten by the snakes of perfidy and embargo, and the roll of the wheel of development might suffer to some extent and to a certain degree but, Iraq, as a land and as an embodiment of pan-Arab civilized, humanitarian and historical roll will remain. What Iraq is losing as a result of the aggression and sanctions will be recompensed from the momentum it gains from steadfastness and resistance as well as from the spiritual lessons and meanings inherited in the history of humanity. This could prove more eloquent for expressing the firmness of human faith and nationalism and may surpass all others.

What concerns us, Arab brothers, is not what causes harm to our people or to the entire members of the greater Arab nation in more than a place or in more than an Arab country including Iraq. The most serious matter that should take precedence over all others is the fate of the greater Arab nation and the suspension of its role to take advantage of the opportunity available for it to keep pace with historical development and to assume its national and human role. This is particularly true for certain societies in the Nation which might not be able to catch another opportunity for development once they lose their historic opportunity of petrol and human resources and lose faith in the capability of their members to develop and defend the nation they belong to.

For these very reasons, we underline again the importance of over-coming, by all of us, the obstacles which stand in our way and which have bled the hearts before the feet. We have to forget our past sorrows now that we have learnt lesson from them. We have to work all, with mutual agreement, for building a better future for the nation after we solidify our present and reinforce it with a faithful creative power which pleases God and the people.

In this speech, which is a recollection of the connotations and lessons of the historic confrontation at the glorious Mother of all Battles, whose major phase of fight started on January 17, 1991, we find our-selves faced with the duty of telling the officials in America a wisdom which we have deduced from that unforgettable battle. Its moral point can be summarized as follows: It is quite possible that one makes an error of judgment when he examines his power prior to its application, and it is also quite probable that he makes the same mistake as regards his enemy's power. As a result, he gives his power one mark higher than what he deserves or what God, the Almighty and All-powerful may permit and gives his enemy's power one mark lower than what he deserves or his firm faith may suggest. But he is considered slow on the uptake if he repeats the same mistake with an enemy who has been put to the test and has countered all powers and potentialities used against it.

It is necessary for America not to delude itself into believing that it can do harm to Iraq in a way that enables it to achieve the goals bequeathed to it by the ancestors other than causing pain to our people and this will be recompensed by God, the Almighty and All-powerful, who will put the Iraqis in their proper place and reward martyrs in his heaven for their sublime sacrifice.

But God, the Most High, is digging pits on the path of the Americans. These pits, covered and dark, may get deeper with the passing of the time when their nervousness and disappointment increase. The Americans will retreat and depart, day after day, from the peak which they think they have reached when they dared to attack the glorious city of Baghdad with their bombs and missiles but the city, nevertheless, has proved to be impregnable to foreign aggression. They should, therefore, re-examine and reconsider what they are doing so that the unjust sanctions imposed on Iraq come to an end. They should also not be misled again or mislead themselves into believing that they can achieve by military aggression what they were unable to achieve by their means of malice, deception and trickery. This is because they have already tested it on several occasions and have thought after or before it that deceit, political deception by means of imposing sanctions and plotting in the dark could lead to their desired aims. The Americans must realize, and this should not be construed as a threat, that as we fought against them and endured their aggression over the past eight years, we have come to know their force and their power for causing harm, in the same manner as we presume they have known the power of the great Iraq and God's protection of it.

Hence, we do not want to fall into the trap of miscalculation into which they have fallen and to vie with them their slow understanding. We only want to attract attention to it and not to embarrass our enemy. Embarrassment is not our aim or goal. All we want to say is that Iraq, as people, leadership and representative bodies at all levels and with different designations are determined, without the slightest retreat, to fight a grand jihad for lifting the sanctions. If the Security Council does not take a decision in fulfillment of its obligations towards Iraq as stipulated in the unjust resolutions which it took alone and without the participation of Iraq as reciprocal commitments, then Iraq has resolved to take a decision consistent with the recommendations of people's representatives at the National Assembly and shall assume full responsibility for it since there is no other alternative course of action. We are firmly convinced that the people of the Arab nation will judge the matter favourably not only in understanding Iraq's situation but also in giving support to its efforts in all fields and at all forums, so that the slogan "lifting the unjust sanctions" will ultimately win and achieve its purpose in breaking open a main gate of conspiracy. We hope and expect that our friends in the world will understand us and everyone, from his own position, will do something to curb evil and support truth. To the peoples of the Third World countries, to their officials and to all countries which share balanced view as regards their relations and interests with this world, we say that America has revealed its true nature as a tyrannical power, selfish and blind which sees nothing but its narrow interests even if their realization of such interest might lead to impoverishing, undermining and destroying these countries and societies after plunging them into a series of crises, wars and disasters.

It is a new disgusting imperialism with all its schemes and policies. It has worn the garb of the people of hell which has a surface appearance of brightness but is actually concealing claws of torture of predatory animals which prey on nothing save human flesh.

Against this background and now that every nation of the world has painful stories, some of them are tragic, of an infringement on its sovereignty, security and vital interests, nothing can save the world but a cooperative and human nationalism in every country of the world especially in Third World countries and forms of solidarity and economic and political cooperation at both popular, official and other levels to contain America's evils and its flames which have spread all over and are threatening the world with all kinds of fire.

We know that this description about America is an expression of what is deep in the hearts and consciences of the whole world, but we also know that not everyone who has this conviction is capable of revealing what is kept in his heart, conscience and mind. We are, therefore, all invited to work together in one direction albeit every individual country of the world has its own course of action in expressing its national attitude at all forums, particularly at international and regional ones and at all opportunities when such are made available for the national will to act in a fair and objective manner.

Let us all remember America's economic conspiracies and its financial dealings which it used against the peoples of Latin America and southeast Asia and even Japan in the last stage despite the fact that most of these countries are its friends until very recently or partners in terms of labour and economic cooperation.

Let them also remember and never forget that America's continuous military aggression and economic sanctions against Iraq are but one manifestation of its selfish and narrow-minded outlook which includes, among others, taking possession of oil and national resources of the countries of the region so that its slogan of controlling the entire world becomes possible.

On this understanding, the struggle of the people of Iraq now is a humane struggle for ridding the world of its disasters in the same manner as Iraq is ridding its people of a disaster. A solidarity by the countries of the world with Iraq for preventing an aggression against it and for lifting the sanctions on it, therefore, a national act and a duty which must be discharged without delay or hesitation. Indeed, a national struggle at this stage which meets with others at common goals for resisting this wild ghoul as an urgent human struggle and a duty to be done by all for the sake of living in a world where no tyrant, oppressor or unjust exploiter can be the sole power, and a world which is both cooperating and secure, capable of seizing its legitimate opportunities without foreign dominion or hegemony.

God is the greatest!

Glory be to martyrs of Arab nation and of Iraq at the glorious Um Al-Marik battle!

Glory be to the nation's martyrs wherever they are!

Long live our glorious Arab nation!

Long live Iraq!

Long live Palestine, a free Arab country!

God is the greatest!

God is the greatest!

Evil be to him who evil thinks!

Speech of His Excellency President Saddam Hussein on the 30th Anniversary of July 17–30, 1968 Revolution, July 17, 1998

IN THE NAME OF GOD, THE COMPASSIONATE, THE MERCIFUL

"Our Lord decide thou between us and our people in truth, for thou art the best to decide" God speak the truth.

Great people!

Brave men of our valiant armed forces!

Arab freedom fighters and strugglers!

Friends!

Peace be upon you!

Moral and Principled Obligation

On this day, every year, we recall with you the two days of the revolution on 17 and 30 July 1968. But today, on the thirtieth anniversary of the revolution we will not engross you, like on traditional occasions, in figures and achievements that acquaint you with what rests you assured of its genuine course and with sincere pledge and promise made to the brave and genuine revolutionists. Rather, it is sufficient to mention some indications of what we can scoop up from its great sea in a manner that makes you more confident and certain that the meanings and spirit of the revolution which broke out at the starting point, on 17 and 30 July 1968, and throughout the subsequent course, are condensing and gathering in an interactive way at every step on its path, as a not-deviated moral and principled obligation, and to highlight at every stage what is new, renewable and ready to leap forward in a manner that angers the enemies and pleases the friends, because talking about figures and achievements does not reflect on the course of the revolution, as the revolution of the new model in Arab life and human life, what is necessary, now its basic achievements have become known to those who follow up its reality and the nature of the battle with the enemies. And because the level of the legendary steadfastness of the people of civilizations and peaks speaks in the utmost eloquence about the level of what assures the sons of our glorious great nation and our friends in the world that the revolution of the new model is continuos and firm, its people and knights are genuine and faithful to their pledge and promise. In the midst of future, it is glorious, prosperous, promising and in the midst of present it depends on its known qualities.

This is your revolution, glorious men and women of Iraq, revolutionists, freedom fighters, strugglers, and sons of our glorious Arab nation.

This is the revolution that you know, friends, and appreciate its true pledge, obligation and position.

It is the glorious revolution of July in great Iraq, the base of challenge, great building, civilizations, position and great Jihad.

The Embargo is Eroding

Great people!

We, all, face the plight of the embargo, threats, conspiracy and the courses of evil coming from outside Iraq. We, all, live up to the honor of firmness, position and the ability to face the threats, relying on God, the Almighty, more confident of the relentless enthusiasm, which cannot be severed from its fountain and resort, of a great people of Jihad.

On previous occasions, we said that the embargo would not be lifted by a unanimous resolution of the Security Council, like it had been depicted that it had been adopted by a unanimous resolution of the Council. Rather, it will be eroded as long as Iraqis hold up to their position, and as the meanings of this position become more clear to the Arabs who increasingly interact with that position as well as to those who bear a serious extent of the meanings of humanity and friendship in the world.

In late 1997, and in the beginning of 1998, Iraqis waged battles and took positions that put the witnesses who have no interest in the embargo, vis a vis the tendentious and evil people in a manner that makes the two lines separated by a clear plain determining unequivocally what is in the battlefield between them without allowing an unexposed maneuver.

Alternative Strategy

If the enemies of Iraq imagine that they are able to deceive a people mobilized with all the factors of national zeal and the experiences of life it has experienced, burned with the fire of its enemies, motivated by the factors of defending life in the midst of its great principles and the immortal legacy of our nation, towards those who wanted and are still trying to assassinate them, a people that made tens of thousands of generous sacrifices of valuable lives every short period of time as a result of the shortage of food and medicine and due to the use of force, we say to them, in the name of the great people of Iraq, that they are wrong and it is better for them to re-read the ancient history and this glorious history carefully in order to derive the lessons that distant us and them from the abyss of their evils and their souls inciting them to evil. We reiterate that the letter addressed to the Security Council and the UN Secretary-General by the joint meeting of the Leadership of Arab Ba'th Socialist Party and the Revolution Command Council on 1 May 1998 is not just a protest cry, but rather it is a will and alternative strategy in case other means and methods fail to return life to its natural track and to put the firm right in its proper place. The Leadership and the Council will meet in a short time to study this subject in depth and to act accordingly with their great people who are always in the pupils of the eyes and in the depth of consciences that pulse patriotism and national zeal.

Nothing will be true but right. God is Great!

The embargo began to erode actually through the steadfastness of Iraqis, their solid adherence to the necessity for the lifting of the embargo and their deep preparation for supporting the assets of sacrifices with additional honour.

This year and the subsequent additional time will be the year and time, God willing, of the serious erosion of the embargo on Iraq. They will be, with the assets of the revolutionary, patriotic and faithful energy as well as the genuine national position of those who take it, the stock of the aquiver and the fountain of the great waterfall to conquer the embargo, break its restrictions, dishonor its masters, the evil and vile. God willing.

Lessons of History

Arabs!

There are always affluent lessons in history, the incitement of which underlines an important aspect of what is possible and not possible at present, when the zeal and faith become active to prepare and mobilize the capability for its role pursuant to the appropriate framework and timing. On this occasion, the thirtieth anniversary of the auspicious revolution, and as some Arabs talk about full and comprehensive summits, and others talk about small or medium summits to discuss the issue of Palestine or the national issues in their comprehensive meaning, and further to our previous speech on the same occasion in July 1997 on the issue of Palestine, we say: The Establishment of the Arab League

In 1945 the representatives of seven Arab states met in Bloudan. The meeting resulted in the establishment of the Arab League which is still existing although the representatvies of only seven independent countries at that time took that decision, not the representatives of 22 states and entities as it is the present case with the political and constitutional division of the nation's homeland. Despite foreign interventions, particularly British and French, were made to make the establishment of the Arab League as a substitute for the Arab unity whose slogans were strongly raised by the Arab masses which called for the unity and by which they rocked the chairs of government and the remnants of colonialism in the great Arab homeland, the old colonialism was not able to control the subsequent march of the Arab League because the Arab masses and their great slogans and struggle were against the colonialist will. Thus, that situation preserved the Arab League and kept some zeal to hold its conferences, including the summits. Had the position of the Arab masses not been as we described, the Arab League would have been abolished at earlier stages of its march after the foreigners failed to make it a colonialist project that could be achieved as a substitute for theglorious Arab un.

In 1967, in the aftermath of 5 June relapse, the Arabs met in Khartoum. The meeting did not include all the Arab officials, on the level of the first officials or those who follow them directly in rank. Nevertheless, the summit took decisions, the most important of which were the decisions which constituted the base of the Arab steadfastness which prepared the possibility of confronting the aggression and the Zionist-American scheme against Palestine and the Arab homeland. The summit was named at that time as (the conference of the three no's). Although some winked at the summit, the rejection of the defeat and the insistence of Naser on liberation constituted the political and psychological foundation of the military position in 1973. This happened because the Arab masses had supported the will of the decisions adopted by the summit and because Naser, God rest his soul, with his patriotic, national and international weight pushed for such decisions. Thus, those decisions remained valid until Sadat deviated from the Arab line by his known position of 1977.

Baghdad Summit 1978

Despite the horrible shock inflicted upon the Arab masses, an Arab summit was held in Baghdad in 1978, which Egypt did not attend and some first officials of the Arab states did not attend too. However, since the convening of that summit and the minimum position required had met or come on the basis of Arab national desire based on the Arab popular mindful position, many decisions were made, a vital part of which was implemented and constituted the basic psychological and practical foundation of others' steadfastness and their non-collapse as expected by Zionism and imperialist planners after Sadat's position.

October War 1973

In 1973, on the margin of the Arab October war against the Zionist entity, a small number of the Arab states called upon the influential international parties to take a fair position, or at least the minimum position after which the evil would be a flood; otherwise the Arabs would be forced to put the interest of the Arab national security in their considerations and their oil and economic relations with the concerned parties. Since the masses' will had supported that call which did not exceed its declaration in the policies of most of the concerned Arab states, or because that call represented an aspect of the genuine position of the Arab masses, the Arabs won in that field without making a serious sacrifice which they were to make at that time.

The Nations Respect and Prestige

In 1980, we visited Saudi Arabia after the Zionist entity put pressures on the states having diplomatic relations with it to move their diplomatic missions and Embassies from Tel Aviv to Jerusalem, and gave them a short respite, otherwise it would sever and terminate its diplomatic relations with them. A number of those states responded to that Zionist pressure. But, only by our agreement with King Khalid, God rest his soul, and authenticating that agreement in a statement which we declared after meeting with King Fahad who was crown prince then, not only the process of moving the embassies to Jerusalem had been ceased but even the embassies which had been already moved to Jerusalem, prior to the Zionist ultimatum, were returned to Tel Aviv. Thus, you see how a brief statement by only two Arab states, Iraq and Saudi Arabia, succeeded in increasing the respect and prestige of the Arab nation amongst other nations. Although it was a joint statement by only two Arab states, its meanings represented the will of the whole nation as well as the whole people. Since the statement had been based on a resolution firmly established in the souls that the warning by the two states to those who would respond to the Zionist ultimatum, was serious, and it was taken to be implemented not just for propaganda, the concerned parties realized that the two states would reconsider their relations with them and that all the Arabs might follow suit. Therefore, they responded immediately and refrained from moving their embassies to Jerusalem, and even those who had already moved their embassies to Jerusalem, before declaring the statement, returned them to Tel Aviv.

Baghdad Summit 1990

In 1990, the Arabs gathered in an Arab summit held in Baghdad. Syria did not attend that summit although its officials were invited. Some Arab states did not attend on the level of the first officials. Nevertheless, its decision had a thunderous impact on the Zionist entity and on the makers or followers of its aggressive policies. The Arab masses positively responded to those decisions to the highest and largest degree because they put their confidence in that summit and built their hopes on it as soon as it had been decided to hold the summit. Before announcing what had been announced of its decisions, those decisions, attitude and the nature of the roles and its known positions had a reflective reaction in the plans of the plotters of the black conspiracy preceded August 1990 against Baghdad, its men, attitude, policy, capability. Hence, the unjust thirty-nation aggression took place.

Cairo Summit 1996

Arab brothers!

In 1996, the concerned Arabs held a meeting on the level of the summit in Cairo. One of its important decisions was to facilitate the task of America and its supporters to continue the embargo on Iraq under the facade that Iraq should implement the so-called resolutions of the Security Council, as if the concerned Arabs were to play the role of a UN office on behalf of America. They also took other decisions, including those decisions taken under the facade of the Palestinian issue.

What did happen after that meeting? Did any of those who are concerned in the Zionist entity turn a hair? Or did the White House, the supplier of the requirements of the Zionist occupation, aggression and expansion at the expense of the Arabs, pay any attention? Did those resolutions have any positive effect on the conscience of the Arabs from the shores of the Atlantic ocean and Mediterranean sea to the shores of the Arabian Gulf and the depths of the Arabian Peninsula?

The answer to this question is clear enough, for us, to take a decisive decision based on a confidence that cannot be rocked by the adorned words of whoever. But, is it clear for those who are responsible for that summit held in Cairo without the meanings that Baghdad represents now in the Arab's position and history? And when discussing Arab issues, did the conference give serious consideration to the Arabs' aspirations and attitudes?

The return to an aspect of the near past may involve some embarrassment to some Arabs. But, we do not mean that per se. However, we are in bad need for such direct inquiries, for us or against us alike, because we are under the titles of the rulers or leaders, each according to his description. In our this capacity, we need those inquiries more than we need them as mere normal citizens in our countries.

Since the walls of government palaces are not always transparent, and as this is their objective description in general, and in order to make everyone of us close to the token, aspirations and the vision of the people, his conscience and principles should be transparent and living.

And because what the transparent and living conscience and principles, that reflect the reality of the nation, mostly need is truth as it is, talking of it and about it and inquiring into it and about it loudly, by us or by others, is an honorable patriotic and national act. Rather it is a sacred religious duty.

Americas Position?

Therefore, Arab brothers, we return to say:

If some ask for America's view in advance, or depend on its view of the acceptance or non-acceptance of holding the summit and of its venue and nature, then how we can imagine their conduct regarding the agenda and the trend of the summit's resolutions, particularly on the issues in which America has a clear and previously determined view. This view is biased, non-neutral, at the expense of the Arabs and not in the middle between the Arabs and their enemy?

Some Arabs have scourtesy to America. Most of them hoped that it would take into consideration their friendship and sacrifices for it during two or three decades. However, Palestine and other Arab territories are still under occupation. Al-Quds, the second holy shrine is still under occupation. There are still some Moslem rulers, including some Arabs, who say that they are Moslems, representing their people and believing in the divine book, the Holy Quran, but they do not feel, in spite of this, any embarrassment or deep wound in their hearts and chests as a result of the occupation of Al-Quds by the Zionists by means of injustice and aggression. Doesn't this contradict the truth, reality, responsibility and faith?

Thirty Years of Struggle and Jihad

Brother Arab leaders!

We have learnt from the experience of thirty years of struggle, Jihad and building in power, and prior to this, from the record of our underground struggle and the meanings of the lofty principles in which we believe and never bargain over them, that it is of wisdom for anyone whom God enable to have some capability, should seek more, depend on God, and not dispense the simplest emotions, capabilities and view of the people for achieving these objectives, because the achievement of the higher objectives requires large concentration, for which the officials cannot dispense with the youngster, the elderly, those who are on the front-line or in the far depths of the battle field. However, if you find that it is in the best interest of the nation and it will mobilize the enthusiasm of its sons, to hold a summit or any other arrangement with a part of its potentials, not its entire potentials, to regain its usurped rights, to immunize the inherent rights that should be immunized and protect them from the threats of the greedy, the malicious and the tendentious, we will be more than happy because this will prove that the nation is well as we believe and see. More importantly, if you, or some of you, are able to achieve that within the minimum requirements that satisfy God and the good sons of the nation, this will prove, for the whole world to see, that the main parties concerned are a living part of their nation. Then, it does not matter, if your dispensing with Baghdad's capabilities and their effectiveness is not an avoidance or ignorance of them but a mere gesture of warriors so that Baghdad may take some rest after its long march of Jihad when there is that who can fill its post on the honorable front of Jihad, although this, even according to this condition and its motivations, does not satisfy Baghdad, its people, lovers and the great people of Iraq who never remain indifferent or accept the warrior's rest on the margins of the battlefields when fighting is fierce or there is a need for deliberation and consultation.

Nevertheless, brothers, you should remember a wisdom derived from this immortal and glorious record, that is that who wants to brandish a sword, which he would not use only if necessary, against the enemy, should brandish it against him without hesitation and with tested and known sword. He who seeks wisdom should ask an experienced man. And he who wants to warn his enemy, his capabilities should be visible with a view to give him a chance to make a choice before getting involved. He who wants to use force against his enemy as an unavoidable choice, should thrust into the battlefields those men who can win one part of the battle by their symbols and the other part by their genuine swords.

Success is granted by God.

On God we depend, first and last.

God is Great!

The Reality of the Arab-Zionist Struggle

Arab brothers!

During the past two years, some Arab officials distressingly tried to falsify the facts deliberately or due to their ignorance of the factors and reasons for the conflict between the Arabs and the entity which usurped their sanctuaries and territories. Moreover, it threatens them with cruelest threats to life, sovereignty and security. It also uses whatever it has and whenever it can use it against their people and territory. No one can ignore the severe suffering of the injured and struggler people of Palestine, the struggler people of Lebanon and the Arab people in the occupied Jolan as a result of the Zionist entity's recklessness of the simplest requirements of right, even in non-Arab perspective. I say, some Arabs began publicly and openly to turn the fact of the conflict between the Arabs and the usurper and aggressor, the Zionist entity, in addition to the great meanings they lost due to this entity's usurpation and aggression, into a mere difference of policies. They also started to minimize and dwarf the fields and meanings of this difference depicting them as if they are between some Arab rulers and Netanyahu on some provisional, tactical and secondary matters, not on basic, strategic and fateful issues which constitute a great concern of the nation. Thus, they gave in to their enemy in advance because the conflict in which one of its parties calls for its entire objectives and reveals them to the quarters that are required to make sacrifices and prepare the strategic requirements necessary for their success, while the other party hides or waive the whole issue by declaring only a part of it and asking only for a mobilization of forces and potentials that are parallel to that part only. In such a conflict, the latter party will inevitably be defeated, rather it is psychologically and actually defeated from the very beginning and before entering the battlefield. This is the case with some Arabs who started to beg the sympathy of the biased American administration to help them by pressurizing Netanyahu for resuming the discussion of the so-called peaceful solution pursuant to the so-called Madrid and Oslo resolutions, while their curses are poured upon Netanyahu only. This negligence by some Arabs is prompted by the Zionist American administration through throwing dust in the eyes of some Arabs from time to time.

Some may say that the speaker does not master the art of tactics because such Arab conduct can help the Arabs win friends in the world, while the Zionist entity loses. Commenting on this, I should like to say: Arab brothers, Tactics is neither (juggling) nor a magic technique in today's international politics. Rather, it is an action comprising capability and time in a manner that serves the strategy designed for particular field, objective or objectives, or for an action calculated for a specific time in the light of a capability allocated and mobilized in the field. Accordingly, tactics is part of a known and understood strategy on the level of the government and people, otherwise it cannot succeed, on the one hand. On the other hand, the enemy masters the art of tactics and the tactic and strategic dealings with its popular quarters, its enemies and friends. It also fully understands the nature of nowadays international politics, as it was the case in the past. Therefore, it will not wait until international politics give it voluntarily what it hopes to get or works for. Rather, it will snatch that from international politics and force it to use some of its concepts and objectives against you in order to force you to give in without fighting and attrition of the enemy. Thus, the enemy never lose from this policy, or rather the non-policy.

Since the enemy masters the art of utilizing tactics as a part of its strategy, it knows that your feet should not be on the extreme edges of the target you defend. Rather, the target should be behind you in order to protect it from the enemy's attacks. The enemy also knows that it is impossible to mobilize a force capable to effectively confront the enemy and snatch from it any target which is stripped of sanctity and the attractive public interest of the people and nation. Therefore, we see the enemy always speaks about objectives which are deeper, larger and more severe than the objectives you talk about and demand. It mobilizes its forces on the basis of the declared and undeclared objectives. It investigates and cits alliances accordin.

Hence, you should return to right, brothers, as it is. Then, right will return to you, under God's patronage, as it is. At that time, tactics will be successful.

At that time, any policy, whatever the minor aspects the Arabs missed, will not cause them a loss of their historical right under variables in which time cannot wait for the helpless and the weak indefinitely to provide them with ready-made gains.

Serious Arab Summit

Nevertheless, Baghdad of the Arabs and Islam, which is full of zeal for the principles, lofty ideals and love for its nation's sons, does not accept for itself to be a cause, cover or an obstacle that impede the holding of a serious meeting of the Arabs on the level of summit to take decisions that put the nation in a better situation towards itself, its lovers and enemies.

What is important, brothers, is that you meet and your meeting should be a serious aimed at deciding on your nation's affairs what satisfies God and the sons of the nation. You should wisely consider your affairs without being distracted from your duty by an obstacle or whim that impede your position.

Your meetings should be regular, with their dates and venues are prescheduled every time irrespective of difference or agreement on this or that matter.

Only then, you can provide yourselves with a strong reason to be a living part of your nation, and your nation will be in a higher status and better situation.

The Price of Rightful Stand and Saying

Brave Arabs!

The Iraqis know that they have to pay the price of any rightful stand and true saying. Nowadays, the price of the rightful stand and saying is not economic, such as terminating an agreement or assistance, diplomatic, such as lowering the relations between two or more countries, cultural or the like, but it is all of this soaked in the sacred blood of the dutiful martyrs. But, Iraqis also know, they remind each other and do not forget, that sacrifices should be on the level of wishes, hopes and goals. Those who have such wishes, hopes and goals should be prepared for their level. There is no way for those who aspire to reach the peaks, not the stagnant valleys, but this level of sacrifice. There is no way out of any plight or impasse created by the greedy imperialist foreigner or the foreign occupier and usurper, through building on a low land since the flood will sweep it off and render it a mere scum. The usurping and greedy enemy does not understand reality and does not respond to what is right and just through shameful submission, but through the adoption of an honorable stance and being prepared for this situation. At that time, the foreigner may retreat without shedding blood. As regards the positions of shameful submission, they will not get anyone out of his impasse, or the impasse in which he has been entangled. They will not open any honorable doors to get out of the plight, doors that get the capability out of the reach of those who besiege it, set it hard punishments or threaten the titles of its components. The Iraqis repeat the following verses of the great poet, Kamal Al-Hadithi:

Bustards cannot escape humiliation by flying away, for the falcon will hunt them.

Flourishing and green is life, and only he whose life is short perishes.

So many are the people who come to our springs that everyone is bewildered when things are confused, We stir them up to our liking and depart, only to drink the purest part which is the best.

God is Great!

Firm Rightful Position

Arab brothers!

The firm position based on the ground of truth and its goals brings us closer to our consciences or brings our consciences to us. It makes us a living part of our people and nation. We provide that position with additional means of wisdom and capability, while it in turn provides us with a great flow of wisdom, capability and love. More importantly, it brings us closer to the Lord of the absolute might and wisdom, God, the Almighty, and grants us the opportunity of God's gratification and forgiveness for the uncountable mistakes of power. However, we neither come closer to Whom we so hope, 0nor He comes closer to us, unless we become a living part of the Arab collective conscience, and unless these considerations become the obsession of all of us, rather than the gratification or non-gratification of this or that of the nation's enemies and those who underestimate its capability.

Only then, and by relying on God and the nation, rather than on any international official, the Arabs can hold a summit with whoever attends it. A summit which polarize the attention and interaction of the Arabs from the Atlantic ocean and the Mediterranean to the Arabian Gulf, whether this or that Arab ruler or leader is present or not.

At that time, the concerned parties will act with confidence. They will feel a kind of love which they do not know before in the eyes and hearts of their people. They will feel the appreciation which fills them with confidence by the states of the world and their representatives when they make their enemies feel the due respect.

In the Name of God, the Compassionate, the Merciful

"Our Lord, condemn us not if we forget or fall in error, our Lord, Lay not us a burden like that which thou didst lay on those before us, our Lord, lay not on us a burden greater than we have strength to bear, blot out our sins, and grant us forgiveness, have mercy on us. Thou art our protector, help us against thiose who stand against faith."

God speak the truth.

Long live the Arabs!

Long live the sons of our glorious nation!

Long live Iraq!

Long live Iraq of Jihad!

Long live Palestine, free and lofty Arab country!

Glory and immortality to the martyrs of Iraq and the Arab nation!

Glory and immortality to the martyrs of Palestine!

God is Great!

God is Great!

Let the despicable be despised!

Address of His Excellency President Saddam Hussein On The Eight Anniversary Of The Thirty-Nation Aggression Against Iraq January 16–17/ January 17, 1999

IN THE NAME OF GOD, THE COMPASSIONATE, THE MERCIFUL

"Say: I seek refuge with the Lord of dawn, from the mischief of created things." God speak the truth.

Great people!

Brave men of our valiant armed forces!

Masses of our glorious Arab Nation!

Peace be upon you and for you, the masses in the Arabic streets, houses and families.

Peace be upon every student, intellectual, solider, farmer, worker, women and men, youths and children. Peace be upon you and for, and upon the people of Iraq, both men and glorious women, the comrades of Saddam Hussein in the leadership, your brother and the son of your people and Nation: Saddam Hussein who is infected with the disease of your love: the disease without which any official in his nation will be sick. It is the disease with which some Arab officials have charged Saddam Hussein when they said that he is infected with the disease of the Arab masses, thinking that this is a defect in Saddam Hussein, but it is a fact, brothers, and it is an honor for us to be infected with the disease of loving the sons of our Nations in the streets, cities, villages, factories, poor districts and countryside. We were sincerely hoping that this disease would infect those Arab officials instead of the disease of loving Zionism and America, submission to them, implementing their orders and responding to their schemes at the expense of the Arab's security and their highest issues and interests. Had this disease, which is health and honor, infected some Arab rulers, the Nation would not have been subjected to what it had suffered from Zionism, America and their supporters.

God is Great!

Long live the (disease) of loving the people and Nation!

Let be despised those who are infected with the disease of loving Zionism, America, their followers and supporters at the expense of their people and nation.

Arab brothers!

Friends!

We remind you, once again, of unforgettable case. On a similar day, that is 17 January 1991, in its long dark night, before the dawn, the blind night covered the shining and bright day. There was a screen separating between them, which God wanted to enlarge in order to include the sins and evil souls of those who committed the crime and evil. The other side of that screen was supervised by a lofty peak of great principles and glory in the Iraq of faith, patience, sacrifice and jihad, a peak which kept itself away from the deep abyss of that screen.

On that day and in its long dark night, some failed and some succeeded. It was a posture, on one of its two sides there were those who attacked Baghdad with their missiles. They were thirty foiled positions which would be followed by shame for ever, and twenty eight armies whose arrows missed their targets, except for those whom God wanted to be destined for the honor of martyrdom as well as the property they destroyed. On the other side, there were those who were inspired with the glorious ancient past, and heightened the status of the Baghdad of history, virtue and lofty meanings. There, the people of Iraq stood with its leadership which loves its people and its Nation to the extent that this love has infected it with the great disease (the health), and it has made sacrifices for its Nation for life and all the time. Thus, it was unparalleled paradox and a tableau of proud faith, virtue and glory which, on our side, could not be measured. And it was unprecedented evil on the side of the devils where those who were led by America, accepted it with submission, obedience and humiliation.

The whole Iraq stood with its enthusiasm, faith, arms, endurance and meanings. With Iraq, the ardent sons of the Nation stood, praying to God, the Almighty, to bestow victory upon the Iraq of faith, Arabism, humanity and lofty meanings in its confrontation with its enemies, the enemies of the Nation, each according to his position and to what was available to him or to what his position enabled him to take as an expression of his position.

As such was the situation eight years ago, namely in the beginning of the first half of the day of 17th of January 1991.

Despite this and the embargo followed it which is unprecedented in its evil and harm, some took positions which were credited for them and some took positions which were registered against them. On the part of those who continued with their malice, malevolence, aggressiveness and evil, all their positions are shameful to humanity which is tortured and oppressed by them. On the part of Iraq and those whom God helped to say the right or to take a right position, the positions honor the good and proud soul that seeks good and virtue and to recover from the filth of Zionism and world imperialism led by the America of evil to the abyss.

Iraqis!

Brothers!

Sons of our Nation, our sole love!

Once again, we repeat the easily heard question: Why did the forces of evil target Iraq only, and focus on it all the time, especially in the first two decades of the age of July Revolution 1968?

The most important characteristics of Man's purity and the level of his seriousness in what he says, declares or promises is to be true. If he is true, he will become honest to what he is entrusted with. The principles and the promise they include, as goals of the struggle of the people and Nation, the power of the state and all its aspects, the mobilization of the people for positions of struggle and jihad against the foreign ambitions during a particular stage before the assuming power, and holding up to its all goals, is a trust which should be bore and protected. The fulfillment of this trust is a great truthfulness and grand struggle and jihad.

The most important sign indicating that the sons of the Nation have abandoned it when any of them assumes an authority of a collective nature, role and mission, is their abandonment of respecting this trust and their diversion from the characteristics of truthfulness and honesty to another level which honors neither the self nor the Nation.

The enemies of the Nation and the greedy for its wealth have discovered that those who lead the revolution and the march of rule and building within it are true in their call and faithful to what they have entrusted themselves with, or to what entrusted to them by the people.

Those enemies have become more ferocious when they realized, through unchangeable evidence, that those who lead the march are capable, relying on God, to translate the declared principles into practical plans, implement the plans, and to turn the capabilities of Iraq, which is rich in its natural and human resources and ancient heritage, from mere general resources buried under the ground or non-utilized resources together with its lands and waters, into live and active wealth and capabilities, and to draw the great meanings of the Iraq's spiritual and cultural heritage and the heritage of the eternal heritage of our Nation, and to activate these meanings, not to think of them as mere cultural material, so that they can actively and tangibly contribute to a new rise of the people of civilizations and roles, the people that a large number of it could not afford wearing shoes. In the countryside, the overwhelming majority was barefooted at that time. Those who wore shoes were the exemption, while diseases, abandoning the role, the contradiction between the ancient past and the then crippled and backward present, had undermined the people's zeal and determination. Baghdad, with all that it bears of the glorious history of the Nation and a great cultural role, was almost a large abandoned village, in terms of formation and services, rather than a city of these historical meanings, living in the 20th century. The State's treasury was empty and those who had jobs were few. Backwardness and inactive attitude on life were devastating the brains. As such or rather less was the situation in other Iraqi cities. After the Revolution, Baghdad and life have become as they now despite the conspiracies of the forces of evil which came one after one with extraordinary actions to suppress the new will that proceeded with building, renewing the role after its rise again, developing the wealth after its creation, enhancing the trust by truthfulness and capability after being built on a solid foundation that does not spoil the consciences and ardor by inactivity and evil example. Hence, the honest have protected the nation's wealth after creating it, turning it from mere natural resources and inactive wealth into an active wealth which has been reflected in every house, district, town, hospital, educational house in the countryside and cities alike. The obsession of those who led the march was and still to enjoy themselves, their eyes, minds and consciences of what they come to know, see and hear about the things that the people have possessed, and the meanings of advancement and progress that the people have, and to cut whatever hand extends to the people's resources and wealth. Therefore, they have deprived the western banks of being packed with the accounts belonging to the officials in the state of Iraq, as was the case in the past times, especially in the monarchical reign, and as is the case with other officials in the Arab homeland. Therefore, the forces of evil have realized that the natural resources, including oil, have been used to strengthen Man's role in Iraq in an ascending manner, not to corrupt him or to simply fatten him up to be eaten by the West. Those forces have realized also that the sincere loyalty to the Nation, people and principles, and the faithfulness to them and to the responsibility for what the guardians are entrusted with, is a case from which there is no retreat neither by the temptation provided by the power nor by the threats posed by foreigners. They have found that the characteristics of truthfulness and honesty are a great danger to their illegitimate interests because their illegitimate interests cannot coexist and grow with the presence of true officials who are faithful to their Nation and people. Thus, the level of danger of the conspiracy and its potential have increased. The plots that some Arab rulers, of the same category, carried out in secret, were insufficient. The schemes were in need for direct roles, some of which were overt. Thus, in the thirty-nation aggression page of Umm Al-Ma'arik, some roles and titles have been uncovered and disposed on the largest scale before the whole Arab masses and the entire world in the page of confrontation on the Day of Al-Fateh. Those roles and titles could not have been disposed unless what the requirements of confrontation necessitate from the wrong to the right. The steadfastness of your great people in Iraq, sons of our glorious Nation, has made such roles and playing overtly to implement them an indispensable state.

Thus, in this respect only, these are the reasons, as well as other known reasons, which pushed the forces of evil which are hostile to our Nation and humanity, to target Iraq and preoccupied with it as a great dam throughout the last decade. For Iraq's collapse, God forbid, would lead to a flood that drowns the Nation for a long time and keeps humanity away from practicing its role in encountering this evil for a long time too. The steadfastness of Iraq, as God wanted it, will make the Nation realize the facts as they are, and to establish its new standards on live examples which are represented by dutiful sons of it, while it inspires its examples in its eternal heritage, rather the examples in our Nation, which we know and read about in the eternal heritage of the Nation, have become more understandable and more believable than before, after the Nation has discovered its potential in life, innovation, creation and the ability to resist, through its deep-rooted struggling titles, at the head of which is the great people of Iraq. So, by God, the evils will not refrain from targeting Baghdad until it betrays itself and its Nation. But Baghdad has never been traitorous. Or they will be defeated and become desperate from the possibility to achieve their evil goals. This is what will happen, God willing.

Tomorrow is very near to those who await it.

Arabs!

People of whole humanity!

Since a known time, when the West got out its borders, states and population centers, to proceed towards the East, with those who came to the East not as propagandists to good, virtue and humanitarian issues of a nature and meanings carrying a common interest of the propagandists amongst the targeted environment, rather the West came as a colonialist, usurper, hostile and to plunder the people's wealth. Thus, the people's sadness, concern and poverty had been increased, and they fell down under heavy additional burdens resulted from the military occupation and colonization. The West did not leave the territories which it occupied and colonized until the sons of those territories made great sacrifices, and when the concerned colonial states realized that there was no way to stay there according to the previous conditions and methods. Thus, some had left (in form) with some of their ground forces whose presence had become impossible and very costly. The old colonization was replaced with a new one that fits the development and situation. After each war in the West because of their competition over interests or other affairs, humanity which is tortured by them, particularly in the East, paid costly for those wars as well as their known old campaigns against Eastern countries.

All this, combined with the level of threats posed by America and its allies to the whole humanity, the maintenance by the West of NATO, increasing its membership and expanding it towards the East after the breakdown of the former Soviet Union which NATO was formed under the pretext of encountering its dangers, in addition to what may be said that the West has its own concepts, interests, heritage, standards and other affairs, and the East has its own location, development, role, the historical depth of this role and its obligations, culture, heritage, foundations, meanings and other affairs, and since the policy of America, Britain, Zionism allied with them and those who support and cooperate with them, has become a danger to the world security, stability and its international and regional interests. Iraq, after a contemplation which is not limited to particular circumstances, sees that an institutional gathering of systems and covenants to be agreed upon, is to be established among the willing states of the world, starting with the East, with a view to establishing serious cooperation in economic, political and military fields in order to maintain balance and peace, first in Asia and what relates to it.

It is natural to say that this gathering is not directed against any one, but it is ready to protect its members, righteously defend, according to correct human standards, the security and interests of its members as well as international security.

Positive cooperation among its members is the foundation on which it is established in order to achieve positive and good results for the benefit of all and for the benefit of international and regional security.

The gathering is open to those who wants to join it in accordance with its basis and conditions.

As it calls for this, Iraq knows that this call will be echoed by the patriotic and honorable minds that are concerned with the security of their people and countries as well as the world security at large. But, it is likely that not all are capable to express their view, either out of fear or intimidation.

Iraq stands ready to hold dialogue, on this basis, with all in order to crystallize the charter of this endeavor, its gatherings and every affair relating to it. On this basis, Iraq will work actively with the concerned parties.

God know the intention.

Long live our glorious Nation!

Long live Iraq and its brave army, the true and faithful army of the Nation!

Glory and paradise to the martyrs of the eternal UMM-Al-MA'ARIK!

Long live free, proud and Arab Palestine!

Glory and paradise to the martyrs of our glorious Arab Nation!

God is Great!

God is Great!

Let the despicable be despised!

Address of His Excellency President Saddam Hussein in July 17, 1999

In the Name of God, Most Compassionate, Most Merciful

Great People of Iraq, Capable by the Will of God, Mujahids, Steadfast and Trustworthy!

The Valiant of our Brave, Honest Armed Forces!

Men and Women of the State!

Courageous Men of the National Security!

Praiseworthy Women and Men, the Conscience and Mind of Wakeful Iraq!

Freedom Fighters and Mujahids Everywhere!

Peace be upon you, and God's Mercy and Blessings!

With the beginning of Man on the life-stage in this broad universe, or after a short time, there emerged in the horizon and in accordance with Man's capabilities, something better than what is common and tangible, more supreme than what is materialized and visible which both rely merely on his sight-range. Concomitant with the above, a thought and a hope were initiated: a thought that exceeds what is visible and tangible, and a hope based on the potentiality of achieving whatever is relevant to them or bridging them by working programmes. Concomitant with this too, there appeared people who stood opposing the thought and the hope. They were thus divided into two groups, or called by two sorts of labels in the conflict: those who aspired after the better and more distant, and those are acquiescent and resigned, being confused or whose will being defeated by items pertaining to the common, tangible and visible, the legacy of the predecessors.

With the new thought and hope, and the degree and level of adherence to the old labels and legacy and to the common and visible or the submission to the status quo and defending it, and to the innovators' persistence in a new thought and a new hope associated with what is more distant, deeper and more supreme than the degree and level can be described. The deeper and the broader the thought and hope, together with their programmes and objectives in their own fields, the wider the gap between various or different labels, and with this the wider and deeper the conflict, and by corollary the more sacrifices.

It is only natural to say that the deeper the thought and the hope beyond what is common and prevalent, the more serious is the transfer of the human surroundings of the thought and hope and humanity in general to a better status. It is only on this premiss, and not on what is common and prevalent that humanity has developed, that Man's role on earth has been enhanced. It has become then possible to perceive the oneness of the Lord of Heavens and Earth with indeed a firm belief in it, since this perception of God's oneness is a developed capability in both vision and conviction. With his liberation from what is only visible to the naked eye, Man was capable to formulate a thought of whatever is better, and a hope of achieving such a betterment, which has been attached to his thought.

With the gradual broadening of Man's intellectual capability, God has bestowed upon him recurrent prophet hood. Likewise, by exercising a limited yet escalating role, Man has realized that he is incapable of absolute perception or comprehension, and with such an incapability despite the progress achieved by his mind and capabilities, Man has encountered a human need to make up for his despair of being incapable of absolute comprehension to keep the thought and hope living, to develop his mind, taste, role and endeavour in an incessant manner except at the divine ordinance which God of the absolute comprehension, Most Great, Most Capable, Most Compassionate and Most Merciful, has cared for Man's incapability so as to salvage him from despair and to preserve an inevitable, moral basis for his progress and development.

Thus started the human revolution, as a thought and as a hope: it has assumed various forms and made different attempts. Each revolution started compatibly with its environment, vision, national and human role and the relevant readiness for continuity, steadfastness and offering sacrifices.

Great People!

Accordingly, our Revolution as a thought and as a hope, even as an embodiment of objectives, in general, is not a new or an exceptional case of the above account, nor of the trend of thought and hope; neither is it so to great people of Iraq, nor to the glorious Arab Nation. We find, here and there, in the people, the nation and humanity various thoughts and hopes and their relevant programmes, objectives and attempts, some went into a certain distance beyond the starting-point, some carried out certain objectives while other have succeeded in conveying a well-developed message, all-including of humanity. Al-mighty God has taught us, through his prophets and messengers, how the general can emerge from the particular and how the latter is governed by the former, by law and by corollary, when He made the Arab Nation and its vast land a cradle of prophet hood and heavenly messages and bestowed upon Iraq the honour of having a greater share when he chose Abraham, the Iraqi, a father of prophets. God has rendered a responsibility upon Abraham greater than the land of birth and growth, so he went roaming about parts of the homeland of our Nation, to communicate the message to where he should and with which he was honoured by God, All-Comprehending, Most Capable, Most Generous and All-Powerful.

What is new and more significant is not the thought of the revolution as a starting-point of change, nor its objectives of unity, freedom and socialism, but its seriousness and honesty: the Revolution has risen from a people known historically of its deep seriousness, a people that has always exceeded what is conventional and common of thoughts, programmes and attempts, and has always aspired after what is more supreme, more developed, greater, deeper and more comprehensive. God, glory be to Him, has eventually rescued the people of Iraq from a continual disappointment in achieving deep penetration or sublimity as He made its land a cradle of His prophets, chose Abraham a father of the prophets and a messenger to the whole humanity, and organized Abraham's endeavour and role to be more universal, more supreme, better, deeper and more comprehensive in accordance with the course chosen to him by God, Most Compassionate, Most Merciful.

Your Revolution is serious, in a serious people; it is honest and true to its patriotic, national and humanitarian notion. It has subjected itself to the test of long struggle, not only to test its own seriousness, but also to test the trustworthiness of its leadership, the great people of Iraq and the glorious Ba'ath, to try out their sincerity after they have been unified into an inseparable one. They have rejected any submission, weakness, servility and bargaining at the expense of truth and right, any replacement of certainty by doubt, rendering the particular as a substitute for the general, hesitation for boldness and intrepidity, any sort of distancing itself from the course of achieving its great objectives or giving in to bargain over alternatives which bring no honour to the people.

In compatibility with the level of the gravity of sacrifices for resisting the greedy foreigners who are hostile to its legitimate objectives, the Revolution has elevated itself to the level of the sublimity, profoundness and comprehensiveness of its objectives, thus coming close to the universal and comprehensive principles, after it has satisfied the Lord of Great Absoluteness, and cleansed the soul and mind of any fanaticism dictated by certain practices of local and national specificity, particularly in the existing circumstances. Such a purification has been an outcome of an action and vision desirous that the good, peace, security, love, justice and fairness based on the principles of truth and eternal heritage should prevail humanity as a whole.

The causes and significance of your patriotic, national, humanitarian, honest, serious and true revolution, capable of long struggle, cannot be explained but in terms of the sublimity and profoundness of its objectives. Thus, amidst humanity, the Revolution has aggrandized in depth and width. Once more, God has honoured our nation after the close of the era of prophet hood and humanitarian messages by making the particu, having been minutely perceived, a starting-point towards the general and its right thought and towards a parallel great hope whose programmes have been subjected to test daily as a pronouncement that implementation is possible by relying on God and the ardour of noble Iraqis, the great example, and by the firm support of the sons of our glorious faithful nation as well as all friends in the world at large.

In the light of a right notion and a sound programme, the Revolution, backed by an unshaken conviction, has steadily advanced. Each step it has made has enhanced Iraqis' conviction in the possibility of accomplishing the successive step for the attainment of all objectives. Only God, glory be to Him, of Whom we seek assistance.

Great People!

Sons of our glorious Arab Nation!

Thus was the conflict, and thus it has always been, set off from these principles between the Arab Nation under various titles of revival, development, and a better role to play on the one hand, and enemies on the other. In the forefront of this conflict, the more wakeful and prepared to play such a role the Nation, the more capable to defeat its enemies with firm conviction and other requisites and by reliance upon God. Regardless of anything else, the enemies cannot assent to the Nation's national and humanitarian role before ascertaining its capability to "snatch" that role and to reject humiliation, submissiveness and weakness now that God has strengthened it by the power of firm belief and the necessity of playing its historic role.

On the basis of these principles, your great people, the vanguard of your Nation, the proud, faithful, and capable people of Iraq, is resisting, as it has so far, all attempts of the thwarted Zionism and the despot of this age: the successive U.S administrations which have employed the economic, technological and scientific potentialities directly on behalf of Zionism, known for its hatred and vengeance upon the Arabs, the Muslims in general, and indeed the whole humanity by means of the U.S Zionized Jewish administrations.

On the premiss of such a vision of the doctrine, such a role of the thought, the hope and the programme, and of such seriousness of the effective action to put the programme into practice, we can perceive the Revolution of the people, of the Ba'ath, which set out on July 17, 1968, to turn into a course of programme and a march after it had been merely a hope and an underground struggle, both based on a thought.

Hence, likewise, we call to memory the significance of the Revolution on the occasion of its birthday, as a revolution of a new and special style, as a beam of brilliant light that dismisses darkness, God willing; now that any one who believes in it and its course has been liberated from the slavery of impossibility and infeasibility and has become free in mind, conscience, programme and objectives in this age, and now that the people of Iraq and its leading party have pronounced in one resounding voice: "Perish be the Impossible", to build, construct and plant the sublime morals and the highest values in the conscience as well as in the mind, so that the zeal may, without the slightest hesitation, overflow onto their fields, and that the sun may rise, yet never set, on the flagpole bearing "God is Most Great", a banner that has embodied the relationship between what is on earth, the Lord of Heavens and Earth and the role of Man, the great and free in his land which is the cradle of early civilizations and first calls for unity of God, and the relationship with the Lord of the World, such calls which freed the Nation from the burden of idols and the intermediaries between the Merciful Lord and Man, the faithful, heedful, true and trustworthy, and capable by the will of God.

Thus, brethren, the forearms have been freed following the freedom of the minds and consciences, and thus they set out to construct and defend the construction. Truly, triumph is firmly certain now that conviction has been ascertained within the souls, minds and ardours. Masks have also been torn, unveiling gloomy, dirty faces with their fangs dripping blood, after they have penetrated deep in the blood of the innocent and martyrs.

Arab Brethren!

On the premiss of these principles, their exquisite significance and their requisites in the struggle and jihad, God has honoured your Nation from which he selected the prophets and messengers in succession. He made them angels of faith and virtue and examples to be followed in the process of change for the better, in setting up justice and fighting oppression and oppressors, for He found them prepared for all this. On these principles and sublime morals God, glory be to Him, selected the prophets and messengers from the Arab land; and he chose them as revolutionary, too, with the hope of communicating the divine messages to the world after ensuring the base of their birth and their starting-point, that is, the Arab Land, and its distinguished people. God prepared them, and developed their capabilities to play the humanitarian role and communicate the message where He wished to be and to the extent their determination could cope within a certain circumstance and capability.

Indeed, the prophets and messengers had revolted to quantitatively change the material world for betterment and advancement. The first lesson from God to Man after creating him is that He taught him how to play his role in life and his obligation to develop it. Yet the most significant lesson relevant to that role was received from the revolutionary messengers and prophets whom God had accorded them a thought and the requisites for its implementation. He had planted in their souls, conscience and minds the hope of firm conviction and great faith that both thought and hope are applicable and spreadable, as they should and as God, glory be to Him permits.

Thus Man in the great Arab homeland is the first to learn the thought which transcends what is tangible, common and visible from the prophets. Correlatively, the first Man who has received lessons in the necessities of the revolution, change and the qualifications for the appropriate leadership is the Arab man, under the sponsorship of God's apostles and their leading role. Accordingly, Man's patriotic and national role in our Nation and in Iraq has been associated with a humanitarian role, which is more universal and more comprehensive. His existence and life in a prior being have also been associated with the duty and obligation of the revolutionary man who has shouldered the responsibilities for constant change and revolting against anything that is commonplace and conventional and thus outdated by time and reality, as a task entrusted to the prophets by God or a direct commission to Man from the successive prophets and messengers. But the timing, type, scope, titles and methods of the revolution are independent judgments from which the fundamental one can be inferred so as to be closely related to life, its kind and condition. Consequently, when an Arab refrains from playing his role in the change to the better and from making the required move to confront stagnation, to remove the rust from life, hearts and minds when they become old and blind, and to replace the obsolete by novelties, such refrainment from playing this role and from revolting against his reality is not only a misjudgment according to the standards of divine commission and law of life as well as a low self-estimation, but it is also a misjudgment when he refrains from playing his humanitarian role by being an example for others to follow, an intellectual radiation and everything that plants the promising hope in humanity.

It is on the premiss of these principles and morals, brethren, sons of our great people and glorious Arab Nation and people all over the world, that the great Ba'ath emerged and led the July Revolution, which we celebrate today. This Revolution has substituted what is existing for what is good, and has proceeded along a course of incessant advancement, a revolution in which the revolutionary men do not bargain over such constant ascent nor over prolonging the struggle without showing any sign of impatience, so as to set up the just society, to unify the Arabs in one will, one potent action capable of defence and advancement and to make the Arab Nation an example to be followed in humanity at large. Having been put to test, the Arab Nation alone is capable of playing this role truly and honestly, and not any oppressive, authoritarian or exploitative role when it becomes distinguished regionally and internationally, in contrast to other nations which have failed to play that role. The Arab Nation's capabilities and potentialities have transcended mere relative comprehension of material life items within its region.

Besides, the favour of the Arab Nation to humanity in communicating the thought and obligations of the unity of God and the heavenly religions which had sprung out of this thought gives this Nation more than any other nation, the priority of possessing these morals and guarantees its steps in that direction.

Such is your Revolution, brothers and friends; a thought, a hope, a working programme, jihad and struggle. It was such when it was a thought in its starting-point and the underground struggle and such it has remained in the conscience of the Ba'athist revolutionary men at the beginning of the change and has been true to this veritable account. It has never substituted the genuine for the bad, nor the good for the evil; it has neither caused the sublime morals sink to the lowest level, nor has it bargained over its course of ascent to bring about progress and change for the better by relying on God, for this Revolution is a descendent of the great Ba'ath which was founded to revive the Nation along its high morals and hence to perform its national, faithful, comprehensive, genuine and humanitarian task.

Arab Brethren!

I realize the sensitivity of some Arab rulers in our Nation to telling the truth or listening to a different opinion as regards matters of destiny and national influence which stretches beyond a limited place into the great Arab homeland, beyond certain people into the glorious Arab Nation and transcends the short present time, fast into the another present which extends into a long time and even into a future whose range of influence may not be wholly conceived. Notwithstanding I realize the sensitivity of some Arabs to telling the bitter truth regarding Palestine, and because we are Arabs, we have relied and still rely upon the sublime principles which we have already stated in the present speech as we did in other previous speeches. Furthermore, Iraqi people has evidenced in all circumstances and time-phases that it has borne, and is still bearing, a special burden and honour compatible to its doctrine and the historic role in reviving the Nation, we have to state the truth and act in pursuance of it, irrespective of the consequences. We shall try to shelter ourselves from the echo of ravens' croak or a stab in the back, by generalizing rather than specifying, so that this topic should be overwhelmed with objectivity and principled motives. We shall also shun mentioning the tokens and their people as we have done in tackling all national issues in general, not evading a certain affair, but hoping for a possible interaction according to the minimum standards of what is right.

Palestine is our unforgettable, national and humanitarian issue. Some may find us insistent on it if relevance is neglected and scrutiny of what has been referred to and stated in this speech as in others is overlooked, albeit it is a vital part of the core of our belief in Iraq's role in the life of the Arabs and humanity as well as the role of our Nation towards itself and humanity. But if anyone scrutinizes a stance which accepts an exchange of viewpoints without being precharged with a counterstance, he will then understand that what we say on Palestine is not a separated view, nor is it emotional; likewise, it is not part of outdated slogans nor is it a forfeiture on the national and human level. It can, however, be a varied view from those thoughts held by some. It is a hope that does not set with sunset nor does it appear only at sunrise, a hope that derives is constant radiation and proclamation from the legitimacy of its premiss and the relevant right and justice.

Brethren!

Palestine is an Arab land, the homeland of the Palestinians, as a part of the great Arab homeland and the glorious Arab Nation; it is the first of the two qiblahs and the third in the hierarchy of sacred places. Is it right for any Arab man or any man who speaks of Arabicism or attributes Arabicism and faith to himself to give up all these morals and principles? Is it possible for anyone who acquiesces and concedes its occupation by the Zionists and al-Quds (Jerusalem) being under the Zionist occupation or captivity to be called a faithful believer and to ascertain that his prayers would be received by God?

We in great mujahid Iraq do not accept this, having relied upon the principles and morals we have just stated. We pronounce in a voice, which means no harm to anyone but performs our duty towards God, ourselves, the Nation and humanity: Palestine is Arab; the Zionists must depart from it. Jews who want to co-live with its people have a right as citizens of one country, and those who have emigrated to it have likewise rights as well as obligations which they must accept. If they do not, each emigrant should go back to where he has come from and nothing else.

Arab Brethren!

Muslims!

Believers in other religions!

It may be said that these thoughts are not realistic, but they represent the historical fact as it is, the truth of what the sons of our Arab and Islamic Nation, and probably other, believe in, albeit they do not act accordingly. As it is itself the historical fact whereas anything else is false or sheer falsification of the statement and deformation of the truth and history, we have to state it as it is and act accordingly. But how to put it into effect is another matter.

Yet, at all events, our endeavour should not contradict the premiss and aspiration. As we wish a just peace for all nations of the world, we ought to adhere to a just peace for our Nation regarding its issues and enemies and to reject surrender and all forms of humiliation, submissiveness and looking down at the Arab Nation.

This is the fact of the matter: if overlooked today and if veiled by deception, dismissed from light by an apparition of fright and failed to elevate itself into visibility due to weakness, there will come at any time, as in the past, someone who will tell the truth as we, and many sons of our Nation, are doing now on the basis of these principles and facts and who will act, struggle and fight in jihad for consolidating the truth and accomplishing its objectives.

Therefore, we see that any treatment, which does not target the core, will be partial, if not deformed or contrary to the truth. It will bring malice to the souls and will incite destructive turmoil more than it appeases them to be calm and peaceful. At all events, any call for so-called peace is merely an opportunity for the Zionists not only to gain time for occupying (the rest) of Palestine but also to cause disagreement among the rulers themselves and even between the rulers and people, which is more serious. When this discord is created between all Arab rulers on one hand and the whole glorious Arab Nation, we mean here the overwhelming majority, on the other hand, it becomes perilous, resolvable only by revolution. Thence, we see that it is better for the Arab rulers to accommodate the viewpoints of the other Arab rulers or leaders vis-à-vis their own, and accept a policy different from theirs as regards the fateful issues on which they disagree, among and foremost of which is the question of Palestine. They should be broad-minded, or at least their minds must be open to accommodate the other opinions of their brothers, the Arab rulers or leaders, when they fail to convince the majority of the Arabs, including the sons of our Arab Nation in various countries, to adopt the thoughts and stances concerning the national pan-Arab fateful issues. Only then and by virtue of taking this attitude, they are able to present a ransom for compatibility instead of revolution which will be ignited by the blazing flame of the disregard of the Nation's opinion and the complete contradiction between one stance and another.

Thus, you see, when we speak of the revolution and its historical necessity, we in point of fact describe it as a means of change for the better; we do not call for it out of an arbitrary, demagogic attitude, nor do we mean certain Arab rulers, still nor out of a personal intention in all events, rather we call for it without labelling tokens and with no prior ill-intention, not even for a subjective, personal purpose but as an objective means when all other recourses fail, as a principled commitment and indispensable cauterization, and as a means for change when all other means fall short, as we have said.

So you see, brethren, that what some of those driven by the lashes of the executioners of information and Western and Zionist diplomacy so call dictatorship in Iraq that actually calls in pursuance of this fair account of the people for the respect of dialogue and different opinions. Thence, through a free and coequal dialogue and good intention, we can be rightly guided to a better way in dealing with information, diplomacy and even armies, should the circumstance requires. The accommodation of more than one opinion in the Arab homeland vis-à-vis fundamental or fateful issues without constraints and without the discord which may cause destruction or collaboration with foreigners, and consultation strengthen the Arabs and is even beneficent to those who hold the view which is close to the appearance rather than the essence of the so-called available, peaceful solutions by this or that concerned and with the spirit of this stance, and the allusion to the Zionists and their allies to the so-called extremists and hawks in the confrontation of the humiliating insolence and arrogance rejectable by anyone with a sound mind and will. So you see Arabs that differences in viewpoints is useful.

Brethren Arab rulers! The haste of some of you for the so-called peaceful solutions which are in essence surrendering, has made the Zionists in Palestine, the centre of Zionism, or in other supporting places, disesteem and disdain the Arabs irrespective of what they say or call for. The plethora of relinquishments have caused the Arab Nation not to trust those who patronize this losing approach.

Let it be known to you, Arab brethren, that the public confidence is vital for any ruler or any leader, be it in peace or in war; it is even more compelling in negotiation with a second party than in any other situation. If the negotiator forfeits it, he may have to offer relinquishments not required by the balance of power, let alone countering principles. He may desist from flexibility under the influence of sensitivity to peoples' rejection and distrust of whoever represents them. Hence it is not wise that any of the Nation's sons should forfeit the trust of the People and Nation except, without regret, the despicable traitor albeit what treason brings to a Nation known to be faithful to God, His holy books and messengers, a Nation which has played a leading role in conveying faithfulness, love, peace, justice and fairness to the whole humanity.

Thus, on these premisses we evaluate the statements by exhausted cravers for the threshold of Zionism who entertain hopes of the so-called new prime minister of the Zionist entity and his Western allies. At the time Lebanon is being destroyed, allegedly as an implementation of the resolution by the former Zionist prime minister, none of the Arabs concerned has uttered imprecations on the former prime minister until they have been given a green light from the U.S Black-House. Thereupon, praise and flattery have hailed down on a new Zionist prime minister in the hope of enabling the flatterer to play a new card on a new horse, not knowing that the exchange of roles, faces and names is merely a circumstance needed by Zionism to gain time, involve those led astray in new mazes and leave them all the time in a trend contrary to the trends of their Nation's opinion and will, and by corollary helping Zionism to utilize despair or revolution triggered by people's distrust of the ruler.

God is behind our intention!

Of Him, be gloried, we seek assistance!

Revolt against oppressors!

God is Most Great!

Long live Palestine, free and Arab!

God is Most Great!

Down with Zionism!

Arabs! We said in a previous speech that "Arab oil is for the Arabs" was one of the Ba'athists' banners, which we had raised and fought for it. On the path of Ba'ath struggle in Iraq, many have died martyrs in the cause of this banner since we were students in preparatory and secondary schools. Days went by. Now we are in the position of responsibility which has given us access to information and now we have assumed authority and supervision, we have realized the rightness of our mujahid party when it had attracted attention in early underground struggle to the significance of the Arab oil to be for the Arabs. Now that it has become explicit that it is for the foreigners as it had been, in the 50's and not for the Arabs, is this then possible?

The Arab oil was seized by the foreign companies of the imperialist and colonialist states whether in extraction, industrial treatment, transportation and exportation, in quality and pricing. Virtually its price was not known then as there was no neutral party to purchase or sell it. The industrially developed world was divided into two camps: communist and capitalist. If any neutral state emerged between the two, it was of no importance in determining the international policy, nor was it aware of this policy tricks but for one exception whose limited potentialities began to grow in the 60's and 70's under the banner of non-aligned states. The world, therefore, was either provided with oil needs from the capitalist states and enjoyed some facilities under (foreign aids) or furnished with similar facilities within the socialist camp or whichever politically affiliated to it under the placard of COMECON, which is an economic group comprising the relevant members.

The first time the real value of oil, the range of market demands and its role in the strategic calculations of the states and their endeavour for foreign hegemony or imperialist-colonialist policy was known when Iraq nationalized its oil in 1972, and when nationalization was crowned with success after nine years of boycott imposed by the concessionary companies backed by their governments then, with the exception of France which took no part in it, but accepted special arrangements made by an initiative from Iraq in the era of the de Gaullist president Pompidou. The imperialist states were then put in an embarrassing situation and were obliged to reconsider their concessionary relations with the countries in the third world at a large scale for fear of the blowing winds of nationalization from Iraq where it triumphed, thanks to Iraq's steadfastness and the world's openness to purchase its oil on a competitive basis and price differential temptations granted to crown nationalization with success and due to the balance policy prevalent then in the two blocks to which we have referred.

At present and after the balance of power in the world has retrograded among superpowers which exercise influence and interest extending beyond their boundaries or among those that seek imperialist and colonialist hegemony, oil prices have been developed in an excessive fogginess. USA together with the Western states which share imperialist ambitions has recoursed to the policy of domination over oil from its resources to transportation and selling via the governance of the balance of offer and demand which is met from the U.S available store a at very low prices, as we explicated on previous occasions. But the worst of it is that USA no longer contended with this ugly imperialism and hegemony over oil so much so that it has become politically valueless or without any effective, strategic significance which might enhance its owners' stance. Indeed USA has imposed on them, particularly in the Arab Gulf, the purchase of the commodities and services it deems necessary, be they civil or military, whether in quantities, kinds, prices and payment schedules, by the help of its fleets and occupation forces in the Arab Gulf. USA has not only dominated all this, but it has dispossessed oil rulers in general of any control, influence or freedom of decision over oil which has turned an ordinary commodity and which the Americans fix its price and decide its influential significance in the Arab land and the third world according to certain terms of description and according to other terms of description elsewhere. The Arab rulers concerned and even non-Arabs are now no more than night watchmen performing sometimes their guard-duty or at others being but crippled rear men and experts for guards brought from beyond the borders and the region.

This tragic situation is in need of a serious consultation among the oil states whenever the will and intention exist, albeit it may start on a small scale and not for all OPEC states which have been penetrated by the foreigners' tricks, because this very small scale may be always appropriate for such a consultation to rescue those who evince the will of rejection of such a situation from being victims to the foreigners' cutting fangs, if not possible to save the others whose strength and will have dwindled under the weight of their inadvertence or slumber, their hatred and rancour.

Thus, it is the responsibility of all those who want to be liberated or preserve their freedom.

The people, each in its country, can play a great and historic role in moving the rulers, supporting them, or putting them in a critical situation if unable to push them forward with the rising current.

Arab Brethren!

One of the strategic objectives of July Revolution is socialism beside Arab unity and freedom of Man, intellectually and constructively, psychologically and mentally, theoretically and practically. As the essence of any socialist activity and its humanitarian and political influence centrally lie within the concept of social and economic justice, establishment of balance in society and fortifying it against imbalance in addition to building it and developing its potentials, resources and kinds of wealth, socialism in our viewpoint and as in our national and pan-Arab progarmmes cannot actually be applied in this particular aspect as it should be and in such a manner as to comply with the principles of great Ba'ath unless and until the Arab relations are truly based on its concepts and not on those mere relations that exist among the sons of the one people within its domestic and national borders. Hence, the good which benefits Iraq, for instance, should, since we are one nation, benefit all the sons of our Arab Nation in one way or another: Iraqis, Egyptians, Syrians, Yemenis, people in the Arab Gulf and Maghrib (Northwest Africa), otherwise, the concept of one nation remains inadequate, unable to cherish the principles of the fateful Arab solidarity among the sons of the Nation to stand in one rank in word, in deed and in trend. We have already proposed various projects and thoughts on previous occasions, particularly prior to embargo, and presented projects and proposals for cooperation to Arab summit conferences in addition to certain initiatives concerning bilateral relations known to many sisterly Arab states and their representatives who are still living, and provided with sustenance.

On this occasion, we would like to attract attention to what we see useful to our Nation to grant it strength, capability and support, after relying upon the Great, the Most Capable. Yet one may say, particularly of those privileged with natural wealth, that a call indeed indicates realistic miscalculations and remains a mere slogan if it targets the distribution of wealth among the Arab countries, albeit they are diverse states with no constitutional bond of relationship which legitimatizes such an action, invites enthusiasm of the original owners and grants them some sort of readiness for sacrifice vis-à-vis the elements of power and the kind of opportunity bestowed upon them by the type of unity, under a certain constitutional relationship between one Arab country and another or among the concerned parties when they are under a tent sheltering more than one Arab country.

These thoughts are not proposed now, for we are a living part of reality. We realize its truth and consequences, and we know what is possible or impossible, but we also see that the reality of the Arab economics, social and cultural relations and the pursuant bonds of the

Arab countries with each other represent a backward reality even in achieving its relative objectives which can be formulated so as to be advanced with respect to the present reality and the Arab status quo. Serious attention should be attracted to the description of the possible and the impossible, since these two are relative, and since the presence or absence of will and awareness behind the true intention plays a decisive role in the account and its applications, for what is not possible in one viewpoint that might be equally possible in another, and each viewpoint is in accordance with the pertinent will, awareness and prior intention. We have experienced in Iraq, even under the embargo circumstances, the possibility of economic cooperation based on the memorandum of understanding with various Arab countries and have found it possible. This cooperation has activated the economic markets, enhanced relations and enlivened social thinking, though perhaps not according to the above account at any previous time. So and by giving priority to the Arab-Arab relations in this respect, by word and deed, the Arab markets will become lively, relations will be enhanced, products will grow both quantitatively and qualitatively, and the weight of influence of every Arab market will be in accordance with its capabilities. Too, one of the most important of any Arab country's capabilities, indeed the most fundamental, is people. Thus we shall see after a while that the market which is more developed will contribute to raise the standard of the less developed in everything, and likewise the country with greater population will participate in making its production larger when it ensures a market for its commodities and services. Only then the whole can benefit and all can genuinely cooperate within the tent of the one nation. The expanding and intricate economic relations will be correlated with social and cultural ones, so that their texture becomes a new shield sheltering the heads of the good men from afflictions of time. This tent with its multiple means of protection and expanding space will be also a new haven for the Arab Nation protecting them from heat and cold, otherwise development and progress in most times, various fields and diverse countries become mere words which others may call nonsense under the domination of the big powers on the world markets of raw materials down to the shaving commodities and services. Furthermore, capitalism which was used to propagating (Let work, let pass) as a type of anti-communist propaganda now calls for a different thing, having become vexed over the simplest things, and the U.S administration which has recently exaggerated the nonsensical talk on freedom, now stifles the free flow of goods, commodities, services and persons to their fields, and even tries to dictate on others what to sell, and before it, what to manufacture, which goods and commodities they have to buy, how and how many; what accruements of money they have to deposit, where and how?

A condition like the above renders economic development and progress merely an unattainable wish for many Arabs, if not all, in our greater homeland and even in the third world countries for some time to come. It also makes thick a burden and a major obstacle to development and progress and by corollary to stability, instead of serving as a decisive factor when cooperation in what we have cited is open to the Arabs on the premisses of the sense of one nation, one market and one will. Besides, the hostile powers may employ under-population in the lands isolated from the depth of the Nation and its great potentiality under the apparition of fear and scare as a means of destruction in the wall, depth and soul of the Nation.

What we call for, brethren, represents the minimum as regards the relations within the one nation, and aims at primarily future results more than those pertaining to a short time. In formulating these thoughts, embargo has not played any role; rather, they have been triggered by the principles of the Arab Nation, its great Ba'ath, and our national and humanitarian responsibility towards the sons of our Nation and its role and our humanitarian duty towards humanity at large. Unless the Nation is in a good condition, it is arduous for any of its countries alone to be so, and it is equally hard for itself to be a good example for others to follow who will find it difficult to accept any effective role it might play amidst them or even to be conceived as a model for a better life.

Iraq has evidenced that it is capable of acting as though it were a nation by itself when it summons the spirit and morals of the glorious Arab Nation, of shouldering the responsibility of bearing the message and of reviving the Nation's role on the national and human levels. Hence Iraq, the strong, is not our main concern in these thoughts, but our Nation at large, including Iraq of vanguard and jihad…

God is Most Great!

Perished be the impossible!

Long live mujahids!

Arab brethren! On various occasions and under different addresses: some are formal, some are informal, many pieces of advice have been given to us from Arab brothers concerning our concept of the Arab masses, our prospect of them and our relationship with them. They told us specifically that you hold out too much hope of the Arab masses, and that you, that is we, attach great importance to the masses and think that they have far too much weight than in actuality, all of which necessitate on your part, that is our part in Iraq, a reconsideration, because the Arab and other masses are either absent or absented from taking an effective stance in confronting events, developments and attitudes in the Arab homeland and elsewhere beside being dispossessed of their will and thus incapable of bringing about any change, etc.

I should like therefore to answer them, partly esteeming their opinion and giving a true assessment of the Arab masses as a phenomenon, a stance and an influence, and partly correcting an aspect of the mistake in those Arabs' advice. The major mistake, however, is that they thought that our appeal to the Arab masses to be aware of their role and realize their capabilities so as to appraise their influence in space, time and direction has been hastily made to take a certain stance. Most probably, those Arabs have gone too far in thinking that we hasten the masses for the purpose of lifting the embargo and that we think that these masses are capable of halting an offensive by the aggressors. Accordingly and being hasty, that appeal may seem to them merely circumstantial in both description and relationship to us.

Brethren! Our prospect of the people's role, its revolutionary masses and its comprehensive, long-term strategy springs from our doctrine which deems the people a sufficiency to our struggle, fight, jihad and construction, and a historical means intrinsic in all the principles and morals we aspire after in the course of the victorious Revolution and its objectives, and not merely an unspecified, temporary means.

Our rapport with the masses is totally different from what some brothers think. As a corollary of the requisites of the legitimate struggle to which we appeal to the Arab masses including the requisite of awareness of their historic role in the battle we fight against oppressors, we do not dismiss in course and ardour, that the masses should defend, to a certain extent or in one manner or another, the Revolution and its right course, which, pursuant to what we have said in this speech as on other occasions, is their revolution too. The sacrifices offered along its course are not only for the sake of Iraq, but also for the sake of our glorious Arab Nation as long as the Revolution remains national and for the whole Nation as it is for Iraq, as it is for humanity in general. The Revolution has proved by word and deed that the above account is genuine, not an allegation, and has been tested by precious blood in the most complicated circumstances.

We look at the Arab and other masses and their role in a historical perspective which is comprehensive but not temporary, not isolated nor circumstantial, principled and disinterested, continual not sporadic, constant not temperamental. Our prospective has never changed whether the Arab masses have acted in accordance with the level of their role in this or that cause or otherwise when their action or influence are below the level of their real capabilities. Indeed, we more adhere to our role and to our national and moral responsibility towards the Nation and its masses when they are weak; and conversely feel happy and rejoice when they promote their awareness and principles to a higher level. Truly, our moral and principled commitment has never changed nor has our hope retreated from its orbit.

Our Nation is not only known for its civilization and humanitarian role, but also as a nation of prophets and messengers from which God had chosen them and selected it to be a cradle and historical depth for them and for their role as well as a scene of action and holy fight, jihad. Consequently, the Nation shall not be held responsible for any negative account stated, attributed or accordingly described both as a historical formation and a historical force capable of playing its role when the Nation is revived. Others perhaps within the tokens of the Nation's items shall be. Definitely they are not within the live historical texture to which the role they have ascribed for themselves is applicable.

Anyone who describes the Nation in negative terms, be he a journalist, a writer or a man of letters, should, before uttering imprecations upon the public or reminding it or his nation of what is negative, ask himself what he has offered as a person in an advanced position. If his reply is that he is apprehensive for the means of subsistence, for himself, his position, title or chair, or is unable to offer more, the responsibility rests squarely on him and not on the people or nation, because those in prominent posts alone bear the burden and responsibility of any defectiveness or weakness which afflict the Nation, people or a collective part, but not conversely the collective part, people or Nation that should be responsible.

Is it right, for instance and for the sake of approximating the image, that the officers should run away from the battle and simultaneously blame the soldiers for defeat? Nevertheless, the officers have enjoyed commandership as well as giving orders and have exercised them on the soldiers, they have even relished and boasted of the military ranks they have and their privileges in all the circumstances prior to defeat. He who enjoys the material and moral privileges of his post should shoulder the responsibility for any weakness in the people's ranks before such a responsibility should rest on a certain, collective part of those ranks. This, therefore, applies to those who cherish a thought opposite to ours, be they rulers, judges, writers, journalists, men of letters, professors and so on and so forth.

We deal with our Nation and People as a historical capability and as a historical formation on the strength of what is possible when other factors exist, so as their role will be great, but not on the basis of an inane description of a situation in the time of the account without depthe role which revolutionizes and sets it in motion, likewise we have delineated the requisites and our genuine role.

Our dealing with the People and Nation is carried out on the basis of a very accurate, humanitarian, revolutionary and principled account of our responsibility towards them, and on the strength of the common action and effect and reciprocal influence, but not on the basis of loneliness, isolation and abandonment. We are a live part in the Nation and People in order to perform our national and pan-Arab role and duty towards them, and indeed towards humanity. We do not presume that our People and our Nation are two piecework contractors who would relieve us of the duty of executing a certain affair so that all we have to do is to wait and receive the keys of an accomplished project. With both, we construct and take the risk of construction just as we share happiness and delight when the construction is completed within its relative utmost. Too, we all defend the construction when it is exposed to danger.

We are a family of one house, and as long as we bear the epithet of leadership, we have the responsibility of initiation, enlightenment and creation of awareness, beside a higher degree of good patience and endurability, so as to be an example worthy of respect and appreciation. We realize the significance of the morals we hold and our trueness to them. Surely we shall be victorious by the people and by the leadership of all prominent titles in our Nation: rulers or faithful leaders, or the heedful educated, self-sacrificers, mujahids and the steadfast of the People and Nation, men or women, civil or military, judges or university professors, artists, journalists, writers, great engineers or others. The young men and women of the Nation will be a tremendous enlightened force in all this. We do not grow date-palms or oranges, nor oats or barley. Thus our patience knows no limits, except when ordained by God, glory be to Him, in Whom we trust and unto Whom we turn.

Brethren who raise queries: such has been our commitment, thinking and our prospect of affairs at the starting point. Yet the experience, which has been replete with the morals of construction and ardour in our fight against the unjust and injustice, the despots and despotism for more than thirty years during which we have lead the great people of Iraq within the Ba'ath responsible, collective leadership, has taught us scientific, practical and social lessons as regards the People and its role with respect top the Nation's vitality as a base and a practical, spiritual and moral profundity, the basis of which is the human morals with which we interact and share our Nation and people.

Like you, we realize that the Nation and People may slug or neglect playing a certain role or roles, but they can never be inadvertent, sluggish or defeated for the whole time, indeed they cannot be negligent, slothful, indolent or defeated if they have a genuine leadership appropriate in mind, conscience, intellect and sword beside other conditions which are prerequisites to their tasks. They cannot be put to fight or neglect except when their leadership is put to rout, is indolent or treasonable. Hence the People and the Nation cannot be held responsible for any shortcoming even when they recoil from playing a role by which they are supposed to advance. Rather the leading, key posts shall be responsible. We have not seen or heard of a people under a leadership whose role has met all principled, moral and practical requisites at reasonable utmost has ever been defeated, sluggish or lazy and has left the leadership alone to bare upper arms in construction. Too, we have not seen or heard of a leader who has the minimal requisites of leadership, has acted soundly and has unsheathed his sword without having simultaneously heard the clatter of the swords of those who fight at his right, at his left, in front and behind, having caused the ears of those nearby tingled when those swords have been drawn of their sheaths aiming at the covetous, despot, occupant or oppressor.

Yet no blame should lie on a people or a nation if it neglects its role in construction when the leader or leaders do not call for construction except at the time their pockets or accounts in the banks grow less than the minimum and hence have to be filled under the token of construction, whereby the slogan of construction and the appeal to it will be but a trickery.

Likewise, no blame should lie on the people, nation, masses and armies when they see those designated with leading titles are whiling away their time, busying themselves in such affairs which are of no concern to the masses, and that they betray them to the foreigners, in which case their call against the foreigners who have ill-intentions and bad-deeds will be no more than a trick-cover.

The masses, like any living being, do not act unless fed, and their essential food to support the ruler or leader is their unmistakable feeling that the leader or ruler has given his life for their cause, pride, glory and welfare. Only then the masses will forgive and indulge the lapses and faults which do not involve relinquishment, treason or prior ill intention. Furthermore, one of the most significant, historical duties towards the nation and people is either to back the one who presides over a leading post and dignify him or else to utter a resounding pronouncement of what is right to attract attention to a deviation or an unusual commission. If he does not retreat, he will have nothing before him save cauterization, i.e., revolution, which will substitute what is bad for good lest the masses' aspirations should be buried alive and their forward movement should be hampered.

When we address the masses and the Arab masses in particular, we do not do so because we deem them a practical substitute from now on for any Arab ruler performing his national duty albeit it is not as perfect as it should be, but as a rear support for any national case and its great profundity together with other tokens including the cases of some rulers as described in accordance with what we have referred to. But the ruler, any ruler, is on his way to vanish, whereas the people and nation are the historical forces that can never disappear even though they might be enveloped in lunar or solar eclipse. In them both, the sun rises from the east, and the moon is full in its due day. Those who never vanish, like the nation and people, are the ones with great acts and stances, which represent the essence of the Nation's conscience and its living mind. Among those who are concealed from the vision and the tangible feel of the masses, albeit they are living and sustained, are the ones who have assumed, at an undated time, a prominent responsibility yet they do not comprehend its significance nor are they trustworthy for it and its honour.

In pursuance with this description, they are merely lifeless carcasses though they are living.

God is Most Great!

Gallant Iraqis, who are a source of joy and delight for your leadership, but a malady for the enemies, who are salubrious to great Iraq, but arrows set at the foes of God and humanity

Praiseworthy, magnificent women whose ardour we call together with the sublime morals when mishaps intensify, when we honour someone highly and preciously and when the soul's great morals are summoned

The fragrance of Iraq and sweet smelling of its battle trenches.

Peace be upon you, and God's mercy and blessings.

Your presence has been brilliant, with all the significance of the model and example, which you represent in every part of the present speech and in what we have been talking about to the Arabs since you constitute with them the sons of one nation and because you have realized from gesture or wink what must and ought to be, what is acceptable or rejectable after this long time of relationship and attitude.

Because we do not defer any act or statement which is of importance, waiting for what to say or act on occasions only, albeit everything has its circumstance and due time to be said and acted, God willing, we have not found it necessnor do we want to burden you with a long speech, reiterating what we have already said or done, what we did in the years past or intend to do in a new year which will come into view with goodness and delight for all of us and our Nation. Thus I find it sufficient to greet you and the revolutionary men and hail your great steadfastness, your high inventiveness for creating an example of life which will enter, for the first time and in accordance with its usual context, the history and action of the Arabs in the present age.

Because we trust in God, our confidence is great in His capability to strengthen your victory as it is already evinced and witnessed without any shade, and to be incessant, God willing, without interruption.

I implore God to bestow upon you more pride, glory, health and well-being, to perpetuate the grace of faith and patience and to rejoice you with whatever delights the soul and brings comfort to it.

Long live our glorious Arab Nation!

Long live Iraq!

Long live Iraq!

Long live Palestine, free and Arab!

God is Most Great!

God is Most Great!

Shame be on the despicable!

Address Of His Excellency President Saddam Hussein in August 8, 1999.

In the Name of God, Most Compassionate, Most Merciful

Great People!

The Valiant of Our Brave Armed Forces!

Sons of our Glorious Arab Nation!

Friends!

As Man is part of his family and social environment in thinking, natural disposition and habits, any phase of people's development likewise constitutes part of their history temperament and customs. Albeit nations and peoples have some sort of common traits, which can be summed up and accessed, each of them has other different characteristics. They take their colours, tokens, level and profundity of influence upon oneself or upon others in the light of the disparity and kind of traits of each people and each nation, their different roles and the kind and level of development with respect to the starting-point of humanity, or the description within the context of its phase. The broader the account and distance between one nation and another is, the more strongly varied and distant are the points of separation.

Leaders and the kind of the part and task or tasks they perform play a decisive role in crystallizing the special traits, level, direction, type of action and influence. On the premise of this account, the level of humaneness or hostility of peoples and nations as well as the level of acceptability of the merits and demerits are affected by the background of these traits and the kind and rank of their historical models in the light of the description of the special trait in both field and occasion...Hence we can recourse to the interpretations of historical phenomena and many periods or even the main trends in the history of peoples and nations, among which are our people and our nation. Therefore, we go back to the past, which is relevant in one way or another to the present speech, and ask, for instance:

Why was Baghdad destroyed in 1258 A.D? Why was Babylon destroyed in 539 B.C? Yet man's spirit in both could not be totally destroyed, nor was the hope for revival anew given up...Why had Baghdad's slumber lasted for eight centuries? Why has Baghdad woken once more, yet has not stooped, twisted, ceased or bargained?

Should we answer in detail, relying upon the special traits of our people and the one who had incurred harm to it, we would find a convincing reply beside circumstantial factors. We would see that these traits explain to us the essence of the positive points being fairly recorded for our people and for whoever has caused harm to it in the past or still doing so, whenever the traits which are in common with the past generation yet associated with its history and people are summoned, or on the occasion of the Great Victory Day in which we are delivering our speech, albeit the difference in time between past and present.

Babylon, Baghdad, Assur, Nineveh, Hatra and Ur were not neutral, in a middle distance between the foot of the mountain and the summit. Thus, when they behold the summit, firmly convinced of the truthfulness and honesty, in addition to other usual requisites, of the leaders, they run fast to it, and occupy it, so they become the uppermost light-house in the surrounding, its radiance is visible at long distances, so that many people would be lit and guided, lest they should stray. Driven by jealousy, envy, feeling of disability and demerits into frantic commotion triggered by the instinct for aggression and destruction, others have sought to sit on ruins, misconceiving them as an upper-most summit. Similarly, selfishness dictates one possibility of taking one general, common direction to interests, which are incompatible with those of another summit and of another description, and by cor-ollary a clash would occur. Conversely, climbing up the summit by means of endeavour and sublime morals is recurrent in the history of Iraq and the Arab Nation, indeed, it is quite appropriate for the Nation and Iraq. When both reach the summit, they often stay there for such a time as to be seen or heard by all, near and far. Due to their own traits, they do not hastily roll down the face of the summit, unlike other peo-ples and nations. Likewise, owing to the profundity and level of the capability and wisdom of their leaders' minds and consciences beside a true love of the significance and course of construction, the removal of such leaders from the summit cannot be brought about except by a col-lision which would unexpectedly take them by surprise at any period in which they become inadvertent or preoccupied with unnecessary mat-ters or fall into miscalculation. Hence, we can expound the reason when Baghdad's eyes are closed, all Arabs' eyes are closed too, and why when it wakes up once more, the sword would be associated with the pen, both being based on wisdom, yet each forming a flank founded on the great morals of civilization and the eternal heritage of our Nation where giant falcons fly to protect the sky and land of Iraq so that Bagh-dad should proceed with its course to the summit armed with the prin-ciples of construction and advancement, and holding the sword to defend the sublime morals. In all this Baghdad expresses the genius of the Nation and People under the protection of the message of the faithful nationalism and immortal humanity. Thence Baghdad has emitted radiance that conveys the morals and illuminates the way with beams reaching all parts of the world under the care and protection of the Most Compassionate. The sword has become a flagpole for the pen, the latter a guide to the morals of construction and faith, a solid base for the former and a streaming banner to enlighten many dark spots of humanity with its great concepts. No wonder then some have dogfought against Baghdad with hatred and envy and have employed forces, some of which are backward for destruction while others have used their accumulation of malice and narrow, greedy interests to portray to the backward of their kind that their destructive approach is right. And as the Mongols and Tatars had burned books of science and knowledge, murdered the scientists in Baghdad and wasted the Nation's opportunity for a long time, some of the backward too pushed by their destructive force and backsided by their evil intents have thought that they are capable of killing men of knowledge and tokens of pen, wisdom, sword and banner in Baghdad, which is rising higher and for the better. Hopeless indeed will be their presumptions, and surely evil are the things they have been doing.

Brothers!

We do not want in what we have said or in what we shall explicate on this particular occasion or on another and on these topics or others to call to memory the mere factors of separation, nor do we like to scrape the scab of the wound which is still wide open; rather we have endeavoured and are still endeavouring to put the facts in their correct, social, historical and faith content and within their scientific context. We would assist others to be guided for what is good as part of our patriotic and national responsibility based on faith, indeed our responsibility and humane relationship whether with Iran or with other nations, out of our constant desire and determination for assistance and initiation so as to build bridges of love and peace, whenever possible or whenever there is a balanced and appropriate opportunity. Thus we state too:

When the ruler discovers in himself or in his people a potential energy that can be utilized but he does not possess the faculty of conceiving the better among which the qualifications for construction and rendering the good, he often exploits it in a manner contrary to the good, love, fairness or construction. A destructive potentiality is consequently produced concerning relations with other nations and peoples, specially the neighbouring ones. Therefore, being busy with construction, values and sublime principles together with a balanced view of the social, economic and cultural life is a strong indication of the ruler's or leader's utilization of the potential energy in himself and his intellect, and in the spirit and intellect of his people and nation, and in a civilized and humane direction based on his love for the good instead of evil, construction insof destruction and aggression. Unfortunately Iranian rulers, particularly the predecessors, and the like up to now, have not occupied themselves with construction nor have they cultivated love and good. Hence, their slogans at the end of Shah's era have been arrogant, aggressive, expansionist albeit they assume the shape of Islamic promulgation. By corollary, the aggression took place and the war broke out.

All this in addition to the authentic records of history may also expound how and why the Elamite Persian King Schuturk-Nachonettihad stolen the renowned Code of the Iraqi King, Hammurabi, and how he attempted to erase Hammurabi's name beneath these laws out of envy and hatred of that great Iraqi king and in pursuit of a remedy for the illness of mind and soul which that Elamite had inherited from his fathers. So, having carried out a destructive operation in Iraq, that Persian King had stolen an aspect of Iraq's cultural and legal history and civilization instead of creating a flourishing civilization, for his own traits had incapacitated him for ascent. Instead he sank low in compatibility with his characteristics and tendencies. Likewise, why and how had the Persian King, Korsch, destroyed Babylon, nearly six centuries later, that is considered the first and most radiant and most influential human civilization then, assisted by the leprosy that had infected the body of Babylon at that time, i.e., the Jews who had been brought captives to it by King Nebuchadnezzar?

Driven by his destructive instinct, envy and hatred, King Korsch had demolished Babylon, not as an expression of insightful capability, but as a blind, foolish disability, thinking by so doing he had treated his complexity externalized by weakness or lack of awareness or by incapability for ascending the right, humanitarian path. He had transferred his hereditary illness to others who would bear it up to the time, as God permit, the hearts, consciences and breasts of those surprised by darkness will be enlightened. By the will of God, glory be to Him, Baghdad shall remain, just as it has always been, inaccessible to the enemies and guarded by pride and by heedful might, true to humane principles. Its gates shall never be open except to the peoples seeking good relations and friendship and to the good faithful, God willing.

Accordingly, peoples with a deeply rooted role in civilization are not the same as those with an insignificant one. By the same token, peoples in whose life, history and tasks the humane aspect plays a great and decisive role in adopting a call or calls for the good and conveying a message or messages in compatibility with the level and kind of the relevant models in the course for the betterment of humanity and sublime morals are not the same as those peoples whose main history is confined to a narrow, limited, selfish and local role. The difference which has also a profound, influential significance in this or that people is between whether the overwhelming probability of playing the role is attributed to material factors and considerations, life items within their own phase or other factors and attributes and whether their stimulating or reminding models of the role are only models for destruction, causing injury to other peoples and nations, transgressing the right deeply into falsehood vis-à-vis other models that summon the good, love, altruism, the great humanistic role and the endeavour for right and justice.

One of the variables influencing the kind and orientation of rulers and peoples in general is: Does what is within their countries suffice them, desist them and distract them from enmity and aggression? Or are they in want of it, especially when they are not rightly guided to the way of increasing potentialities and life items instead of another way, factors and right humane reasons for the significance of man's creation by God? Thus we have found the neighbouring barren hills had been rolled down to fertile, sedimentary plains by some who were evil, armed and aggressive and also by others who sought easy living after a hardship. Manifestly, the radiance of the Rafidain plain has formed a column of immense radiant light illuminating the surrounding as well as the remote distances whenever its strength has escalated to its due level.

As every man has energy, feelings and thinking, nations too have their energy, feelings and thinking. The results, their kind and level depend on the direction in which the energy, feelings and thinking are oriented. Here, leaders play their role and shoulder their decisive responsibility in determining results in the light of selecting objectives and manner. If they release potentialities and their traits in the direction of destruction and evil, they will reap what is relevant to both, for this is the very road that descends low though it might appear easier or the only one. The destruction and evil instinct would be employed when the mind fails to grasp its wide field, the justifications of the great principles and the interdictions of the sublime morals code. Indeed, the failure of a lofty imagination causes energy to slope downward to where it collides with the lowland. One of the most perilous matters is that those of this kind of fancy and its course misconstrue that they score triumph even when the have been wrecked by the acceleration of their lowermost decline of energy; they are unable to imagine the ascending paths and thus are drifted towards the slope, as we have just mentioned. But if they direct their energy towards the good and its accesses, they will reap what is relevant to both too.

On the premise of these morals and the level of the summoned models relevant to the two ranks or opposing ranks, the different throngs can take one direction, or else contradict and collide with each other. On account of the principles and morals we stated in our last 17 July speech, we can expound one aspect of the conflict that broke out in the glorious Qadissiya battle, after a series of offensives in which the Iranian officials concerned had released evil and depleted the potential energy of emotions which the revolution against Shah of Iran had liberated and released from its bulging long-necked bottle.

Iranian peoples had not then waged a war for a long time and had faced all sorts of humiliation, coercion and hunger under that regime. So they sought another way for self-assurance. The new Iranian officials concerned have triggered or released that energy into the wrong, destructive direction, now being deprived of its humane and spiritual principles in the simplest terms of description, albeit it had merely assumed a formal, flimsy and verbal cover from the spiritual standpoint, as we have said. It had made its spirit and morals targets at which destructive weapons and energy are aimed. Great Iraq, however, has repelled it with a breast full of faith and with a balanced prospect of life, endeavour and responsibility. Such were the happenings: victory has thus been ascertained within and without the soul of Iraqis at the starting point and likewise in the ultimate result and as a natural outcome of this kind of conflict.

For more confirmations of that account of the two parties in conflict each according to its worth, we cite certain examples from a huge amount and enormous heap. Iraq, for instance, released all Iranian prisoners of war (POWs) a short time after ceasefire, except one POW who was later set free just as we stated in our speech on the same occasion last year. We have released them, guided by the principles which we believe in and relying on the great profundity of the morals of the True Islamic Religion and the principles of the glorious July Revolution. All the time in the cages of captivity, Iranian POWs had been in contact with International Red Cross; they have enjoyed all the POW's rights in accordance with their proper context. Conversely, Iran, up to now, has retained thousands of Iraqi POWs, and has even refused to register some of them at the Red Cross. Our heroes of POWs have received and are still receiving various kinds of torture and pressure, many a time thehave been murdered inside the captivity cages, for no reason except they respect their humaneness, patriotism and the principles of their nation. They do not betray or do evil to their country or people; they do not speak ill of their symbols and principles. Therefore, Iran's conduct is unprecedented. Thus we have only to search for a certain aspect of history so as to be rightly guided to its causes and accurate description and to say that any account of this conduct lies squarely within a description contrary to that of the people of Iraq, its system, principles, leaderships and their morals. Because each token of the two countries, Iraq and Iran, has now had an explicit description, action, policy and course after such a long period of governance and conflict, any one, near or far including the Iranian peoples can be assigned a special description for each as well as the pros and cons of each.

The second example is that Iraq had deposited civil and war planes in Iran, some of them prior to the encounter with the thirty states in Umm al-Ma'arik (The Mother of All Battles), others during the battle, for we misconceived that the Iranians concerned might share a common property with humanity and wend the way of the good on the account that Iran is no longer an enemy of Iraq. God had made us triumphant over the evil rank on August 8, 1988. Fighting had then ceased through the two parties' agreement. Based on what was suggested by our memory of the Iranian officials' slogans in the past era and present, among which the slogan we recalled concerning USA which they called then the Great Satan, we thought, wrongly, that there was some possibility of a minimal adherence to those slogans, because we did not imagine that whosoever, especially those who claim that Islam is their religion, could express differently from what they concealed and could abandon overnight their slogans and even coun-teract them, particularly the battle was between Iraq under the protec-tion of the Most Compassionate on one hand, and what they have labelled then "the Great Satan", i.e., USA, and its ally Zionism and their allies or those siding with them on the other.

These two examples, brothers, are of many others which occupy vol-umes on the party opposite to Iraq. They also unveil some of the mor-als of the two direct parties of the conflict whose consequences cannot be expounded except by recoursing to what we have stated and what we are saying in our speech today and to the profundity of July speech which we delivered last month on the occasion of the glorious Revolu-tion Day in addition to the facts that have emerged from two neigh-bouring marches and two experiments separated only by geographical boundaries. Indeed, the Iranian officials pushed their peoples and kin-dled in them all elements of repression and energy which had not been rightly employed with the Arabs in general. So they collided with the Nation's great insurmountable dam and well-fortified citadel on the eastern front, Great Iraq.

Despite all reiterative calls, before and after the encounter, for delibera-tion and detachment from the motives and spots of evil and despite all appeals for peace released by Iraq from the highest and various levels, the slogans, drums and guns of aggression and war had persisted beside the slogans of hopeless, greedy ambitions which were all defeated. The slogans of invasion and its premeditated and preplanned intents were also frustrated. Right had triumphed over falsehood; it was a victory for the sublime morals of humanity at large, including those Iranian peo-ples that believe in an anti-aggression course of policy.

Thus, brothers, the sword and pen…or the arm and wisdom of mind are two parallel counterparts in a balanced action in the history of Iraq and the Nation and their immortal heritage. They have also been in equilibrium in this conflict. So we did not gloat at mishaps or act perfidiously when fighting came to a halt, because our wisdom dictates that the sword should not be a substitute for the pen, nor should the arm replace argument, conviction and interaction. It does not live on land without a sky nor does it manipulate weakness by clutching verbally to heavenly morals, which have no faith or solid ground. It does not hesitate to use the sword when it turns to be an inevitable way to validate an argument and when the mind fails to convince the one who is guilty of falsehood not to commit an offense of aggression by falsifying his stance.

God is most great!

On this premise and its morals, we call back to mind the day of the great victory when God has rendered us triumphant in a capable and powerful manner on August 8, 1988 in the second glorious Qadissiya. The victory, its preludes and the concomitant delivery in addition to what we have stated help us understand why embargo on Iraq has lasted for more than nine years now; why the states bordering Iraq, including Iran, have performed the task of field embargo in such a manner as to covetously encourage and support the aggressive Americans and Zionists to continue committing genocide against the Iraqi people by hook or by crook, and why the Iranian peoples have been refrained from visiting the holy shrines albeit they were incited for intrusion into Iraq by force. That might have suggested then contrary to reality it was as though Iraq were preventing the Iranian peoples from visiting the holy shrines so as to act as a cover for the slogans of expansion and aggressivity, which reveals too the reason behind Iran's collaboration with U.S intelligence, Zionism and their supporters in the occupation of Sulaimania in northern Iraq following the 30-state aggression against Iraq in addition to other known examples of hostility such as Iranian air raids on Iraqi targets deep inside Iraq as well as missile attacks for the same purpose. Indeed these examples of aggression and aggressivity help imagine the offensive against Iraq that took place in 1980. By corollary, the answer will be explicit to the question:

Do the disclosure of falseness and humbug and the revelation of the right and truth not render a good service to humanity and not only to Iraq or the Arab Nation? It has also become clearer and clearer how and why the day of the great victory, August 8, 1988 is worthy of celebration and rejoice by us, the Iraqi people, the Nation and all good and peace loving peoples. It deserves to be called back to mind all the time as a wonderful, humane outcome albeit all happenings.

By God, indeed, it is an eternal, humane day; and everything, which is dissociated with or contrary to it, is hopeless and cursed.

It is truly a great day that God has wanted it to be an evidence, a token and a banner.

God is most great!

Long live Iraq!

Long live our glorious Arab Nation as a humane example, radiant with love, good, sublime models and a great capability!

Long live the friendship of our people and our Nation with the neighbouring peoples and all the peoples of the world!

Fie on the aggressors' hostility!

Shame on the despicable!

Brothers! Nations and peoples are the brainchildren of their particular and general history. Despite the existing linkage, in one way or another, between the staring point and the final, or any representation in the development of peoples and nations, any phase in history, qualitatively or situationally, cannot be a replica of the one or many representations antecedent in development. This is not only because time phases are phases of development, or such they ought to be, but because one major aspect of the portraits of history within its rising or falling decades represents those of leaderships in one form or another. Therefore, we can say that history pillars are either general or particular. The general represents a description, action, trait and influence of the collective state formed historically as a general characteristic of the people and nation. It is also a description, action, property and influence of the particular state of those who lead the people and nation, within their phase. The deeper the conviction and the more profound and serious the interaction on a wides between the leaders of the people and nation on one hand, and the people and nation on the other, the closer the general; viz., the leader or leaders. The differences between the general and the particular become merely those of their relative phase, that is, differences of historical development between one phase and another with the concomitant consequences of the transferred customs. The phase becomes as though it were, in one way or another, the general traits of the leader or leaders in addition to all that had passed down or desired to be connected with the traits and customs of the previous historical phases.

Hence, it has become manifest to us how and why a leader leading other leaders can transform a nation or people in morals and reality into a state of great ascent, upward and downward, when the leader or leaders are congruent with their peoples through sublime humane principles. Likewise, a ruler and other rulers can turn a nation and a people into a state of retreat, implicitly, from its opportunity and role after they have distanced themselves from their people and nation. They become unable of activating the capabilities of the people and nation at the level of what ought to be and must due to the ruler's feeble influence, deviated treatment of affairs or to his weakness of polarizing them to the right course. Thus we comprehend now why and how the happenings took place in the two Islamic states concerning their proclamations or beliefs and between two subjects described as Islamic states, namely, Iraq and Iran.

The religious description, brothers, applied to nations and peoples whether these peoples are of Islamic doctrine or affiliated to it or under a description and tokens of other religions, cannot annul the history of the nation before and after conviction or affiliation, nor abolish the influence of their general history when it opposes or contradicts the new doctrine which is in the light of broad promulgation, level of commitment and profundity of its effect, introduces new morals into the history of nations. It can even bring in entire historical phases stamped with the new principles or their essence in accordance with the level of faith of the leader or leaders in these nations of the new doctrine, and not only the peoples in addition to their readiness to consider its fundamentals a basis of their thinking, action and moralities.

Hence, if the requirement of genuine association with the collective state of the public and the elite of the people and nation, more specifically with the ruler or rulers of the new religion, to position themselves in fancy and reality in accordance with its standards and to act ethically, is not met, then the history of the nation in the final outcome would cease to persist and to interactively serve as a link between old and new. The new religion becomes merely formal and general, as a placard for propaganda, and not for commitment and genuine interaction. Here, the description depends on the congruence or discrepancy between the collective state of the nation and the particular one of the ruler or rulers in this respect.

Brothers!

Iran was within the Islamic State, led by the Arabs in general who were for some time its leaders, rulers or guides. After that, there emerged local rulers, leaders or assistants to others in Iran from the very peoples who did not entertain anything good for the central authority in the Islamic State. They publicized that they were worthy of a better treatment, frequently evaluating and deeming their worthiness on the basis of Iran in the past under the leadership of Persians and Khosraus who had occupied parts of the neighbouring countries, be they to the east or the west, and not on the basis of their fusion in the new state under the banner of its faith and principles, and under its leadership in pursuance of the explicit Islamic principle in governance and administration, i.e., "And obey God, and obey the messenger and those charged with authority among you." Instead, they often dissociated it from its context, rendered it inoperative or attempted to interpret it incompatibly with the Pure Prophetic Tradition or the consensus of the Islamic nation. Sometimes, they had given a narrow sense to "those charged with authority among you" so as to confine it to the governor of the province at that moment instead of the Caliph or the Commander of the Faithful "Amir al-Mu'mineen" for the purpose of facilitating the task of the provincial governor in Iran and disputing with the Commander of the Faithful or the Caliph or rebelling against them.

This situation had found its other level in Iran in the light of abolishing the fundamental periods in the history of the Islamic State as well as the greatest part of its representative symbols. It is now restricted to certain bright periods yet dissociated from its foundation and the context of continuity and profundity. They had been put in a frame of contrariness that accepts no compatibility or interaction with all other great bright periods. The Iranians concerned had given an opportunity to all these notions and the situation to incessantly perpetuate the history of Khosraus in Iran without taking into consideration the history of the Islamic State. Thus they were severed from this profound history and the jurisprudence (fiqh) of the State, the better of which cannot be perceived then except by considering the development nowadays, because it had been matured and developed at that time by the Islamic State.

In Iran, a new jurisprudence has been encouraged since long time ago to grow not on the basis of an independent judgment ijtihad which is right, indeed it is a duty as well, to deal with a certain case, circumstances and by-products of the development within its successive phases, but on the basis of a new birth dissociated from its profundity and lineage. For about eight hundred years, the link has been severed from the point of birth and its subsequent development and from the whole jurisprudence and legislations of the Islamic State at the period of the Rashidi (Rightly Guided) Caliphs and from the history and representative symbols of the State, its banners and jihad, and by so doing the Iranians offered an opportunity for the Iranian history, in pursuance of a certain conception, to perpetuate without disruption and for a new jurisprudence detached from the profound jurisprudence of the Islamic State and symbols including the sons and grandsons of Caliph Ali (May God be pleased with him). Some people were fought or dismissed from the course of linkage on account of their stances or even their names. A case in point is that names like Abu Bakr, Omer and Uthman were excluded from the lineage of descendents of Ali and Al-Hussein (May God be pleased with them) except for some selections according to a particular purpose or purposes from the jurisprudence of Caliph Ali (PBUH), most often cited or intentionally wedged into a certain frame for a certain object or objects or at least according to a formula which was intended to appear as if it were in contrariety rather than conformity with the jurisprudence of the Islamic State and its history.

At all events and no matter how bright the periods are within the whole course and its genuine origin, their ember often fades when separated from its source, their influence wanes like a fragrance of a sweet-smelling perfume which vaporizes when it is no longer confined in its flask or when the glow of a kindling live-coal faints as it is detached from its brazier.

The description given above concerning the conduct of the Iranians concerned towards the Islamic history had encouraged Shah of Iran to celebrate and rejoice the 2500th anniversary of the Persian State, transgressing Iran's history within the Islamic State and taking no consideration of the Iranian peoples' stance or even the elite then. It is the same account behind the Iranian rulers who, when the great principles of True Islam were absent or absented, sought to destroy Baghdad in 1980 and to occupy Iraq, just as Krosch had destroyed Babylon in collaboration with the Jews in 539 B.C.

What we have stated expounds why Iranian students are not taught the history of the Islamic State. Why do even the religious schools there not teach the history of the Islamic State and its jurisprudence at the time Iran was part of it? By corollary, how and why did Iran launch aggression against Iraq? The war subsequently broke out and lasted for eight years. From these considerations we can arrive at an explanation for the reason behind the offensive triggered by anti-Iraq leaders, for the continuation of the war for eight years and the failure of all efforts including those exerted by the Islamic Conference Organization and its Committee formed to stop the war and bring about peace between Iraq and Iran at that time. The war had ceased only when God has ordained so in the battlefields. He has bestowed victory upon the faithful who have a history rooted to its base of great faith and associated with the virtuous models and symbols as an inseparable whole. It is a triumph over those who have endeavoured to make Iran's history dissociated from the sources of perpetuity of the Islamic history and have dismissed the elements and virtues of love to be replaced by hatred which has been wedged by their own manner and thus distanced them from the stream of the principles of great Islam to continue uncleansed by the water of its upright principles.

Therefore, we can explain why and how the US administrations which claim association with the principles of Jesus Christ (PBUH) have allied with the abominable Zionism, the aggressor upon the land and the rights of the Arabs and Palestinians and have supported the Zionists to murder women, elderly men, children, indeed the whole people in Palestine, the cradle of Jesus Christ (PBUH), and other Arab parts too. Why and how do US administrations ally with some countries to kill and cause famine to the Iraqi people and destroy its cultural structures and even archaeological monuments?

Hence we can say how in every period following destruction and stagnation Baghdad, and indeed the whole Arab and Islamic nation in general with few familiar, relative exceptions, seemed as though it had been as frozen as it were in the previous period in all walks of life and in all domains including socials relations then. For about eight centuries, development had come to a halt, in fact it had receded incessantly in another direction because the foreign Ottoman ruler, albeit his claims of ruling in the name of Islam, was in reality running the State through a narrow prospect relevant merely to the legacy, apprehensions and aspirations of his nation and people. He had neglected the Arab Nation as a nation of morals, holding a sword and a banner, of great leading cadre of faith and its banners, of construction and other sublime morals and as an authentic reference to interpret Islamic principles and whatever is relevant to them and to offer words of advice for selecting one or more appropriate approaches. That ruler had overlooked the history of the Islamic State and its great models. If a reference was made to a certain aspect of its heritage, it was treated separately, selectively and formally to, on the basis of the ruler's liking of this account and not as a faithful, responsible, far-sighted and deeply rooted in the fateful association and profundity of the legacy of the great principles. Therefore, the people and nation did not interact with the Ottoman ruler who was kept isolated from the people in opinion, stance and decision. Likewise, the people's attitude, opinion and aspirations were far from operation, but mere theoretical hopes. All this took place when the ruler's traits either did not exist or interact with the people, and indeed when history discontinued or was inoperative in the best terms of description, as if its final episode prior to the fall of the Ottoman rule were identical, again in the best terms of description, to the one that had by a single day anteceded the Ottoman domination of Baghdad and by corollary all the Islamic states in general.

From the above and from the qualitative level of the sublime morals warehoused in Baghdad and the capability of being insightful on certain, familiar conditions, we can expound how the sun had not shone on the people of Baghdad and others during the reign of the State run by the Ottomans in the name of Islam when Baghdad faded and how now light shines on the foreheads of many sons of the Islamic community and all Arab sons, people of the sword, pen, banner and great principles when the rays of light are beamed from Baghdad, the city of great history and glory.

Brothers!

When we celebrate and rejoice the Great Victory Day on August 8, 1988, we do not only mean to affirm the worth and importance of heroism which is closely connected to its genuine source, the base of deeply rooted faith and the morals of a nation that has always been mujahid, holding a banner, faithful to the Most Compassionate, Most Merciful, trustworthy of the value and effectiveness of all relevant principles and shouldering the responsibility of playing the leading role of development as a decisive element in the conflict. We also want to stress the significance of the principles of construction and the leading role of man as a believer in life progress and in boosting love over hatred, exalting the object or objects, means and morals of construction over backwardness and the spirit of destruction and endeavouring to connect the present to its genuine sources of faith and deeply rooted past. Such a man has achieved two triumphs over the side of opposite description and tokens: one victory within the soul derived from one's feeling that man is a living part of a whole rather than a cast-off, acting in such a manner as to satisfy the soul in performing his duty towards the One worshipped alone; and another victory over the enemies when only the impossible conceals them from death. It is not just one victory. When achieved by any of the above descriptions it either introduces the melancholy of feeling of loneliness into a road shared by no one else or the gloom of despair, which no matter how intense is the feeling of self-content, preserves in this case the sense of defeat in the enemy, thus burning their backs with the lashed of triumph and perhaps the consciences and minds with scars and bruises caused by the triumphant's gun bombardment.

We would like to say to the whole world including the Iranian peoples that the victory won by the Iraqis is a great humane victory because it is a victory of progress over backwardness, of faith and truth over falsification and of construction over destruction. Had this victory not been accomplished, God forbid, and had another, different thing been achieved by the stoned Satan's act of strike, materialism, promulgated by the West under the leadership of USA in the Middle East region and perhaps in other places, would have created a horrific situation of destruction caused by the backward condition that is secluded in a lacerated image albeit dressed in religion or in some aspect of it. Faith would have been defeated after being shun by the people's souls and minds as a result of what would have befallen them under the slogans of religion. Zionism and USA would have won through people's recourse to their protection, clutching at a false hope for peace and stability, which they can provide to peoples in the face of the ghoul of backwardness and destruction beside the war drums of sectarianism. Iranian peoples would have remained captives of deception for a long time after they would have wasted their energy, suffered subsequently bitter disappointment and immersed in the crimes of aggression and destruction. Indeed, victory has salvaged the Iranian peoples from all that and rescued the peoples of the world from the domination of Western materialism whose view and way of life would have had the upper hand at the expense of balanced, spiritual principles and the right moral and living aspects for a long time to come.

Therefore, it is the right, indeed the duty too, of peoples and nations, not only the Iraqi people, to chant: "Long live August 8, 1988" as a day of victory of all peoples, for righteousness over falsehood, sublime morals over the abysses at the lowest bottom.

Long live the people holding the victory's banner, principles and sword!

God is most great!

Great people!

We realize that we have burdened you with the style of this address. But as you have been familiar with what you have listened to or read on such occasions you realize too that we endeavour, as best as we can, to make our speech of simple style, be it for the young, middle-aged or elderly. Yet the simplified style, dear people, is not always capable of expressing the meaning of what we want to state once our statement assumes an intellectual course and sets off in accordance with this description. Furthermore, our problem does not lie within the Iraqi people, but with others, you know. It is with the people who allege that through their aggressivity they can express a thought. Thus, it is inevitable that we deal with the wrong premise of their thought and replace it by a correct one, as we think or believe in. We also deem it appropriate, even at the level of the general humane standards common to all people wherever they set or act on a fair and objective basis. Our apology, valiant men and praiseworthy women, beloved boys and girls, is that, on this occasion as well as on others, we, in Iraq, have begun to communicate by gestures and by eyes and not only by speech which these two support. We also communicate when our consciences meet in the space of great love and become so exalted that a constant pledge is held to build our country, boost the faithful men and defend our dear homeland and the great principles of our glorious Nation. Therefore, I hope you comprehend what we say for you are capable of comprehension and you are the Arabs' cranium. The simplified speech, brothers, in this respect, might take a course that could fracture the foreheads and split the hearts of your opponents. However, this is not our intention. Now they have come to know that you can, in the name of God, cleave foreheads and tear livers in the battlefields. Instead, we try to cure the sick souls and hearts and open, in the best manner, the eyes to the facts as they are, whenever the minimal guess is possible. We are performing our national and humane duty after seeking the assistance of God, glory be to Him. Based on the knowledge of more than eight thousand years of civilization and eternal heritage of our nation, we state (quoting the Quranic verse): "Go, both of you to Pharaoh and speak gently to him."—Truth is the word of God—and maintaining, concomitantly, the essence of the mujahid people's stance and its leadership, as a believer in God, homeland, nation and people. God is most great.

Glory and sublimity to the martyrs of glorious Qadissiya!

Life of pride and sublime morals to our wounded and the living who are provided with sustenance: "Among the believers are men who have been true to their covenant with God; of them some have fulfilled their vow by death, and some are still waiting, but they have never changed in the least." Truth is the word of God.

Greetings to our POWs in the cages of captivity in Iran, and great pride of their patriotic stances there!

Greetings to the true believers wherever they are!

Long live our glorious Nation!

Long live Iraq! Long live Iraq!

Long live Palestine, free and Arab!

Long live the people of Palestine and the mujahids of the great stance!

Glory to the families that had the order of honour for the loss of their sons, our honest sons, in the fields of honour and jihad, families that have patiently endured the pain and hurt with hearts replete with faith and sublime morals.

Long live friendship with peoples!

May God help all the Iranian families which were stricken with the calamities of the war, yet they are still adherent to and entertaining a good-intention and love for relationship with Iraq because they realize and understand the significance and causes of the conflict and those who had triggered it.

God is most great!

God is most great!

Shame upon the despicable!

cided with cleansing the pure land of Iraq, Daughter of the Euphrates and the Tigris, and restoring to her great, just and faithful Arab face. The cleansing of Persia followed. Before the banners of righteousness and her great edifice, the banners and edifices of falsehood and those who had upheld it were crumbling to dust.

Yes, brave and faithful men of our armed forces, men of the great and loyal Army of the Nation,

Yes, ardent sons of our Arab Nation, and sons of the great people of Iraq, the citadel of glory, faith, righteousness, virtue and justice,

Today, the Sixth of January in the year 2000, corresponding to the year 1420 of the Hijra, is the prime of this year and of all other years. It is the day when we recall and do not forget, for we never forget, and when we welcome and celebrate the feats of valour of our army on the day of its establishment.

It is the day on which our army began, soon after its birth, to fill its great chronicle with glorious deeds.

May God keep it the source of honour for its people and its nation!

It is the lofty flagstaff for the God-Is-Great Banner, which has become proud of what is written on it and proud of the high level of influence it exerts on the souls, conscience, minds and hearts of the people.

With this banner, and with what supports and forms the depth of its memorable feats, stands and struggle, our army has become the devoted son of the people and the nation. It has become the quiver for the arrows of right against falsehood and the pride of the faithful military career of our nation. It has become the nation's living example in this age and the constant inspiration to its endeavour to achieve sublimity. It has become the source of great honour for those who join it and those who love it for endeavouring to please God, History, the Nation and the People.

This army has fought in defence of righteousness, virtue, faith, and noble objectives not only as it should, but also with a spirit and valour for which eyes were dazzled, heads bowed in respect and hearts amazed and awed—even the hearts of some of those who lined with the enemies of our nation and our people.

We take great pride in our Army Day because our army has linked without breach in exemplary values, our remote past, which is the beacon of our road to the future, with our present. It has won this lofty position through the high calibre of its performance, its forbearance toward adversities, the sublime level of its faith and its virtues and manners which are those of men with a mission.

The virtuous example we are talking about—the example set, in the name of God, by our army—was not set under favourable circumstances. It did create this ideal characteristic and its underlying significance all by itself and for itself. It wrenched it away from the claws of predators to whom many, many heads, on this Earth of God, have bowed. Some of these heads are honest but powerless, some are dishonest and ignoble. So, too, from among those who are counted in the list of Arab rulers and holders of titles of responsibility, are some who have weakened and some who have abased themselves through treachery.

Blessed be our valiant armed forces on their Day, which is anointed with purest virtue and decorated with the noblest of feats which are recorded in their immortal and glorious annals. To preserve the purity of their virtuous qualities and to defend them, our armed forces have had to wade through a lot of blood—pure and impure.

Blessed be the martyrs!

Blessed be the martyrs who illuminate the flagstaff of Iraq!

Let our nation take pride in its great army, the bearer of its mission!

Let our people, the great and loyal people of Iraq, take pride in their faithful army, their true and dutiful son!

Great People of Iraq!

Sons of our Glorious Nation!

Brothers!

After this brief talk on this highborn occasion of ours, some of you may ask: What about politics and politicians? What about the embargo and those who impose it? How should it and what must be done for the present and future?

Here I will say, briefly too—for we have already discussed this in details and elaborated on it on occasions other than this—that very early, since 1991 and 1992, we have been reiterating that we should not expect the powers of evil and vice to fulfil a pledge or keep a promise. Pledge-fulfilling and promise-keeping are not characteristics of them. They have no other characteristics but treachery, aggression, breaking promises, cancelling covenants and doing everything that is vile and injurious. We have said it with certainty that the embargo will not be lifted by a Security Council resolution but will corrode by itself. Even if a Security Council resolution will one day be taken in this respect, after all evil attempts have failed and all nests of poisonous wasps have been shattered before the Will of the strong, faithful, truthful, just and honest Iraq—such a resolution will come as an expression of this failure and not as the fulfilment of a promise or the discharge of an obligation.

This has become obvious to you generally and in detail after all that has passed by you and all that you have passed through.

As for now, it pleases us to say to you briefly and without going into details, that the stage of embargo corrosion is no longer something which we predict or wait for. It has actually started, thanks, after thanking the Almighty God, to your great fortitude and endurance. Therefore, and after having dismissed what is false in what has been presented to us as hopes to build upon, we have nothing before us but to keep on the path we have taken and cling to the spirit of fortitude and endurance we have been upholding in our state of becoming. Thus, God may grant us a great victory on every day and every while. On each flagstaff of this victory you will have a lofty banner of honour and an additional asset of potency to lead life successfully and to keep you the foremost model for the nation and for humanity at large.

In the field of politics and politicians, we say that, originally, we did not start with politics; rather, we started with principles. Principles have their own way, which is one of strife and struggle. Their basic means is justice, and their end, after pleasing God, is to please the People and the Nation. Therefore, we have never had any role in the world of acrobatic acts on tight ropes, and we have never participated and will never participate in the slave market of this world, bargaining away honour, virtue and the interests of the people and the nation.

The beginning and the far line on the horizon, or the line at hand, ought to, or rather, must be based on the principles of the starting line, while interacting genuinely with all colours of life so that we may find what relates to the colour we have chosen since long and have given, as a glorious nation and a great people, generous sacrifices and gracious patience.

Principles are the alternative of the politics current in the international and regional arena. From our principles emanate our politics, whether it pleases some or displeases others.

The End is for the righteous who strive and fight and persevere in patience and shall have the lofty rank of Truth with the Lord of the Worlds.

The politics oozing out of our principles has become the ideal for every virtuous, free and honest individual in the Arab Homeland and outside it. It has become the guiding landmark for everyone who strives sincerely in defence of his nation and people and puts politics at their service.

In the field of political activity, our relation to what is going on in the region and the world is not other than fending off evil or siding with anyone who needs our siding to sharpen his endeavour for himself and ease his feeling of loneliness on the road—a feeling that has dispirited him and rendered him incapable of crossing to the safe shore. This is done with all the senses of honour, glory and obligation to faith that ought to or must accompany the actions of those who shoulder the obligation faith demands of those who have it. No change have we in this. Anyone who wants to harmonize with us or understand us will have to alter what is wrong or ill in word and deed. God will bear witness to what he really wants.

Therefore, Great People, I say that you are the prime of the present, that the future is yours, and that your enemies and adversaries of your principles and their objectives and ways will have nothing but shame.

God is Great!

And long live the Sixth of January of every year!

Long live those who bear the banner, title and honour of this Day!

May our Nation, our People and our Army enjoy prosperity on this occasion every year!

Congratulations and best wishes to you, Brothers, on the occasion of Ramadan and the Feast of Breaking the Fast!

May we all keep on the way that pleases God and consolidates the position of all believers!

May God disgrace the unbelievers and the aggressors and provide the weak with the capability that may guide them to what they ought to do to follow the track of right!

May He crush the traitors and the oppressors!

Long live our Nation, the Nation of the Message and Messengers of God!

Long live Palestine—free and Arab from the Sea to the River!

Respectful salutation to the martyrs of our valiant armed forces and to the martyrs of the armed forces of our glorious Nation!

God is Great!

God is Great!

And let the debased be despised!

Address of His Excellency President Saddam Hussein On The Ninth Anniversary Of The Grand Battle "Mother Of All Battles", January 17, 2000

In the name of God, the Merciful, the Compassionate.

Wondrous People!

Great People of Iraq!

Men of our Valiant Armed Forces!

On a day like today—on the night of January 16–17, 1991, evil-ridden humanity delegated you to act for it, after history had called upon you, and you and your valiant army responded to the call. You responded in the name of your nation and in the name of the history of Iraq, which is rich in glorious deeds, sublime values, meanings, symbols and wisdom. As true believers that you are, you stood up to oppose the tyrants and the renegade oppressors of the age and all those who took ignominy as a stand, and accepted shame and disgrace as epithets of their character.

Thus took place the Grand Battle—the Mother of All Battles. It faced up to a new challenge, and looked up to a new ascent to the lofty summit of a mountain erected on glorious feats and built on the firm stands of faithful men and faithful women. It was the most rugged ascent with the most complicated path. But God, glorified be His name, was with us to uphold true believers and have His angels bear witness to their struggle, convey the message, keep the secret and sustain their effort with additional fortitude so that the Battle may become an eloquent lesson to all its parties: each according to the values and stands he represents. Its fields were anointed with the fragrant blood of men and women believers and with the Birds of Paradise, our beloved little ones. Paradise opened its widest gates, and I do not rule out that Bilal [the Muezzin of our Prophet (Peace be upon him)] called to prayer anew in the spirit of the situation and that the armies of Khalid, Aba 'Ubaida and Sa'ad took part in the Battle. Thus honour hovered over the situation and the future opened wide before the steadfastness of resolution and determination and before the sublimity of the stand and its justice. The Iraqis faced up to the Battle, in the name of their nation which elected them for it, spearheaded by armies that believed in their God, His Books, His Messengers and in jihad a path to honour and a means to win the satisfaction of God, the Compassionate. There arose great confusion: echoes reverberated, guns pounded, aircraft buzzed, and remotely controlled bombs exploded. But a thundering voice towered above and overtopped all of these sounds, a voice which has become the new means of announcing that the faithful Arabs are coming—the voice of "God is Great". Meanwhile, above the heads of men waved a banner, like an amulet carved by God of the great faith of those who believe—the new, truthful, proud and striving banner of the Arabs, the God-Is-Great Banner. Everything got mixed up with everything else. Faith remained in its trench which stretched along the battle field, wherever there was a heroic heart of a man believer or a splendid, glorious woman believer. Facing the trench of Faith was the trench of Disbelief—a foul-smelling, swindling, evil-scheming, sinful, aggressive and renegade trench. This was assisted by the efforts of shameful, lowly and debased turncoats who sold out their honour, the history of their nation, and the right, healthy stand.

Despite what happened on this day and the days following it and throughout the forty-three days and the days that followed the cease-fire, on which air-raids were made on the Republican Guard formations in the customary treachery of the aggressors—we say, throughout these days and as the Battle became more intense and the stand of righteousness got firmer and the stand of falsehood persisted in stubbornness, the trench of Disbelief and Evil never mixed with the stand of faith, right and honour. Your heads, Arabs and loyal Iraqis, remained uplifted before God, before the history of your nation and before humanity at large, proud of your struggle and endurance. While the heads of the believers never bent, some of the disbelievers, the renegades and the ungrateful prostrated themselves abjectly. And while some faces were blackened with disgrace, God, glorified be His name, rendered the faces of the brave Iraqi men and glorious Iraqi women more luminous, whiter and more lustrous. These are the whiteness and lustre of this life and the second life. The Arabs, spearheaded by the Iraqis, re-recorded the symphony of their glorious history and played the tune of life so as to record for this life and the other life exemplary standards of conduct and new stands of heroism. They recorded this for the age and for all those who aspire to lead a life free of humiliation and rich with a creative ability to get them across from one edge to another, from one shore to another and from the glory of faith to the dignity of life. For this and under other well-known conditions, the gates of paradise will open for them in the second life. Thus we reiterate:

God is Great!

God is Great!

And let the debased be despised!

Great People of Iraq!

Arabs!

You know that the value of things derives, in general, from the price and, sometimes, from their rarity, as well as from their role and their effect on our life and on our spirit. It may even derive from the degree of our clinging to them and the level of our desire to acquire or own them. The value of the high principles, practiced in our life, and the level of their effect on us and the degree of our clinging to them are measured with the quality of sacrifice we render them and the degree of our conviction in them and our understanding of them which are implanted in our souls, minds and hearts.

People, thus, have adopted gold and other precious stones as a standard to measure the value of things against. But you know that matter and material things, whatever name they may take, do not rank highest in value during the lifetime of man. They may continue to exist after his life, because man dies and leaves them behind, unable to exchange or use them after he passes to extinction. You also know that he who does not pass to extinction is that human being on whose life, in thought, spirit and conduct, matter and all things related to it have the least effect, and he who is least avid for them. That is because those who leave a good name for the stands derived from the high principles they cherish during their lives will live on even after their bodies vanish. They will live on maintaining the rank and the memory they deserve on the same level as that of the high principles they recorded while they were alive. They also keep the place in Heaven God the Compassionate assigns to them for winning His satisfaction, while they were alive and not after their death. The result of reckoning is resolved by the Almighty God in the light of what a human being recorded during his lifetime in a record which closes with the extinction of his body.

The value attached to what man loves or whom he loves ranks on the same level of the sacrifice he renders to them and according to or commensurate with that sacrifice and its effect on his soul. Regardless of details, we love God as much as we sacrifice for that love and endeavour to win His satisfaction with us. You have sacrificed, noble Iraqis, all that is dear and precious, and have shed your blood seeking the love of God and in hope to win His satisfaction, praised be His name.

You are now the nearest to Him and ranking highest in His love. Your chance of winning His satisfaction, glorified be His name, is greater than that of any other people, that is because you have sacrificed so much for your high principles out of love for your people, your homeland and your nation. Pioneering your sacrifice, to guide it through to the sure arrival and to throw bright light to embody forth its significance, colour and shape, is the blood of our dutiful martyrs—our beloved, the beloved of the people, the homeland and the nation, or rather, the beloved of every truthful and loyal believer.

You have sacrificed so much, and I have never doubted, not even for a moment, that you love God and that God loves you evenmore for your nearness to Him has been proportional to the degree of your faith in Him and your love for Him and your sacrifice to win His satisfaction with you.

Now, you love your nation even more, and your nation loves you and appreciates your role even more. You love Iraq—you love its earth, sky, water and air. Keep up your love in order to reach your target, for you are definitely reaching it. By God's permission, happiness after suffering is at hand, at hand, at hand.

Know that a ship's speed in sailing is proportionate to the quantity of water it cuts and pushes away on both sides as it moves. So, keep up your sailing unburdened and undistracted from the necessary effort you should exert to cross safely. Push aside from your path all obstacles put by the daily affairs of life, because giving them much attention may waste your effort, endeavour and resolution. Your illustrious ship will then move to its anchorage in the harbour of honour, virtue and glory where you will breathe the musk of sacrifice along the course.

And know, Men of Iraq, and Women of Iraq, that nothing is more capable of weakening resolution and blurring the ability to see things in the right perspective and evaluate them correctly than avarice and greed to acquire unnecessary food, clothing, drink and other things.

Defer, exalted Men of Iraq, defer, glorious Women of Iraq, anything on the list of demands. By deferring them and wisely managing, at least on the level of unnecessary or unneeded details, you add a decisive factor to shorten the time of arrival and determine its quality and its level. Thus arrival will be secure and the ship will lay anchor safely—without damage, scratches or deep wounds.

Great People!

Sons of our Glorious Nation!

Mankind!

God creates human beings along the same line and sets them on the same course. But He, glorified be His name, creates them unequal in many characteristics. Of these characteristics is the ability to transform dispersed or scattered will into an organized and controlled capacity that marches or halts in degrees, acts or refrains, advances or retreats, works and sacrifices for itself only, or works and sacrifices for others or for all the others. To each He gives what is ought to be given of strength and weakness. The source of ability in man is released by Faith from the inside of himself and directed to the right directions. And since man was created among other living creatures and among his own kind, and having been created by God in the best of moulds, it is the type of behaviour derived from the nature of his reasoning that determines the degree of his farness from other creatures or his nearness to them. He, who submerges into things only, out of need or just

Address of His Excellency President Saddam Hussein On Army Day Of The Year 2000 In January 6, 2000

The 79th Anniversary of the Establishment of The VALIANT IRAQI ARMY On January 6, 1921

In the name of God, the Merciful, the Compassionate,

Great People!

Manly men of our armed forces—the active weapon and loyal stand for our people and our nation!

Comrades in doctrine and comrades in arms in our Valiant Army!

It is the dawn of your renewed anniversary. It is your Day, and it is our Day too, for your glorious chronicle indicates that you have been performing the duty and the honour of your military career in the same spirit and on the same line as those of your ancestors. They had the honour of bearing the banner of righteousness and revolution high. They commenced by cleansing the lands of Hejaz, Nejd and Yemen of abomination. Then, after they had consolidated Islam in those lands through crushing the apostates and stamping out the spirit of apostasy, they headed for Syria and cleansed the whole land, and for Egypt, Daughter of the Nile, and broke the power of Byzantium. That cointo acquire them, and he who, mainly or to a great degree, concentrates his attention, effort and ability on them, will get nearer or closer to other creatures, including animals. When he limits his role, for instance, to eating, drinking and procreating, and works for this only and moves in the sphere of securing his physical needs only, he gets nearer to animals than to his self which God has cast in the best of moulds. Even plants feed, take in water and propagate. They do many of the functions the human body does. They breathe, they accept or reject by implication in response to the harm, care or benefit entailed. But plants lack the willpower, so they cannot transform rejection and acceptance into a course of action similar to that taken by man.

Iraqis, therefore, have been thankful to the Almighty God, obedient to His will and loyal to what He likes when they decided to think and exercise their will on the basis that of all God's creatures man was created in the best of moulds. Thus, they have met the conditions under which God created man. They have never allowed life to deprive them of the basic characteristics of man. They love others as they love themselves or rather, they love others more than they love themselves, as attested by the martyrs when they sacrifice themselves for the stand they take in loving God and loving the others, and in rejecting falsehood and clinging to right.

The Embargo has cut down from you, Iraqis, things which do not harm your humanity, and deprived you of things which, if man does not balance his needs for them, may cause him to lose high values and cease representing his true self.

In any case, Iraqis have not, by choice, deprived themselves or others of things, save those that God has forbidden. But man, under certain circumstances, one of which is our own circumstance, finds himself facing a difficult test to choose one of two alternatives. He either secures for himself all the things or most of the things he desires to acquire and thus loses many of his values and moves far away from his humanity, when he accepts that, and comes closer to the characteristics of creatures that live on things only. Or, he sacrifices all of the things or most of them and thus upholds the values he cherishes. On this basis, those who take and believe in the second alternative, never deal, essentially or most of the time, with things save those that are necessary to sustain life. Man, generally, and man under a certain circumstance like ours, loses of his freedom an amount equal to the weight of the things that burden him. But the lighter he is of those things, the faster he finds his humanity and the more agile he becomes to be a leader of a movement in life and not a heavy wagon fastened behind a train locomotive.

You have chosen the way of values and rejected, noble Iraqi Men and glorious Iraqi Women, the way of things which are immersed in poison, disgrace and humiliation. Had you accepted life on this basis, you would not have really received even what is exhibited of these things, or what is being waved before you in exchange for a stand of humiliation. But you have chosen the other way and rejected this way. You have thus gained confirmed certainty and a stable state resting on high values, with all the provisions that come with them to sustain you on the road. God willing, you will keep both your values and the things, or plenty of the things you desire to have. Thus, and only by this way it becomes possible for you to keep an essential thing of the ones which help material life and part of the social and cultural life to develop and advance forward. Together with these things and ahead of them all, and forming their waving banner, will be the high values you have attained and kept and safeguarded to put as a crown on your heads, by which you will be identified and distinguished from other peoples. You have thus won the shore and its sea with its ebb and flow, life and its sky and God's satisfaction and His earth.

And God is Great!

We, in the Leadership, are fortunate, for God has honoured us with the Iraqis whom He prepared to measure up to the honour and responsibility of carrying the new message of the people of Iraq and the nation for themselves and for humanity at large.

No other case or other people will be able to shoulder this responsibility unless they acquire the same essence of your characteristics. That is because the endeavour needed on a long and exceptional road differs from the endeavour needed on a short and usual or traditional road—exactly as the honour, significance and results achieved differ. The people of Iraq has come to be the son of this new message and its leader. It is the son of the transitional period in the life of the nation. It is the dutiful son of the nation and the leader in this period of scoring new records for its present life and for some time to come. It is scoring records in various fields of life and on all levels of values that endear man to himself, to his nation, to others in humanity and to God, the Creator of ability and the Director of its course towards achieving deeds that will disgrace evil-doers and the cursed Satan.

Let all know that this has been the decision of the people taken since the beginning of the Grand Battle in harmony with the spirit of the message and the call of history. It is still the people's decision, and there is no other way but preserve the essence of the significance of this decision.

Honour belongs to God, to the people, to the nation, to the homeland, to sovereignty, to security, to stability.

The right of option and decision belongs to Great Iraq and to our Glorious Nation.

Long live Iraq!

Long live Iraq!

Long live our Glorious Nation!

Those who delude themselves into believing that the prolonged march may break the willpower of the Iraqis have to stop relishing that delusion. They have to wake up and learn and remember that after the conflict they had planned to make long in order to break the back of Iraq in the Glorious Qadissiya Battle, Iraq emerged at the end topping the summit of glory, with greater capability. Therefore, the prolongation going on now in the Immortal Mother of All Battles, no matter what colour the schemes take and the more wicked and cunning they become in this or that means, including using threadbare and flimsy covers bearing the titles of international organizations—this prolongation will not make Iraqis change the course they have taken after they have given all that they have given to maintain it. It has won the satisfaction of God; and God's satisfaction is nobler and dearer than anything people may offer in this respect.

The evil-doers will have to acknowledge this fact and prostrate themselves before God, after first they believe in Him, and beg Him to forgive them for the crimes they have committed against the people of the Divine Messages, Prophets and pious believers. They will have to beg God to make the people of Iraq accept to forgive them.

Glory be to the Martyrs!

Glory be to the Martyrs!

Long live Iraq the Great—immortal for its values and the significance of its deeds!

Long live our Glorious Arab Nation!

Contempt and shame for the enemies!

Long live Palestine—free, proud and Arab from the Sea to the River!

Long live Freedom Fighters, the Sons of our Nation!

Long live every free, loyal freedom fighter everywhere!

God is Great!

God is Great!

And let the debased be despised!

Address of His Excellency President Saddam Hussein In July 17, 2000

In the name of God, the Merciful, the Compassionate

Great people of Iraq!

High-minded men of our valiant armed forces!

Masses of our glorious Arab nation!

Honourable people everywhere in the world!

Having set it as their eternal National Day, Iraqis annually celebrate the 17–30 July Revolution.

What is this July Revolution?

What have its repercussions been up to this day and all days to come?

It is not possible to describe the effect of the act accomplished between 3o'clock at the dawn of July 17, 1968 and 3 o'clock in the afternoon of July 30 without describing the state as it was and without recalling the aspirations of the freedom-fighters and the revolutionaries—both those who are still alive and those who passed away.

The reality of that act is present before our eyes. Its minute details have been extensively researched. Many writers have already written about it, for occasions like this one have become a common and well-trodden road. It can be taken by anyone who may like to talk about the occasion and its direct circumstances, or describe its condition in the narrower or wider horizon.

But the July Revolution is not a common course chosen from among many possible courses. Rather, it is a state of evolution and ascent towards what is deemed to be almost impossible. I am not referring to the circumstances surrounding the early days in the life and time of the revolution. What I am referring to is its spirit, its ability to guide life and renew it along the best path there is. And I am referring to the intent of faith in the hearts of the men who caused the noble fount to gush out and who mustered up all the potencies in the hearts and minds of the people so that they may plant all that is useful and healthy in the womb of life.

The July Revolution has not been a traditional course taken with the intention of weaving for the people an overall to cover blemishes that show through their tattered dress. It has been the sowing of healthy seeds where they should be sown before irrigating them with the water of life so that they grow green and blooming and fruitful. Its yield of fruit will spread the zeal rendered in sowing the healthy seeds. It will thus spread and extend the cultivation of life to a vast homeland—the Arab Homeland, and will activate the zeal that lies idle—the zeal of the Arabs—to be companion to that of the Iraqis.

The July Revolution has acquired the experience of the road and has developed eyes that never miss the target. It has cherished a heart that has never known anything but faith as the base and regulator of its beats. It has nourished a mind that has invoked the great history of a nation made thirsty and a people who were on the verge of starving and standing naked after vicissitudes of time have torn their dress to tatters.

Before the July Revolution, the condition in Iraq can be described as follows: It was a wasteland that had no agriculture to be taken into account and no livestock to be proud of although it had much water. Is it possible that life and land suffer from thirst while water exists?

The Iraqis knew that they had the potential, but they did not know how to muster up that potential. Their rulers did not take the responsibility on the basis of that potential. The leader and the guide who was able to put that potential on its right course had not yet emerged from amongst them. Even when some had discovered that potential, they did not know how to deal with it. Nor did they direct it where it should be directed so as to enable it to evolve into an effective act that could make life pulsate and fill hearts with happiness.

Each thing and each element in Iraq then stood isolated in its properties and characteristics from other things and elements. No reaction between them took place, since that reaction required first the presence of a catalyst to enable the principal elements to release the sparks of life. That reaction would have purged souls, revived zeal, removed the veil from eyes and hearts and sent life flowing into limbs that had gone dry and paralyzed.

That was how Iraq was then.

But a breeze blew on it. It was like indignation voiced by a gentle patient man. It was like the smile of a baby whispering to its mother, or playing with itself in celebration of life. It was like a prayer of a hermit giving God the adoration of great love. That breeze dipped out of the Great Sea of Omnipotence, after the Great Master of Omnipotence, the Merciful, the Compassionate had permitted that.

And there was rain!

It was clement rain, filling the sky of Iraq and falling abundantly on its parched land. The idle wells filled their beds and water overflowed all around. The immortal Tigris brimmed and so did the Euphrates. The main flow filled its tributaries. Life crept into every living thing and every dead thing was removed from the field. Together with that relieving rain, their blew pollinating winds. They speeded up the shaking of the date-palm trunks. Pollen was strewn over the heads of palm trees. Similar pollen was sent to every tree and every plant.

And there was life!

Life streamed after it had revived all veins and crept into everything that could harbour it. Does not pollen pollinate palm trees so that dates will later fall fresh and ripe?

That is how the July Revolution has been: lightning which God meant to be the pollen for everything capable of being.

And there was birth!

It was birth that came after calm, though prolonged pregnancy. The newborn baby could have lost the power to be, had not the revolutionaries made it possible for it to be.

We, our people, our comrades and Iraq have reached the state you know us to be in, after we had been in the state which we were honest in describing to you—or which you already know.

Is it possible that he who stands at the bank of a river gets thirsty?

Is it not strange that he who spends the night in a temple does not pray?

Is it acceptable that he who has the ability to benefit his family, himself and his fellow countrymen does not do so?

Can he who lives with his date palms starve?

Can this happen while the land of Iraq is rich in oil and while it has the Euphrates and the Tigris?

Can the womb be barren while it is well and healthy? Or is it that the loins are barren?

Thus connected were each thing and each element after they had been isolated. With their connection, and with the presence of the right catalyst, the great reaction took place. It goes on to enable life to go on along the lines we aspire for so that, God permitting, building towers up, health is restored and birth takes place under favourable conditions.

Thus, too, the people and the nation achieve victory and the evil ones meet defeat.

And thus the free, exalted men and women win victory over the invaders.

Long live the July Revolution!

Long live July, the Seed of Life!

God is Great!

May God have mercy upon the souls of those who were martyred or those who died!

Long live our glorious Arab nation, and long live its Eternal Message!

Long live Palestine, free and Arab from the sea to the river!

Down with the Zionists in their usurper hateful entity!

Peace be with you, brothers!

God is Great!

God is Great!

And let the debased be despised!

Address of His Excellency Saddam Hussein On The 12th Anniversary of The Great Victory Day (The Day of Days) 8.8.1988, August 8, 2000

In the name of God, the Merciful, the Compassionate

Great people of Iraq!

Loyal freedom fighters of our valiant armed forces!

Masses of our glorious Arab Nation!

Peace be upon you and God's mercy and all His blessings!

Every year, the eighth of August towers above us like a splendid moon in the skies of our people and our nation, or like a morning star that guides those who follow the right path in a dark night which has obscured the dawning of day. The masses of our nation await this dawn and all Arab freedom fighters seek it to model their present on it after the image of their true worth was shaken in the eyes of their enemies. These enemies fight the nation because they are covetous of its wealth and contemptuous of its potential which they imagined to be merely the potential of its rulers and nothing more.

The dawning of the eighth of August, and God's manifest victory on it come as a reward and a prize for an eight-year battle with those who wished our people ill and our nation harm, backed by international Zionism, imperialism and the wicked Jews in the occupied land and in their accursed freak entity. Today with the splendid moon of that day and its morning star there line up stars whose sublime stands express the true potential of the nation wherever chances open before it. The significance of the Day of Days is backed up by days in Palestine and Lebanon and by stands of honourable Arabs wherever the conscience of the enlightened and faithful youth of the nation is spurred on. It is spurred on towards a horizon that enlivens their spirit to express its firm stand and true level of worth. They can, thus, openly reject what should be rejected and couple aspiration with what they really want to achieve for their nation, our nation—for its thirsty land, its withheld waters and its potency which is detained in the cells of occupation in Palestine, in the Golan Heights, in our sacred land in Saudia and in the Arab Gulf. This potency is also detained inside the cells of weakness in the minds of those who have become accustomed to abasement to the degree of addiction from among rulers and kings who have no concern but to appear on their chairs and thrones as if they really rule.

Is it not shame and disgrace on those who harbour shame and disgrace that the planes of the aggressors take off from their land and territorial waters to bomb the citadel of the Arabs and the cradle of Abraham (peace be upon him) and to destroy the property of the Iraqis and kill them all, women, men and children? Is there any other way than this to describe treachery and disgrace?

May evil befall them, for evil indeed are the deeds they do!

It is they who have sold out their souls and have appointed (the occupying foreigner) to rule over everything that is dear and precious in the values and wealth of their people. Whatever they find saleable they have sold to the U.S and Zionism, thus becoming mere agents getting commissions deducted from the wealth of their own people and getting ignoble authority chairs to sit on.

Glorious Iraqi men and glorious Iraqi women!

You have become the yardstick of values, potency and highminded-ness. You have become the guides on a path that discerning eyes can-not miss. It is a path that has become continuously trodden by those who have faith in their hearts and minds since that day of yours, the immortal Day of Days in the great record of the glorious Qadissiya, and these days, the days of the Grand Battle, the immortal Mother of All Battles and its greater record.

In this we do not explore, we only point to the meanings which the faithful will and the healthy conscience can achieve when present in the hearts and minds of the glorious men and women who have the volition after they have entrusted their souls to the Great Omnipotent.

That day of yours, Iraqi people, which we now welcome and celebrate, has become a day for all the Arabs and for all those who bear in their hearts the true meaning of humanity as opposed to what the forces of evil planned it to be. They planned it to be a pitch-black night in which bats turn into ferocious beasts to wound every virtue and to rip open the abdomen of every woman expecting a baby to be born and to speak Arabic later and to believe in what the Arabs believe in.

They wanted to twist your tongue and swerve your path. They wanted to break the flagstaff of your banner, God forbid, after they trample on everyone who has dignity and honour. But God stood by right against falsehood after the banner of right was stained with the blood of free-dom fighters whether in the battlefields or in the POW camps in Iran. To those who sacrificed themselves and to their families we extend our highest appreciation and the appreciation of Iraq. This appreciation comes to you with every gentle breeze and every sublime stand of honour and dignity and every dainty and lawful morsel of food eaten by the people in peace and security.

The Highest Heaven and God's blessings to our martyrs!

Happy Paradise with our Merciful God as an everlasting dwelling for them all!

Glorious men of Iraq!

Glorious women of Iraq: mothers, sisters or any relationship you may have with those brave men who fought in the legions of right against wrong and to whose heroic deeds the battlefields bear witness from the land and waters of our beloved Basra to the Minshaf headland in our dear North, if we were to give details of your stand and the stand of your sons—our sons and brothers and brave illustrious comrades—, the pen would not be able to give them their due. But we found it appropriate to change the style on this occasion and for this year, and to present to you the lessons deduced from honourable fighting and from honourable building which convey all the meanings of virtue and bear witness to the loyalty of the sons of our people to their fatherland. These lessons may help him who is in need of them so that the radiance of the future intensifies in his soul and the capabilities of the present consolidate in his mind. This will strengthen the stand of right against wrong in a march before which only the banner of wrong and wrongdoers will tumble down, and, God willing, the banner of right will remain fluttering high, sharing with the truthful believers all their pride.

Here is what we found to be the gist of great lessons from the experience of our people.

These lessons are addressed to you and to all the patient strivers and freedom fighters in our glorious nation:

Do not provoke a snake before you make up your mind and muster up the ability to cut its head. It will be of no use to say that you have not started the attack if it attacks you by surprise. Make the necessary preparations required in each individual case and trust in God.

Do not take him as companion who thinks that you despise him.

Do not pay those to whom you are under no obligation more than their due, for if you do so out of charity, they will fancy it to be their due. If you lower that level later on, they will regard it as a shortcoming on your part or as an unfriendly attitude. You will thus lose those to whom you have been charitable instead of winning them.

If you do not intend to go all the way, you will have to enlighten your enemy on the consequences when it is your intention to avoid a conflict with him. Perhaps he has not decided to take the conflict all the way, and his action which suggested to you that he intended a full scale conflict was nothing but stupidity on his part which veiled the possibility of his seeing the consequences. Your enlightening may stop him from going all the way. But if you decide to combat the enemy, expose his reality as an aggressor and let the big blow come from you and the decisive blow be yours.

Hasten and hurry in doing good, but tarry and take your time in doing what may cause harm to others. Do not hesitate to execute right in its field and to strike at wrong wherever it shows itself.

Do not put on an equal footing: the cowards and the braones, the loyal and those who have not settled on a clear stand, the clean and the defiled, the truthful and the liars, and do not equalize summits with mere landmarks on a level ground.

When you judge, judge with justice. Do not allow whims to burden a sentence or allow an unreformable criminal to escape punishment.

When you cannot be present in the field of work or fight for a good reason, do not let your shadow be absent from the place or your voice be unheard in it.

Draw your general plans in the light of the capability of the majority, but put them on the alert for higher deeds.

Let the elite lead them and guide them towards a perpetual ascent. Let the first man in the file see the last one and the last one see the first.

Let mercy be the crown of justice. Let resoluteness take the place of hesitation, wisdom the place of rashness, and reason the place of foolishness. Do not give your enemy any chance to get the upper hand of you.

Let not your enemy hope for your forgiveness, nor your friend be hopeless of it.

If you find that your anger may lead to a decision which you will regret taking, wait so that you take your decision in whim-free circumstances. Whims may cause your decision to deviate from its target or may close the path of mercy in your heart.

Do not put your friend and your enemy on an equal footing, even when a reconciliation with the latter takes place, lest your enemy should slight you and your friend make light of the meaning of friendship and its rights. Give each his due according to the description he deserves.

Your conscience and your mind are your sovereign—not your tongue and your whims. Curb your tongue with your mind and let your conscience be the controller over your whims.

Seek not to wrong anyone. It is better that you let him who deserves punishment escape it and lay the blame on yourself than to wrong a human being and rebuke yourself for doing it.

Trust him who presents himself before you in adversities and does not talk about himself. But beware him who stands in the file and works only for himself.

Guard your secret carefully. Do not divulge it to anyone. Entrust what you deem to be a necessary part of it only to him whom you have already tested with a similar secret. Do not make your secret the starting point or the key to test the reticence and loyalty of people.

Do not underrate the simple person who may smear your reputation. Many are the small stone that broke huge glasses.

Keep peoples' secrets. Do not put them into other peoples' mouths, nor use a friend's secret against him.

When you take a decision, do not regret it. But when you find a mistake in it, do not hesitate to rectify it. Let not easy paths lure you when you find that the paths that cause your feet to bleed lead to the summit or to the choice without which life does not ascend to where it should ascend.

Count on the men who do not falter before difficult tasks which may seem to you at first sight to be higher than their ability. Do not count on those who select the tasks that fall below their ability.

Do not take as an introduction one attribute in the character of a person whom you depend on and overlook to test. Do not allow the branch to take the place of the trunk. Reserve for each his role on the basis of his attributes and stands.

Keep before your eyes the manner in which a person behaves in ordinary life and the manner of his behaviour under difficult circumstances, making the latter decisive in tipping the scale.

Your word is your stand. Do not humiliate it. Do not exaggerate a promise you cannot fulfil or a threat your ability cannot support.

Let generosity be your path against stinginess, frugality against prodigality, union against estrangement, forgiveness against revenge and love against hatred. If you have to choose between two contradictory paths, let a middle path be your choice as a contingency you pass through temporarily without making it a permanent law in your life and dealings.

Do not use your full military potential when you take the offensive in a conflict with an enemy unless you calculate that it will achieve a decisive result; otherwise, the result of the conflict will turn against you and your enemy will triumph over you.

Do not keep the starting point of your potential and means in a conflict with an enemy as if they were your constant image before him in later times. Constancy here is nothing but stagnation and the movement of your enemy meanwhile will give him an advantage over you. Update your means, measures and potential with everything that increases and enriches them if you want to win the conflict.

Do not measure your capability only on the basis of what you have inside you, but on that and on the degree of your influence on others too. If he who is your concern, or he who shares with you a collective act weakens, do not build your glory on his corps or on his weakness. Try to turn his weakness into strength by supporting him and protecting him from that weakness and by the encouragement, protection, enlightening and strength you grant him. Know that collective work, whenever action is based on it and whenever the situation requires it, is highest in rank and quality and it has the greatest potential. And know that the Hand of God is with the group and the hand of Satan is with those who stray from the group and with the selfish ones who do without their society.

Know that nothing is better than renewing hope in victory and that the human relationship between superior and subordinate revives optimism in the soul and gives it steadiness to continue in circumstances of war or conflict when victory is won through endurance, patience and determination.

Principles are not only life's means of advancement, they are also its crown. So, do not lower principles to the level of inferior means, and do not let them hang in the air without a cord to give them the vitality and the ability to renew themselves through their connection with life.

Do not make matter the base and resource of the spiritual and moral values in your soul. Do not let these values remain without a concrete capability to accompany and take care of them. If you were given the choice, choose that which satisfies your soul because your soul is the source of your capability.

Do not employ but a person tried in a field whose full extent you cannot explore at the starting point, and do not deprive others of their opportunity to be tried in a new situation or field.

Do not wound a friend's feeling with a piece of advice, but do not deprive him of it so that he may know his mistake.

The trodden road is not always the best road, but it is wise not to neglect it completely.

Keep your eyes on your enemy. Be ahead of him but do not let him be far behind your back.

Let your concern be with the chance you grab, not with the chance given you.

Let not your chance be at the expense of yourself and thus lose yourself. Win yourself if you are forced to lose your chance.

Real chance is the chance you take, not the one you merely imagine possible.

Ward off regret with wisdom lest regret should become a reality that burdens you.

Gluttony in food and drink is gluttony in life. Gluttons, in general, have the heart of fish. So, do not give them great authority over people. The leadership of people requires a person who has a human heart, i.e., who loves people and hates hateful acts, who can get angry and can get satisfied, who can be agitated and can be appeased, who frowns and smiles, whose moustache shudders at the sight of an inadmissible thing and blooms at what pleases the soul, who is well balanced in his view of life and his behaviour in it, and who is moderate in food and drink.

Do not give authority over public wealth to him who builds his fame on wealth, nor over the media to him who builds it on ostentation, nor over the army to him who builds it on conquest, regardless of the nature of the conquest and the degree of right or wrong in it, nor over national security systems to him who is light in weight and influence among people or to him who acts treacherously in the dark and who is not afraid God. Give each and all of these posts and titles to those who are strong, truthful and trustworthy.

People's tongue is a book written on the ground. Do not neglect reading it, but do not believe everything you read in it.

He who feels no embarrassment in praising himself before you, without first praising the good deeds of others, becomes his own depreciator. You should know this and recognize such a person.

Do not make little of a simple person who builds himself a good reputation, nor of a simple person who defames you. Know that a big fire starts with a spark and one drop of scent fills a whole court with its fragrance.

Put your foot firmly on the ground while extending your vision to the horizon. Do not deprive yourself of the connection with both earth and heaven for neither of them alone is enough as a substitute for life.

Benefit from the lessons of others before you pay their price. If you cannot do this, benefit from your own lessons lest you should be burdened with the accumulated price you pay for them and then you will get drowned. If you cannot do this either, beware of being described as stupid or foolish; otherwise misery and ruin will be your fate.

Avert evil. Do not win it on your side. Ward it off by fair means whenever possible without paying any price to its source. But be on your guard against it. If evil attacks you, do not bend before it but face it with all that it requires to face it. Expel the devil of weakness from your soul because God loves the brave and Satan fears them. Evil is the devil of the foolish and the arrogant. Weakness has another devil. Expel all devils from your soul with active and faithful potency, and from the battlefield with the same potency. Break their codes on the anvil of your strength, after trusting in God.

Do not make your past all that you rely on as a source of your capability and effect of your action. By doing this, you have merely leaned on it. Make the past the root of your capability and action but be vigorous and effective in the heart of the present while extending your vision and the ambition of your thought to the future as a whole.

Beware of yourself before you beware of your enemy. Pay attention to your friend before you pay attention to your adversary.

The foundation of the true and noble nature of men is that they disdain to commit any failing. Do not entrust a mission of good will to anyone who is not ashamed of a failing, but have him argue with your opponents and enemies only.

Do not do all that you are capable of doing, but only that which is regarded to be right and legitimate in the light of the principles you believe in, after trusting in God.

Do not demand what is not your due, but do not waive what is your due unless you relinquish it to someone who deserves it more than you do. Balance rights against duties or obligations for he who seeks rights without fulfilling duties and obligations is a parasite, and he who fulfils duties or obligations without rights may put himself in the position of the exploited weak. Neither is an attribute of a true and faithful Iraqi and Arab person.

If you want to minimize your wrongdoing and maximize your justice, remember that Satan tempts weak hearts and nests in chests empty of faith. Put yourself in the place of your opponent or adversary to learn whether right is on your side or on his side.

Always remember that you may regret an action or a word that are immaturely or inaccurately directed towards a person. But you will never regret patience, no matter how long it lasts if it has as foundation the planning of an action that requires patience.

Do not select for posts of leadership those who claim higher roles for themselves in success or victory and disclaim their responsibility for failure or defeat.

Select for positions of supreme titles those who have prepared themselves to be better equipped for the task of serving the cause of the people and the nation, but not those who look at the post as the means of their chance to rise at the expense and interests of the people and the nation.

Young people!

If you are outrun by those who surpass you in material things and appearances, do not follow them. Choose your own honourable path if the path of those who outran you is not honourable. Outrun them towards what is spiritual and moral through culture, steadfast stands, educational attainment and honourable and legitimate work. Your clinging to these principles will be deeper in effect, firmer in stand and higher in position. Everything else is transient.

Great people of Iraq!

Faithful men of our valiant armed forces!

Men and women comrades!

Bearers of the trust of the great Ba'ath principles and banner!

This has been part of what we found it appropriate to refer to on the occasion of your manifest victory on 8-8-1988. These lessons have been inspired by your march, a march that is proud of its faith and proud of you. It is proud of you because you are the faithful and truthful custodians of friendship, sincere affection and every virtue and value that rise above any weakness and frailty. They are the fruit of your great endeavour and struggle in the fields of work, construction and defence of right against wrong for more than thirty years. They have undergone fermentation in the heart and mind of the writer before he committed them to paper to be broadcast to you in this address on the occasion of the Glorious Day of Days.

Extended to you are the sincerest gratitude for your sublime character and the noblest, God-loved pride in your nobility of descent and in your great stands.

From us and from you, the affection of one passionately in love is given to our glorious Arab nation, the nation of prophets, and to every Arab man and woman who are truthful in intention, stand and call.

Long live Iraq!

Long live Iraq!

Long live our glorious nation and its eternal message!

Long live the people!

Long live the army!

Long live the comrades!

Long live Palestine, free and Arab!

Down with Zionism!

Down with the Jews of the occupied land!

May evil befall every traitor, hireling and cheat!

God is Great!

The Highest Heaven for the martyrs!

Glory to the martyrs!

God is Great!

God is Great!

Let the debased be despised!

Address of His Excellency President Saddam Hussein on the 80th Anniversary of the Establishment of Iraqi Army, January 6, 2001

In the Name of Allah, the Merciful, the Compassionate

Brothers!

Sons of Our Glorious Nation!

Great People!

Sons of Our Valiant Armed Forces!

Before we speak at length about today's occasion and why we celebrate and honour this glorious day, the Sixth of January of every year, we pose the following questions:

Is it high-mindedness that creates the fighting army or is it the fighting army that creates high-mindedness?

Does consciousness precede experience or is it experience that creates consciousness?

Does a deep-rooted nation, that is great in its role and in its history, create the leaders who rise up to the level of its qualities or is it the great leaders who create the nation in accordance with their own qualities?

Does a task create its means or is it the availability of the means that determines the nature of the task and its objectives?

Does history create a nation or is it the nation itself that creates its own history?

Questions like these may go on. They may be extended along the same line of inquiry. They all seem to presuppose the existence of that which is "root" and that which is "branch". If we elaborate the presupposition that the root has its qualities and that the branch has other qualities which are not connected to the root, we may arrive at results that are far from true and which we do not believe in. Every root, in one of the stages of its historical formation, begins as if it is the inevitable result of the factors of its formation. Birth out of it in subsequent stages is also an inevitable result. Therefore, no root is of any value unless it is suitable to be the basis for the continuation of the essence of its qualities in later stages. This is how nation and leadership create history. In both, nation and leadership, history plays its role, and each creates the type for the other. Thus, nation, army and leadership create history. History creates them through their true and legitimate affiliation to it and through its inspiring them with its sublime meanings. The more inspiring and asking for inspiration are possible and able to create high qualities on the basis of their meanings, and the more related they are to a foundation for a new creation, the more correct the connection is and the more expressive of the decisive historical correlation, regardless of the predominance of the role in the creation and description of the result, in this stage or that, of any of the names we have referred to and any other names analogous to them.

From this, Brothers, it follows that while we are celebrating the birth of our Army today, we are celebrating and honouring the potency of the great people of Iraq in the fields of struggle and armed jihad. The great people of Iraq are ready to be. If the Iraqis have their historical chance, they are capable of creating an army, undefeatable and powerful, by right, to break down falsehood and defeat it always. Accordingly, we are celebrating and honouring the armies of our Sumerian, Babylonian, Akkadian and Assyrian ancestors, or the Armies of Victory which had Iraq as the base of their great reinforcements in the direction of the East or wherever a battle became necessary to decide the potentials of the Iraqis. We can also say that we are celebrating and honouring the Army of the Glorious Qadissiya and the Immortal Mother of All Battles, our modern, mighty, powerful and loyal Army whose birth was a patriotic one in the conscience of its sons in this stage on January 6, 1921, when its first battalion was established, regardless of the nature of those who ruled the country then.

We celebrate special meanings of a specific kind and a specific description. We will pay no attention to the low meanings that tried to oppose the sublime meanings. The failure of those opposing meanings bore fruit and yielded the meanings of endeavour, virtue, courage and glory in a splendid tree whose crown is the battle helmet, whose decorations are the battle equipment and whose characteristics are the characteristics of its heroes who have immortalized the description and the position of glory and honour to their people and their nation in all fields, under all names.

Why have the sublime meanings won and yielded fruit? They have won, Brothers, because they alone are capable of representing the true quality of our people and their faithful native and national will. They have won because they have represented the stand which formed the great and glorious historical meaning of all the armies of Iraq, under all of their names and under all of Iraq's names. They formed the great historical meaning which the great leaders willed. That meaning materialized in a cordial interaction between the will of the leadership and the will of the people, bringing together the unity of stand and expressing their potency whenever action was sincere, effective and loyal. That meaning, thus, uplifted the position of the history of Iraq, its role and its qualities, while making of all that had passed a firm and a true starting point for marching forwards and upwards.

Thus, too, the branch was fused with its root in the Second Glorious Qadissiya and in the Immortal Mother of All Battles. The fusion was so complete that it became impossible for any, other than its sons, and the sons of the people of Iraq and the glorious Arab Nation, to distinguish which was the root and which was the branch. The branch bore all the meanings and the true essence of the root in quality and attitude. This happened to the extent that each single quality that uplifted our people and our army showed itself as if it were the root, while it was but a branch if measured by the yardstick of its stage. The branch, thus, came to bear the qualities of the root and to represent it. And the root came to be alive within the stage during which the branch gave it a true representation with the highest meanings. That root had been cut out of communication for a long time before the zealous sons of Iraq, the sons of their glorious nation, became masters of the test through which they successfully proved to be the loyal sons of the history of their people, their nation and their army. They became masters of the chance to decide the fate of their peoples' will, the direction of its action and the stand the people and the army take. Meanwhile, all the meanings of potency and all distinguishing characteristics were born out of the womb of the nation and the loins of the people and the meaning and fragrance of history.

Now, we can address our Army and say to it:

You, brave, heroic, loyal, trustworthy and great Army!

You, son of your people and your glorious nation, their sword and lance and shield and armourplate!

You, Army of the Qadissiya of the faithful Arabs and Muslims, the Army of Abi Bakr in the Wars of Apostasy, of Omar Al-Faruq [he who distinguishes truth from falsehood], the symbol of the sword of Ali bin Abi Talib, ever drawn for the cause of Allah, the Army of Sa'ad and Al-Muthanna, the Army of Nebuchadnezzar, of Hammurabi, of Sargon, of Shalmaneser and Ashurbanipal, the Army of the Glorious Qadissiya of Saddam and the Immortal Mother of All Battles, the Army of Iraq, the Army of the Arab Nation, the Army of Palestine, and the Army of the People and of great difficult tasks.

Allah's greetings to you! You are the might and the potency that trusts in Allah. By Allah, you have represented all the sublime meanings which came under all the titles and names we have mentioned. You are the arm and the forearm in battle, the heart of steadfastness in adversities and the conscience of history. You act in the name of your people and your nation, without whose depth and meanings you would not have been what your are now.

We honour your Day, you brave heroic Army, on the Sixth of January of every year to celebrate all the sublime meanings. We celebrate the brilliance and radiance of faith, jihad, civilization and the stand representing all of these titles, not merely the abstract meaning nor the general descriptive mean of that day in the year 1921, nor only its meaning within that stage.

We celebrate and honour you under all of those banners and under the crown of the meanings of all those great historical stages. We do this in order to restore the role, the cause, the stand, the high-mindedness and the spirit of sacrifice and selflessness, with all that fortifies the nation and the people and all the past history they created for them. It is a history which looks brand new while connecting all of its great steps forward and its high morale with the past of our nation and our people, in all the previous stages.

Greetings, salutations, high regards, pride and glory to you!

Veneration to you and pride in all that pleases Allah of your stands and sacrifices, while you take your jihadic and heroic steps carrying the Allah-is-the-Greatest Banner, ahead of your great people to record for them and with them a new history that fortifies the nation, raises its place and brings shame on the treacherous unbelievers and their self-abasing followers.

A loving greeting to you for every stand in which you have chivalrously responded to the call of right and the meanings of manhood and struggle in the Iraq of virtue and glory. A loving greeting to you for every chivalrous stand that fortifies the Arabs and the Iraqis. Thus chivalry, on the basis of that stand, becomes a great historical act which sheds light upon any darkness, dispels any dimness, guides the marchers on the tracks of the road leading upwards. While pointing to any weakness, cowardice or abasement, chivalry arouses determination to cling to the meaning of the principles and the stand of the faithful men. It expels from the chests and the souls and the ranks any inclination to retreat and any stand that may bring shame upon history and give the enemies false impressions and embolden them to call Iraq names that are unbecoming to its history and the history of the nation.

Greetings and salutations to the martyrs!

Greetings and salutations to the martyrs!

Glory to the martyrs!

Glory to the living while they bear the sublime meanings!

Long live our glorious nation!

Long live Iraq!

Long live Iraq and long live its Army, the Army of difficult tasks, of great zeal and of heroic stands!

Long live Palestine, free and Arab!

Long live Palestine in whose battle Iraq has represented, with the assistance of Allah, the potency of faith, side by side with the heroic Palestinians and the armies and the will of the Arab nation wherever the banners and the true stands endeavour to fortify the nation and those who take those true stands!

A special greeting to the heroes, the vanguard of the striving people of Palestine while they carry the banner of struggle to liberate Palestine from the River to the Sea!

God is the Greatest!

God is the Greatest!

And let the debased be despised!

Address of His Excellency President Saddam Hussein In January 17, 2001

In the name of Allah, the Merciful, the Compassionate

Great people!

Exalted men of our valiant armed forces!

Glorious men and women who have volunteered for Palestine and its crown, Al-Quds, to be free and liberated from the filth of Zionism!

Arabs!

People, wherever you are, you whose hearts are filled with faith, and who have made justice and fairness the path towards what pleases Allah!

Peace be with you and Allah's Mercy and Blessings!

On a day like this day in the year 1991, a marvel happened on both sides of an encounter. It was the first encounter of its kind in the history of mankind until Allah decrees a similar one, in a similar situation, on two sides, each on the basis of his description and what he deserves.

At that time, on a day like this day ten years ago, Evil and all those who made Satan their protector lined up in one place, facing those who represented the will to defend right against falsehood and who had Allah as their Protector. They chose the sublime meanings and jihad, with hearts humble in prayer to Allah, glorified be His name, as their path towards His good pleasure, to win His forgiveness, pardon and satisfaction through faithful obedience.

Do you know, brothers, who deserved the latter description? I do not think that you do not know him who identified his name through the quality of his action on the path of jihad and virtue and the path of every human meaning which is sought by all those who seek it to achieve even a part of it.

On this side of the encounter were the people of civilizations, the cradle of prophet hood, the torch of Allah's messages and the anvil on which all hammers broke. Thus, through the power of their endurance and the power of their fortitude to reject injustice and oppression they became the cause for many a government to tumble down, and for the sun to turn away from those who are so much disposed to evil that they have become the representative type of Satan in their actions and in their lack of character.

On this side of sublime meanings and the true free stand were your people, you Arabs. It is your valiant army, you faithful freedom fighters. It is Iraq, you good people in humanity at large. It is the son of the immortal twin rivers, the bearer of the greatest mark in honour, character, principles, faith, stand, sword and banner. It is he whom you have known for the last ten years defending the principles of faith and humanity and defending the principles of his glorious Arab nation.

Some of you may have forgotten, and I do not think that many of you have forgotten who were on the other side of the encounter. They were the debased, the enemies of Allah, and those who had Satan as their protector for he had their character. They were those who missed no chance to confirm their character with what stamped it with the stamp of disgrace and shame whose marks will never disappear till Doomsday. So, those with the highest attributes, the attributes of dignity, honour and heroic stand, and with them the people of great Iraq had their chance to be at the zenith while the debased and the treacherous had theirs at the nadir.

Don't you know who the debased and evil are?

Shall I reiterate in their hearing and yours who they are? Or would you say that you know them by their ugly and debased faces? Those ugly faces lined up dishonourably against and in front of faces beaming in beauty and brightness while looking towards their Lord with the marks of the People of Paradise, the faces of the pious martyrs and the faces of the living who have never changed their determination.

To refresh your memory, I will count on the side of the base act and the disgraceful stand those who represented the U.S, those who represented Britain, France, Germany, Spain, Holland, Argentina, Belgium and Australia…Shall I continue counting or do you still remember the number: thirty-three states, twenty-eight armies, taking the first place in the aggression upon Iraq, and more than forty states taking charge of supporting the direct aggression in addition to world Zionism and its freak and accursed entity?

As for the Arabs. O you Arabs, you who are our pride, our honour, our wound, our wound, alas! Shall I count? How can I give names and count? How can I say and open the wounds? I will say but not count. I will say that the Arab nation is our nation. We belong to it and it belongs to us. It is our pride and our strength. It is our depth and Iraq is its depth. In its name was our call of chivalry, and in the name of its great ideals, our great ideals and its principles, we assaulted falsehood and knocked out its brain and caused it to perish. It is the nation of prophets, of martyrs and of holy men, it is our nation. Other than this I will not say. Let every coward or censurer hear me. It is my nation. No individual, even though he may say he belongs to it, can ever do evil to it or to its character. Will a rivulet with stale or stagnant water change the properties of the thundering sea?

No! The properties of our thundering sea will never change. And those who represent it in the sublime and principled stands are the true representatives of its properties. Everything else is accidental and short-lived.

Long live every stout-hearted and every faithful and generous individual in the Arab nation who is ever enraged at falsehood, discontented with it.

But did you know what happened in that continuous encounter then, and in this one which is going on even now? Did you know what the injustice and the embargo did to the people of Iraq? shall we engage and burden you with the details of what happened and what was said, or is it enough that we describe part of what should be described?

On the side of Evil, they showed on television part of what they did, boasting of the atrocities they committed. Do you know, brothers, what they did? Have you seen (the doing) of a reckless, spoiled and light-headed child who takes after his father who was one of the kings of old times, but the like of him may exist even now too? Consider what this heedless child can do when he feels jealous of a rich museum and finds that he has the means to destroy it. None but this description fits those who waged and are still waging aggression and inflicting destruction upon the museum of faith, virtue, civilization, noble stand, the museum of the brave men and glorious women, and the great tree of life in the Iraq of the Arabs and the Muslims and the Iraq of faith. But what they destroyed, brothers, excepting human lives and blood, was but a copy of the original. The museum of civilization has remained radiating its meaning and keeping its original patterns safe, for they lie latent in the deep faith and in the true viability inside the souls and inside the giant tree of life, whose roots go deep down in human history, to the nation and to people everywhere generations after generations.

Isn't this the proper comparison on the side of evil with those who believe that they are destroying man while they merely destroy what is material in his surroundings?

The missiles and bombs of aggression hit everything material and suitable as target for their weapons. Much dear blood of the dear ones was shed. But they have become the flagstaff of Allah-is-the-Greatest Banner. They have become the candles that dispel darkness before the march of great Iraq, generations after generations, and whenever darkness tries to veil the luminous light before the great march of the Iraqis who have sworn by Allah, by the blood of the martyrs and by every great name to make their crossing unquestionable.

Thus, Iraq has remained, the people have remained, the army has remained.

Long live the people!

Long live the Army!

Long live the Comrades!

Now then, one may ask: who was lining on the side of Iraq? shall I describe and tell you, and this is my belief, how Allah, the Omnipotent, was watching over Iraq with His attention? And how He turned their fire cool and a means of safety for the Iraqis? And how the conscience of the Arab nation with its splendid history, its great faithful ideals, its meanings and its sublime symbols stood by the side of Iraq? And how Iraq was fighting and moving freely in the battlefield?

Have you seen a mountain in a state of furious rage and eruption?

Have you seen the waves of a huge, roaring and thundering ocean in a state of a great flow?

Have you seen the Tigris and how it floods in April every year?

Have you seen how the believers love Allah? And how people love people when they love deeply and with sublimity?

Have you seen how a lion in its den defends its cubs when in danger?

He who has seen and known this knows how Iraq was and how it is now. Iraq faced hate with love, weakness with strength, despair with hope, cowardice with courage, dishonour and treachery with honour and loyalty and truth of the honourable stand. The Iraqis loved their people, their civilization and their glorious history. They loved their nation and its great principles a love surpassed by none before. And because they were born free, they loved the right of every nation in humanity to be free, unyielding to the might of tyranny and exploitation of greed. That is how they came to be what they are, and to be what you know them for.

From these significant examples and meanings you can understand how an Iraqi loved his nation and loved Iraq, how he forbore, fought and held his ground, how he built towering buildings, how and why he plants trees and flowers even while the blazing flames of fire were and still are scorching his face in the continuous aggression of the evildoers and the injustice of their followers, how and why he sows the seeds of life and smiles to them and how and why he builds and elevates the building after removing the debris of destruction.

Iraq has triumphed over the enemies of the nation and over its enemies. It will triumph in all the remaining rounds with the help of Allah because it has achieved its triumph inside its soul, its conscience, its heart and its mind.

As for you, striving and struggling Arabs, this is known, too, by anyone of you who envisages, remembers and never forgets the maturity of the bills of the great principles of faith as a debt becoming due and as an assignment entrusted to him by Allah and by anyone of you who remembers that his ancestors were the pioneers of faith and the principles of human civilization and the lofty banners to the whole mankind. Anyone who can recall the image of how the Companions of the Messenger of Allah used to fight, preceded by the sword and banner bearers: Al-Hamza, Abu Bakr As-Siddiq, Abu Al-Hassanain Ali, with his sword, Dhul-Fiqar, Omar Al-Farouq and Khalid bin Al-Waleed, and how they used to hear the voice, the call and the prayer of the Prophet (Allah's blessings and peace be upon him) for their victory—anyone who can recall this, knows how the Iraqis fought led by each brave hero who has been true to his Covenant with Allah. He also knows how he should strive, struggle and fight too in defence of his identity, the principles of his nation and the meanings of the True Religion. Thus, he fortifies patriotism and the homeland, uplifts, with right, the position of the nation, the people, the nationalism and faith. He defeats evil and weakness, and strikes down degradation and falsehood and every foreigner encroaching on the right of the Arabs, on the meanings of their faith and on their right to sovereignty, security, life and the protection of the principles of honour and dignity.

Moreover, and after the Immortal Mother of All Battles, and after the children, youth and the aged of Palestine, men and women, have faced the weapons of the U.S and Zionism with stones, is there any Arab who may ask: How? After this and for a thousand or thousands of years to come, can fear find its way to the heart of any Arab in a position of responsibility unless he is a fear-ridden coward or hopelessly unpatriotic and lacking the virtue of faith in his soul? Can anyone who is faithful and zealous for his people and nation be excused when he does not rise against the injustice of the foreigner and the injustice of the unjust, and does not force and help himself to get rid of the weakness inside his soul?

Long live our glorious Arab nation!

Long live Palestine, free and proud from the River to the Sea!

Long live Iraq!

Long live Iraq!

Long live the people!

Long live the army!

Long live the comrades!

Allah is the Greatest!

Allah is the Greatest!

Allah is the Greatest!

And let the debased be despised!

President Saddam Hussein's Address on the 33rd Anniversary of July 17–30 Revolution

In the name of God, the Merciful, the Compassionate

Great Iraqi people!

Courageous armed forces, pinnacle of glory and our upholders in adversity and combats, and whenever our march needs grand willpower so that, God willing, our edifice becomes higher, our glory greater and our crossing over achieved!

Revolutionaries and Mujahidins!

Here comes a new anniversary of your revolution that adds yet another bright star to your sky in which God exalted you by way of your glorious revolution. You celebrate the advent of the revolution and its new anniversary galvanizing your verve, reorganizing your ranks to enhance your march and to enlarge, deepen, extend your wisdom and patience, rendering them more effective.

Iraqi people!

You are the source of your pride, the succor of every honest and free man who calls upon you, and the defenders of all aggrieved people.

You have been just as I imagined you in the year we are bidding farewell to, but I have come to have a new perception of you, the advanced standards of which are based on your high level of fervor toward Palestine, your people, and your Quds (Jerusalem) in Palestine, in addition to your other stands. Am I not right, dear beloved ones, to draw my perception of, and my hope in you on the basis of your earnestness in construction, succor, patience, sacrifices and glory.

God bless you all, for you have maintained your faith in God and you have pursued your virtues in all your action, the forefront of which is your great stand of defense you have taken to repulse the villains' schemes and to disillusion their abject wishes?

Yes, by God you are the people of sublime distinction that exalts faithful men.

Great Iraqi people!

Glorious men and women!

Writing this address to you, I asked myself: does destiny choose for people the roles they play? Or do people themselves choose their roles in the light of what exalts or diminishes the faith, awareness, and the verve of this or that man amongst them?

Let me point out the gist of what I want to say: being the living essence and the authentic representatives of the Arab nation, did the Iraqis choose their role, or is it destiny that chose their role for them, after having shown their preparedness and their fervor and mindfulness?

When we look deep into the background of any result attained before giving it the marks it deserves, and before saying anything about it, we must first say that we think that, being the advanced example of their Arab nation at this stage, the Iraqi people have taken a stand which is the result of a ravishing mixture of the destiny's choice for them and their own preparedness to play their role in line with God's will to make the Arab nation the forerunner of humanity in all commendable deeds.

Hence we understand that, after believing in God's faith, man chooses his role, and declares his faith. Then he works in such a way that reminds him of his duties, history and role. Destiny chooses the roles people play only when they rouse from their lethargy, be mindful of their roles and of the patience and sacrifices their action requires to become fruitful.

The spur of your verve, mindfulness, and determination to undertake your role is your authentic history, your stand, your role within the Arab nation and the role of the Arab nation within you. You have carried faith to your Arab nation, in one of your roles. Then came your nation of the descendants of Abraham (peace be upon him) to play another role, to undertake whatever novelty or renewal God wanted.

One might ask: why are the Iraqis recalling their role now and not before or after? Here, too, interferes the will of destiny in the choice, the maturity of man's mindfulness, his high verve, perspicacity, wisdom, and agility at the moment, so that things can be decided, God willing. Hence was the revolution with all its events and subsequent development including our present day situation.

Dear Iraqis!

A seed does not grow but at a certain time and a certain season. If it ever grew at the wrong time, it wouldn't bear fruit even if it flowered and blossomed. If it did bear fruit, the fruits would be of a kind to which the soil or the seeds are not used to. Consequently the seeds would fall into lethargy to recover its capability of growing, flowering, blossoming and bearing fruit according to the quality of the soil along with other factors. It is just like when some trees shed their leaves, staying alive only at the minimum level of being. After a period of lethargy they regain life in their proper seasons and after bringing together their capabilities during their lethargy in order to peruse their role and mission.

Iraq has gone through something like this metaphor taken from nature. The moment of the role destiny chose for you coincided with the moment of the role you chose for yourselves, after a long period of lethargy. This is why your verve was so great that God has bestowed upon you and your Arab nation glory and grandeur.

Iraqi men and glorious women!

Great people and army!

Its your historic opportunity, and along with it, your Arab nation's opportunity in as much as the role you play within your nation and your nation's expectations of you.

Dear Iraqi people!

What can we tell you about your revolution, you who are its authors, guides, source of its capabilities and verve along with your great faith?

Shall we tell you how Iraq was and how it has become now?

Can anyone in an address of an occasion like this, elaborate upon how Iraq was on the eve of 17–30 July revolution in all walks of life, and upon what it has become now? shall we tell you how the evil forces were mobilized against the revolution, and how they resorted to the most debased schemes to deter the revolution and discourage its authors from their choice and route?

Can anyone enumerate the types, history, and the level of achievement that have reached every household, cottage and family?

Shall we say that a great number of our Iraqi people were barefooted, and only few of them thought that their life would be better the next day? Should we compare the number and the level of students in schools now and before? Should we talk about what we used to manufacture and how and what we used to import, from which countries and how? Or should we count down the number of workers in the countryside, and in the industrial and services sectors compared to their numbers now despite the unjust blockade?!

Should we mention the high level of the standard of living of the Iraqis prior to the build-up of the forces of the evil and the mobilization of their fire against Iraq in a timing and a way that made them think that they would indubitably destroy Iraq, its people, inspirations, role, and destiny?! No, I will not burden you with these details, because you already know them. You are the people of all virtues, stands, and verve that have carried Iraq to the summit. Your enemies, before your friends, know now who Iraq is, and how is its faith, determination, verve, stands, and capabilities. But, we say to the Arabs and friends, and by so doing we will exasperate our enemies and please our friends and brothers: the reason behind all that took place against Iraq and its revolution is that Iraq made its choice on the national, pan-Arab, and international levels when its great faith reached its summit, to be totally free, to play its role and to be firmly settled on its route. Any contrary action would not curb the Iraqi people's will, after having seen its route and after the fact that not only the vanguard, but all the Arab nation have come to know that this route is the route of true freedom and the route that safeguards our dignity that no Iraqi or authentic Arab would have it stigmatized or touched upon by whosoever.

We are arriving, with the help of God the Almighty, at what pleases our friends and strikes our enemies with one disappointment after another. Our willpower and our capability to build and to make better choices, are with the help of God, stronger now than before the beginning of the confrontation in the eternal Um Al-Marik (Mof all Battles).

Although petroleum is an essential part of our great national resources, it is not the basis of our potential and willpower, and it will certainly not be a doorway to weakness in us, nor a breach in the fortifications of our country or in the patriotism, fervor, and the virtues of this loyal people of Mujahidins.

Nevertheless, we must tell you, men and glorious women, of the great people of Iraq that you are part of a great nation, and that the values of the grand role you represent for your great nation have blossomed in you. They are not the fountainhead of hope for the Arab nation only, but for part of humanity as well. The enemies' schemes to get hold of the spirit of the Arab nation can not be achieved, God forbid, but by humiliating you. God the Almighty, the Merciful, will disgrace them. Your enemies, the smaller ones, their servants and attendants, and the bigger ones are still contriving against you. Their despondent designs, before they breathe their last, continue, and the Zionist malignancy continues to support and encourage them on evil doing. They are hoping that in this way they will domesticate the Iraqi people and be able to decide what and how much this great people eat and drink before, God forbid, slaughtering them. May God disgrace them. The illusion of your enemies reflects their despair, and is still leading them to forget their qualities, just as they have forgotten the qualities of the noble and dauntless Arabs, and consequently fell into the trap of your heroic people in Palestine, of the heroes of the resistance in Lebanon, and before that in the trap of the revolutions in Iraq, Egypt, Algeria, and on all the Arab territories.

Dear Iraqis!

Dear Iraqi glorious women!

You are the fountain of willpower and the wellspring of life, the essence of earth, the sabers of demise, the pupil of the eye, and the twitch of the eyelid. A people like you cannot but be, with God's help. So be as you are, and as we are determined to be. Let all cowards, piggish people, traitors and betrayers, be debased.

Dear beloved ones, speak to those abject evil doers in one voice. Show them the fervor that God has bestowed on you so much that even sore eyes can see it just as you did in all the vicissitudes of the revolution and the people's combats. Confirm, not by reverberating voice but by your grand verve, your statement that you are the people of Iraq, the people of a great history and stands that you are the cranium of Arabs, their conscience, their indefatigable swords and willpower, and that you are the mentors of the world not its domestic fowls. Speak out strongly, and do the same thing you did before confirming your statements with the action they require. You are the people of construction, virtue and principles, capable of confronting and ascending all difficulties. Those who fight you will gain nothing but disappointment and defeat. With God's help, your enemies' schemes will end up in abyss, and your fervor and willpower will not diminish. God is with you and no one but the devil will be with your enemies. Those who are befriended by the devil will end up in hell whereas victory will be the lot of the patient and faithful believers.

God is the Greatest!

Arab nation!

Best family and best home!

You are the best people in faith and in rising. You are the conscience of humanity and their mentor. You are the people upon whom God bestowed all goodness. You are the instructors of the great lessons of chivalry, sacrifice for great principles, and enjoying victory within yourselves when you are right, prior to attaining victory in its field, by God's help.

Rise up dear ones for whom we are ready to sacrifice anything, except honor and our stands of honor. Say to your enemies, the enemies of our Arab nation who are the foul Jewish usurpers, their covetous allies, and all the colonialists and their abject servants: stop abusing the Arab nation, the nation of prophets and God's messengers. It is now the right time to say this and to work on it, for the situation has become intolerable, and injustice has settled down and reached its climax. Now it is the right time for you to seize your opportunity to be and to play the role God chose for you, otherwise, the enemies of Arab nation will inflict more injustice and tyranny upon you, instead of being thanked by the good peoples of the world, after thanking God and his prophets. God will stand up for the believers who stand by Him, and will bestow glory upon the courageous Mujahidins and all free and honest men who fight for the freedom of their countries.

Glory to our martyrs!

Glory and heavens to our martyrs!

Glory and heavens to the martyrs, of Palestine, Iraq, Lebanon, and to the martyrs of the Arab nation!

Long live the nation of Arabs and its eternal message!

Long live the Arab Mujahidins!

Long live Palestine!

Long live Iraq!

And long live Palestine!

Down to hell with all conspiracies and evil schemes!

Down with all the debased resolutions of America, the enemy of peoples in the world, its allies, supporters, and servants!

God is the Greatest!

God is the Greatest!

Let the debased be despised.

President Saddam Hussein's Address On The 13th Anniversary Of The Great Victory Day/August 8, 2001

In the name of Allah, the Merciful, the Compassionate

"Our Lord! Let not our hearts deviate now after you have guided us, but grant us mercy from your own presence; for you are the Grantor of bounties." Holy Quran (III. 8)

"We hurl right against injustice, it strikes at it then it will be frustrated" Holy Quran

Great loyal people of Iraq!

Godly martyrs!

Manly men of our valiant armed forces!

Noble women of Iraq!

Sons of our glorious Arab nation!

The days and the months revolve, and once again we are in the presence of August to give it an account of what we have achieved, after extending our due reverence and veneration to it. We would like to reassure August, having first endeavoured basically to win the satisfaction of the Merciful, the Compassionate, and to reassure with August all the people we have just addressed and all the good people in the world. We would like to reassure them and reassure August with them that its spirit of victory is still alive in the great and lofty construction carried out by the people of the summits and in the great struggle in the Grand Battle, the immortal Mother of All Battles, and that the harvest of victory is progressing along the lines of the promise we gave to it. And none will suffer frustration but those who are frustrated of their purpose.

Brothers!

While thinking of addressing you, I wondered: Is victory achieved only when the elements of strength are gathered, organized and mobilized, and when the timing of each action is chosen to suit its right moment according to the property of its objectives? Or is it the translation of faith, after it rises to its level together with the readiness for sacrifice, into items in a realistic and successful working plan, that achieves victory and renews itself and its means after developing the available strength to create what is additional in it and not merely using it as it is, as the first hypothesis postulates?

Victory, brothers, is achieved through both hypotheses when they fuse and interact under the supervision of an experienced, devoted, open-minded, potent and faithful leadership that cherishes its deep roots. The energy that nourishes victory and the guiding light on its main and subsidiary routes spring first from the hearts and the souls before looking for them in the field of things and other conditions. But feeling them inside the hearts and souls of their pioneers and those who hold titles of leadership in them, each according to his responsibility, power and authority, and the inner feeling of the possibility of achieving victory inevitably in the light of the faith inside the hearts and souls alone—this feeling is the foundation without which total victory cannot be achieved. Hand in hand with this inner feeling goes good management, arrived at through the accumulation of experience, knowledge and the trust of the people and the army in their leadership, after having tested their leadership in all rounds of struggle and jihad and in other fields of life.

From this trust and with it, after the trust in Allah, the Great Omnipotent, and on the basis of justice, fairness and care for people's lives on the part of whoever leads the people and the army, spring elements that merge with each other and, Allah willing, undergo a great interaction to produce the fundamental factors that make victory possible. Or rather, with the gathering together of the attributes we have mentioned and their active presence and genuine interaction, victory becomes decisive in the hearts and in the souls. The certainty of victory and the absolute feeling of its presence are not cancelled out by any partial disagreement with its final results in this front or that, in this partial time of the battle or that, when the causes of victory in the hearts and souls of the opposing adversary forces are not of this quality—even when they achieve superiority in things or in some partial results which come contrary to the wish of the true freedom fighters and the patient, faithful people of the just and fair stand and of the high sense of honour who are on the opposite side—they will not turn into a decisive result which counters the expected victory. The thoughts of those who line up under the opposing banner will be confused, their faith in what they were expecting and working for will be shaken, their lines will be dispersed and their power will depart with the prolongation of time and as endurance and patience in the lines of the faithful go on until Allah gives leave for the preponderance of the line of faith, the right stand, the wakeful management and the renewal that is not cut off its necessities and its circumstance.

Thus should be understood the preponderance of having victory spring first from the soul basically, and impose its image through factors called for by necessity to be united and interacting with what is inside the souls, hearts and minds and their outer surroundings to render it,

Allah willing, decisive and final and to have it as the inevitable result of what we have referred to.

This is precisely the inspiration we, your brothers and comrades in the leadership, have received from your great history, great people of Iraq and high-spirited men of our valiant armed forces, and from the history of your glorious nation and their immortal heritage before examining closely the state of things at that time but, or rather, while examining it too. And this is what we exerted ourselves to do under all difficult circumstances for eight years, from September 4, 1980, when the Iranian aggression started as an organized military aggression with the shelling of towns, villages and economic establishments, to August 8, 1988, on which Allah favoured the people of Iraq and their free loyal army with His manifest victory along its description. Described thus, it is also a victory for the righteous people in Iran as it is a victory for the Arab nation and for the true believers. This is, brothers, the description of the victory achieved on August 8, 1988 and this is its nature, its foundation and the type of faith in it from the starting point until it became a final fact in the record of history.

On this basis, and along the same central concepts and their genuine constants, together with the required revolutionary compatibility and continuous renewal in styles, means, concepts, potentials and methods of treatment and behaviour, the proud and loyal people of Iraq and their valiant armed forces will win victory in the final results of the immortal Mother of All Battles. With them and through them, good Arabs will win victory. Their victory will be splendid, immortal immaculate, with brilliance that no interference can overshadow. In our hearts and souls as in the hearts and souls of the high-minded, glorious Iraqi women and high-spirited Iraqi men, victory is absolute conviction, Allah willing. The picking of its final fruit, in accordance with its description which all the world will point to, is a matter of time whose manner and last and final hour will be determined by the Merciful Allah. And Allah is the greatest!

Great people of Iraq!

Arabs, the best of all those who have struggled or sacrificed, descendants of the best of mothers and the worthiest of fathers,

Knowing the facts of life and dealing with them rather than with illusions, important as the two are for the revolutionaries to implement their practical programmes, including their great struggle to achieve victory over their enemies, may become a heavy burden for them unless they deal with these factors in the spirit of the faithful and optimistic revolutionaries who are capable of creativity, innovation and ascent. It will not do to deal with these facts in a shaken spirit and trembling, unsure souls and to succumb to their appearances as they are, and not with the spirit of confidence in the possibility of changing them radically and deeply to make them as they should be.

In any case, there is a clear between the mentality of that who deals with things in the light of their present possibilities only, and that who deals with them in a spirit connected to the deep-rooted past on the one hand and to the future desired to be promising on the other hand. It is an energetic spirit which revolts against any feeling of weakness or impotence to look up to the whole future and be a living part in it. As the facts of life stipulate that they should be viewed as they really are so that the plan of changing them may succeed, the history of peoples and nations, the possibilities of additional creativity through constantly renewed high-mindedness and the desire for soaring up through strength on the part of those who want it—these are all facts and not illusions. The spirit informing the history of the nation and the people and their immortal heritage is the most important of the facts of life. It is, rather, the source of the main light in it, especially if it is interconnected with the faith and high-mindedness of those who believe in it in the present so that it comes to those who work on it like a glorious sunrise filling the whole horizon with brilliance, provided that it is preceded by a genial gleam inside the soul and a definite and total belief in it until victory becomes a fact at hand, seen by the naked eye.

In this spirit and on the basis of its laws and its relation to what ought to be and what should be in the manner and necessities with which the high-spirited men and glorious women of Iraq dealt, the manifest victory was achieved on August 8, 1988. It was achieved despite the predictions of those whose vision or resolution weakened or collapsed or was exhausted to the degree that they could not see it even in the remote horizon, while those who believed in the cause reached the end line in it carrying its banner and each according to the order and degree of their arrival, feeling as if they were taking the first step in the race, or rather, feeling as if they were unwounded or as if the ointment of the result had healed all their wounds. Thus this victory was born. With its birth, all the powers of evil in the world were provoked and mobilized after having seen that what the nation had been lacking was achieved on August 8, 1988, not only in its results but in its spirit also. The people and armed forces of Iraq started a new round with all that is required of the accumulation of experience, determined resolution and comprehensiveness and depth of conviction. The result, Allah willing, will not be but a brother to August. And as August was a brother to July, April was their sun, which dawned with the birth of the trustworthy nationalist Arab thought. It was the first faithful, truthful, virtuous and honest step on the road. July and August will have full brothers, as they had their sons in all the rounds of construction, in the spirit with which right encountered wrong with resolution, awareness, competence and faith of the high-born people to render the description of July and August and their sun, April, harmonious with the description with which Allah graced the true believers and disgraced the evil doers. The months of April, July and August will not be the only months of the Iraqis and the Arabs. With them will be all the months of the year because they are the months through which Allah has willed it to grand prosperity to the good and has made the shooting stars in them as missiles to drive away the evil ones. In these months, and for the first time in the history of mankind, the Babylonians devised astronomy and fixed the calendar of the year, the month, the week and the day, and the number of hours it contains.

And none will be despised but the debased!

Based upon all of this, brothers, we ask once again: Is victory achieved through mustering all potentials and directing each of them towards the target defined for it, and through choosing the right timing for any action? To this we answer:

A victory like the victory of August, which we celebrate and receive cordially and in which we salute the godly martyrs and the brave men and glorious women, or rather all of the great people of Iraq and the whole Arab nation and the Arabs who contributed to it—a victory such as this is not of the type or the description of the victories achieved by a technical condition and a ready-made strength only. It is rather achieved by a vision of the conflict in the middle of life as a whole. Only then can victory be potency for life, connected to its significance and necessity by deep faith.

The victory of August 8, 1988 was a victory of the faith we had and the way of life we chose over that which they affected and chose, imagining it to be faith and were deluded into believing that it would lead to it and that it was the right choice. Victory is the gist of a conflict with a list of comparisons full of items along the path of life and under all its titles, with each title, on our part, conflicting with its counterpart on the opposite side. The result of this conflict came precisely under this description: a manifest victory. Victorious in it were the faith we have and the quality characterizing our great people and their loyal representative in the front lines of the conflict, our valiant armed forces.

The manifest victory was achieved over what they had invented and called faith. Our life with its visions and concepts won along the path we chose. Before it and with it our faith won over their falsehood. Allah, Lord of the Worlds, was a witness, watching, with His wakeful eyes, over those whom He deemed worthy of a good reward and for singling out by His will, glorified be His name, those who deserve success and those who should fail. Thus came the victory with which He strengthened the Iraqis in their faith and their choice of life.

Along the same line will be the description of the victory in the immortal Mother of All Battles. That is because the eleven-year conflict with the evil aggressors in the Atlantic Pact, Zionism and its accursed freak entity and with those who allied with them or followed them like a hair in the tail of a treacherous biting dog, that conflict has defined all the titles of faith as we have them in the whole of Iraq. With them are defined the titles of our life and what we have chosen for it as path, image and condition, which are all conflicting now, as they conflicted for eight years in the Glorious Qadissiya, with their counterpart titles in the lines of the thwarted opponents. And then, the final victory on our side will not be the victory of massing a ready force and mobilizing it with technical success. It will not even be mere massing of a ready capability or a mere technical one only. That is because he technical list of comparison of what was ready on both sides of the conflict from the starting point till now, whether in strength or capability, in their technical sense points, from a narrow point of view, to the superiority of the enemy to us. But why do the Iraqis prove superior now, after trusting in the Great Omnipotent, and will prove superior in the final results too, Allah willing? They do so because the titles on the plane of faith and life, supported by the potency and the necessity of mobilizing the national and Pan-Arab spirit, will surpass the empty counterpart titles because these titles have lost, at the starting point, their legitimacy and the basis of justice and fairness in that legitimacy. They have lost the minimum requirement needed by a normal person to convince himself and others of the necessity of going on, exactly as it had been lost before by those who had chosen the conflict with us needlessly and whom we faced in the Glorious Qadissiya. Therefore, brothers, we will be victorious in the immortal Mother of All Battles too, as our people and our armed forces were victorious in the Glorious Qadissiya after faith won its victory over imposture, inventions and illusion, and after life won its victory over those who wanted it to be nothing but decayed bones in Iraq an, perhaps, the whole Arab nation.

In the light of these concepts and in the light of the facts of the conflict which we have been experiencing for the last twenty years in the Glorious Qadissiya and in the immortal Mother of All Battles, we find that it is our duty to address to you some observations about politics and some specific precepts on faith and life, on the methods of dealing with time and capability and how to develop potency and use it under certain circumstances, on how right wins victory over wrong after establishing right as the base for faith, justice and fairness and on all other things which were our guidelines in victory and patience.

And, brothers, because the Palestinian cause and the conflict in its field with the criminal Zionists, the usurpers of the land of Palestine and the lands of the Arabs, backed openly by the Black House and by certain people amongst the Arabs who are guided by personal interests and in whom both man and manhood died, because this cause is now the most important field in the Arab-Zionist conflict and because Palestine is the full sister of striving Iraq and the immortal Mother of All Battles, we find that what we know and what we want to give as precepts to the Arab strugglers and freedom fighters should start with a letter addressed to Palestine and to my brother, the freedom fighter President Yassir Arafat and to all the Palestinian strugglers and freedom fighters, men and women, and through them, this time, to every honest and zealous Arab and to every free and trustworthy believer:

Brothers and bother President!

Leaders of the people of Palestine!

Do not look for victory outside yourselves and outside the circle of your people. What is outside yourselves, Palestinians, is of little manly qualities under the official titles and their related nomenclatures. It is covered by misleading darkness on the whole. So, like the avant-guarde amongst you, be a lamp to guide and be a beacon to whatever pleases Allah and pleases the honest people in Palestine and your Arab brothers and people all over the world. Be like your brothers and sisters in Iraq, where leadership and people have become one and where official titles are no more than an additional honorable commitment towards good citizenship and towards serving the people and uplifting the voice of right and the nation. Be on your full guard against anything that divides you, because if you are divided, Allah forbid, you will loose the foundation of your strength.

Be as you should be, brothers, and as you vowed at the starting point to have Palestine victorious through you. Your victory, with what support you get from the Arabs, will be a victory for the whole nation. Remember this, and remind those who forget it, and on the basis of what you are supposed to be: strugglers who hold the principles of the revolution and who fight on the side of their people and in the depth of their nation in defence of the principles and to confirm these principles through fairness, loyalty and honour.

Prove to everyone that presidency and leadership are a trust, a stand and a sacrifice. Thus you may add a new layer to their new model initiated by your people in Iraq and by your brothers and comrades in the leadership who are the people, the brothers and the comrades of every honest, zealous and loyal person in the Arab Homeland. Presidency and leadership in Iraq have acquired a new meaning connected by an honourable and a solid bridgehead to the conception and meaning of presidency and leadership in the Arab-Islamic history.

In any case, do not pay much attention to the terrorist statements circulated by the defiled Jews and Zionists in the world, supported by the criminal administrations in the Black House. Do not make these statements a passage to weaken the unity of your people and their national force which is mobilized entirely to liberate the whole of Palestine after it has been baptized and has performed its ablution with pure blood.

And do not give any weight, which may affect the struggle of your people, to those who call for the extinguishing of what they call fire at the expense of your revolution and the revolution of your people. Your struggling, patient, zealous and faithful people are being burnt daily. Yet, that by which they are being burnt is but the perfume of Paradise with which they cleanse themselves and thus draw nearer to their salvation from the Zionist presence. This presence has been sitting heavily on the chests of the Palestinian people and the chests of every faithful, honest and ardent Arab and Muslim since the criminal Zionists occupied the land of Palestine through the scheming of the criminal world Zionism and the execution of England and its politicians.

Do not fear a fire with which they intimidate you and intimidate your people. The real fire which leaves corpses to decay in their place is surrender. But the fire that leads to Heaven and to victory, if Allah wills it for his striving worshippers to pass through, will be turned cool and a means of safety for them by Him, glorified be His name, and He will make mercy and the uppermost Heaven the martyrs' reward.

Let him, whose garment is bought with ill-gotten money or ill-gotten oil or ill-gotten stand, burn without extinguishing the fire. Do not accept it from those who try to extinguish the fire to turn the Palestinian rifle into a fire extinguisher and thus open with it a road of death by suffocation, not only for our people in Palestine but also for the people of our entire nation, leaving the corpses of the suffocated without perfume from Paradise and without angles to enclose them and bless them in the name of the Merciful Lord.

Finally, tell them, brothers under the leadership of brother President Yassir, together with your brothers in all the titles of leadership and its hierarchy on the land of Palestine, and let every honest and loyal Palestinian freedom fighter and every faithful and ardent Arab tell them this: Death is right and for those who struggle and fight a jihadic war, it is supposed to be an expected state at the starting point. Tell them that the death of a loyal, truthful and striving freedom fighter is a better life not only for him but also for all of those who share the same stand and faith with him. Tell them that the struggler President and all the strugglers do not fear the death schemed by the enemy if there is only one choice between dying as martyrs and surrendering or accepting whatever weakens the march of the people.

Do not give any chance to those who try, in line with what is called thwarting the plans of the Zionist entity, to bargain with alternative slogans such as saving the lives of Yassir Aaraft and the leadership in exchange for extinguishing the candle of resistance or dimming it or distracting it from its basic objectives. We will not accept it from anyone to wrong the strugglers, and you are strugglers, brother Yassir and my brothers in the Palestinian leadership. So, I do not believe that you accept to be wronged as we and every honest and ardent Arab do not accept it for any of you to be wronged with such misleading and flimsy calls. Manoeuvre them in politics, brother President Yassir, whenever necessary. You and the brothers who help you have an attested experience in political manoevring. But do not leave in your political manoevring any gap that may thwart the people or eliminate the unity of the strugglers.

Brother leaders of the people of Palestine, tell those who say to you (either the continuation of the revolution or the lives of Yassir Arafat and the leadership), tell them: We will have both: the continuation of the revolution and the lives of Yassir Arafat and the leadership. And then, you will live and with you, or in the forefront of you, lives brother President Yassir, as the martyrs who are alive in the conscience of their nation live, and with you will live the people of Palestine too. The remains of whoever chosen by Allah for martyrdom will be the perfume of Paradise and the niche for a glistening lamp that lights the path for those who walk on it now in the future till Allah decrees what He decrees for his good worshipers.

The supporters of Satan will reap nothing but that which they have sown. The freedom fighters will be the perfume of this life, its lamp and its banner, and they will be the perfume of the second life and its fragrance.

And Allah is the greatest!

Brother Arabs!

High-minded Iraqi men and illustrious Iraqi woman!

I think that you have heard or come to know the hostile statements against Iraq, made there, across the Atlantic, in a place imagined by those who live in it and by the unmindful and those deceived by lies, to have become, in a moment of negligence on the part of time, the centre of polarization and illumination in their new world or for their imperialistic globalization. Yes, made there, in the house the Iraqis called (the Black House) in the U.S. And here we have to apologize to all our brothers in humanity who have black skin because by describing it as black, we do not refer to the colour of the skin of its masters but to their deeds and to the colour of their intentions.

They deserve this description because of their criminal deeds against the whole of humanity and because of the evil burden they inflicted upon the Arabs and upon Muslims in particular.

Do you know the pretext under which the masters of that house prepare themselves this time to commit new crimes against Iraq? it is not the allegation that there are concentrations of troops near the Saudi borders, as they alleged in August 1990 or after. That allegation was shared by some who were misled and some who behaved wickedly out of joint evil purposes. It is not getting Iraq out of Kuwait, as they replaced their first lie by a new cover. It is not even getting rid of mass destruction weapons, which they wanted to be a cover for continuing their aggression and their aggressive intentions, even after Iraq pulled out of Kuwait. And it is not incompliance with the so-called U.N sanctions.

Do you know what the pretext is this time? It is saying that Iraq is threatening the American aircraft of aggression which break through its air, trespassing upon its skies, the sanctity of its sovereignty, its land, its people and its wealth. Yes, this is what their master-magician and his associates in the American-Zionist mass media band say.

How strange it is that those politicians still imagine that people can be deceived by these lies! I hope that this does not astonish you, brothers, Do not they who advocate this illusion hold big titles? Moreover, isn't it the attribute of those who share with them this title in these times to lie, to quack to slander and to wage aggression against people? Isn't this the attribute of those who are deemed big by the propagators of the globalization policy, led by the Black House? Or rather, isn't this the pivot on which turn the dealings with the world of this House which is a nest of poisonous wasps?

Doesn't this make you laugh? It does. The worst affliction is that which makes you laugh. Or rather, this low level of what is called the politics of our times drives people even to nausea.

People of rank in the United States, if you really care for the lives of your pilots and for your people, for whom you have widened the prohibited grounds, including your embassies, then you have to stop your harm and your evildoing against the world.

Stop the harm done by your cat's paw, the Zionist entity, and stop its crimes against Palestine and the Arabs, and against the sanctuaries of the believers. If you care that your pilots and your aircraft are not harmed by the fire of the high-spirited freedom fighters of faithful, trustworthy and great Iraq, take your aircraft and your battleships and go home. Stop your aggression and your aggressive attitude towards Iraq, and let the American people live peacefully and deal with the world respectfully and establish balanced interests with other peoples. If, however, your aggressive policy against all peoples, including the Iraqis, the Arabs and the striving Palestinians continue, you and those who support and encourage you will alone, and no one else, bear responsibility before Allah, before all peoples and before the American people.

Remember that your aircraft, of whose safety you talk, do daily drop, by your orders, elements of death and destruction on the people of civilization, faith, stand, principles and zeal. The Iraqi people and their leadership will not stand hopeless before that, because they were born free and have kept their sense of the value of their attributes and their role. And none will be despised but the debased evildoers. May evil befall every arrogant transgressor who persists in doing wrong against right.

And Allah is the greatest!

Now, brothers everywhere, we present to you some precepts which grew out of our experience in life and our struggle against falsehood, and as follows:

When you reach a post of authority, deal with the post and the decisions issued from it or in its name in the manner of one who is put to the test by authority and the responsibility of the post in it. Exert yourself to succeed in the test. Thus you will be well-pleased and well-pleasing before Allah, your self and the people. Otherwise, you will deal with authority as if it were a personal gain where you do not find yourself unless you use it deviantly or pervertedly and coercively. So, make the distance between you and the post clear, with a well-defined base for it. From the dictates of necessity and from several choices, choose the least harmful one. Otherwise, the best choice is that which brings you nearer to Allah and to the people.

Remember that the channel of evil is like the channel of stagnant water: the deeper it is, the more suffocating it becomes to those who wade in it, and the broader its unpleasant smell travels. So, perfume the channel of life with good deeds and leave the channel of evil to those whose benefactor is Satan.

If you have commendable attributes, do not imagine that all of those with whom you deal have the same, but do not imagine either that they are incapable of having the same or even higher attributes. In the first case, you may be frustrated when you discover the opposite of what you imagined about them. Doubting or neglecting the good attributes in them may make you miss the chance of dealing with them in a positive and a well-balanced manner. Always remember that your people deserve to be trusted by you, and that you should make good will and good faith in their actions and stands your starting point, provided that you guard against the evil elements and prepare the needed measures to protect yourself and your people against them.

Do not block the road at all times before an opponent who tries seriously to correct his mistakes. But do not draw your plans and organize your potency on this probability, for your opponent may surprise you with the opposite. You always have to prepare all that enhances your capability to protect yourself against an existing evil and an evil, which may take you by surprise. Open your door to whoever knocks at it asking forgiveness for an evil action or an evil design he intends to correct. Base your ruling on what Allah has ordered you to do and what He has forbidden to be done, and on the sublime principles you believe in, backed by the social practice which is stable on its right base. Take lessons from the past, but open your mind and your heart to the future. Be on your guard lest you be taken by surprise or trick. Trust in Allah in all of that.

Remember that the triumph of your enemy over you is bitter. So, do not delude yourself into believing that your strength is greater than it is, nor delude your enemy into believing that it is less than it really is, unless you want to trap him. Remember that if your enemy belittles your strength, he will inflict his evil upon you in a manner that it becomes impossible for you to avoid it. Strike the right balance between this and that. Endeavour to make your strength equal to your word or even higher than it is. Avoid evildoing, without leading your people and your friends to imagine that are weak. Make of you right a fence to secure your protection justly. Back out of a mistake if you make one. Know that Allah is the benefactor of the patient and the brave who believe in right against wrong.

If Allah grants you the ability to defeat your enemy, do not humiliate him. Just take your right from him or pardon him. If you humiliate your enemy after defeating him you will regret it when you realize that your opponent in that is the Great Omnipotent Allah. Thus, you will make your enemy, in his turn, regret his stand against you and try to take another stand in the light of his endeavour to enhance his strength and capability. The conflict continues with alternative success, in the light of strength and chance rather than right against wrong.

If you expect or desire to heal broken relations with an opponent, do not widen the enmity to the extent that neither he can bridge it to his advantage nor can you to yours. The enmity will thus turn into a total rupture. Attempts to heal it become mere cover to a wound whose pus increases by neglect or by applying the wrong medicine. The more pus a wound has, the more difficult it becomes to treat.

Make doubt an exception to the rule of trust and confidence in your relation with your people. But make it the rule of conception and behavior in your relations with foreigners at the starting point, and keep some of it all along the way. While the foreigners demand, as you do, that some steps of relative confidence be taken so that your dealings straighten within the limits of the relations you want to have along the description and the extent you both decide. Your people are worthy of your trust. You only have to prove to them that you are worthy of their trust and confidence in you at the starting point and all along the way.

There is an essential difference between a man who works hard in order to govern and a man who endeavours, strives and struggles in order to realize his objectives in the light of the principles in which he believes so that he may serve his people and his nation. The first likes people to say to him: You have spoken the truth—even when he tells lies. The second is concerned that people tell him the truth. When he does something right, they say to him: You have done this right, or dispense with that if it does not win the satisfaction of the people. When he does something wrong, they help him with truthful advice and sincere work to set it right. They do this on the basis that people and leadership are one historic condition within its stage.

Therefore, if you are of the second type of men, unite for life with your people, open your heart and your mind to them on your mutual course of life, and trust in Allah. This is how you win the satisfaction of Allah, of the people and of self, and thus become a popular landmark on the course of the history of your people and your nation, even if you are merely a struggler or a citizen among your people, with no other titles.

A judicious mind is a treasure. But not all of those who have it, in its scientific standards and attributes alone, can find its true significance and true power. Not all of them develop its comprehensive and deep properties and set it on the direction it should take in order to have an effective presence.

Mind, according to this description, is not that with which you convince yourself alone, but that which convinces people of you and of your mind thus describe.

Find the jewel of your mind. Develop its properties. Use it in the right direction on the right way to achieve that which you want to achieve. With this, and with the presence of the live conscience and noble human meanings inside your self, you will find that regret will diminish and self-satisfaction will take its place, optimism will take the place of despair and pessimism, vivacity the place of laziness and wise courage the place of hesitation or rashness.

Bear in mind that a victory, which is true and meaningful and whose significance and effect are of an everlasting nature, is not that for which you look outside your self. It is that which, in the first place, you find inside self, for self is its first and last testing ground and the field that precedes every other field.

Bear in mind also that victory inside the self will become the guiding model for any other successive victory, provided that one is capable of keeping up its requirements, maintaining it on its right base and shaking off it the dust or rust that gather on it in the course of its progress or as a result of the changing circumstances and their factors.

And then, victories of what is inside the self become victories outside it too. On the basis of the description, field and title of each of them, they become foreseen results, if, during their stages of birth and becoming, they are backed by the requirements of good management and by other capabilities, after trusting in Allah, the Great Omnipotent.

Keep in mind what Allah, glorified be His name, said about patience and its significance, and remember the way the prophets and messengers of Allah led their lives, and the sayings of the Noble Messenger of Allah, Muhammed bin Abdullah (Allah's blessing and peace be upon him and upon them all). And consequently remember that the least self-chiding people are the patient ones.

If patience does not imply the mustering up of strength for what a more effective and a more successful action requires in the direction of the predetermined objectives, or if it does not imply the choosing of the right moment for an action which is greater in effect, deeper in extent and lesser in sacrifice, then it is nothing but despair in which chances are lost and dignity may be wasted. It should be described as submission and servility instead of being describe as graceful patience.

Patience is wealth. In order for it to be living wealth, used on the right occasion, under definite titles and on the basis of right timing, it needs a captain. That captain is you, man. Know, then, how to find it, how to develop it and how to use it. Otherwise, it will turn into what looks like wealth buried in the ground and is unretrievable. It may even turn into a heavy burden to you.

Rights are like wealth, the more they outgrow the size, type and extent of the duties set against them, the less control the captain has over them and the less balanced their use is. Nothing is more important for the legislator of rights and for him who demands more rights, after considering that which satisfies Allah, than balance between these rights and the rights of society and the duties that ought to or must be carried out by whoever makes use of the rights. Otherwise, imbalanced rights become a burden to the individual and to society. And if they do not lead to catastrophes, they will certainly disturb the balance until things are brought back to their right shape and right course.

Any imbalance in rights to the advantage of duties can be adjusted without endangering the safety of society or altering the flow of life in a radically negative way, provided that the imbalance is neither serious nor intentional. But the serious imbalance of granting rights at the expense of duties will cause society to miss great historical chances and may lead to its collapse if it becomes comprehensive and if it extends over a period of time which exceeds the temporary circumstance. Whoever legislates for life and society or leads in both of them must bear in mind that whoever encroaches upon rights to the advantage of duties which do not have the form of a legitimate obligation or are not called for by necessity, will have Allah as his opponent. And he whose opponent is Allah is heading towards an abyss.

I add the following to what I have said so that everything becomes clear. A ruler who lacks the qualities of leadership and principles is often enticed to impose on the people and the nation more and greater duties and obligations than the rights he decides or are decided for them. Many ordinary people, on the other hand, are enticed to talk about and try to gain more rights, even if that leads to an imbalance between rights and duties.

Do not sow for today only and do not content yourself with what you sow for tomorrow but work on both. Give each the special care it needs and the attention it requires. Remember that the best work is that which makes today's sowing lead to the fruits of tomorrow's sowing, provided that neither of them infringes upon the other so that each yields the good fruits the sower desires. Do not let tomorrow distract you from you today, neither today from that which you hope for and endeavour to gain tomorrow, after trusting in Allah.

Neither wisdom nor virtue has he who is ungenerous; and undiscerning is he who is without divine guidance.

There is no good in him who bases all his weight in life on the title of authority he occupies, whose appearance and action are derived from his feeling of superiority to people, whose wealth is built upon ill-gotten gains and whose endeavour to win people's loyalty is based on their fear of him.

Man gains and enjoys as much freedom as he liberates himself from the weight of things on him. He will be guided to truth along the best and shortest routes when he deals with life without gloves and when he knows as much of divine omnipotence as concerns him when he trusts in Allah and deals with His Omnipotence without mediators.

Great People of Iraq!

High-spirited men of our valiant armed forces!

Arabs!

This is what we wanted to present and say before August that emerged victorious by the will of Allah, while we welcome, celebrate and commemorate all the days, months and years of the long battle and its complicated circumstances in the Glorious Qaddissiya and in part of what we are undergoing now in the Grand Battle, the Glorious Mother of All Battles. We affirm here to the sons of our glorious nation a vow we, as strugglers, made early in youth when we were still in the secondary school, a vow which the heroic people of Iraq, exalted men and glorious women, have now made with us that we will remain the dutiful sons of our nation, shouldering loyally the message before Allah and history. We will foster every good deed and defend with honour great Iraq and the sanctuary of the glorious nation.

Long live Iraq and long live Palestine!

Long live Palestine and long live Iraq!

Long live our glorious Arab nation and long live all the strugglers and freedom fighters in it!

Shame and disgrace on the enemies of our nation and our people. Disgrace and curses upon the criminal Zionists, the usurpers of the land of Palestine and the land of the Arabs!

Glory to the martyrs!

Glory to the martyrs!

And Allah is the greatest!

Allah is the greatest!

And let the debased be despised!

First Open Letter From President Saddam Hussein to the American Peoples and the Western Peoples and their Goverments, September 15, 2001

In the name of God, Most Gracious, Most merciful.

Once again, we would like to comment on what happened in America on September 11, 2001, and its consequences. The comments we made on the next day of the event represent the essence of our position regarding this event and other events, but the aftermath of what happened in America, in the West in particular and in the world in general, makes it important for every leader to understand the meaning of responsibility toward his people, his nation, and humanity in general to follow up the development of the situation, to understand the meaning of what is going on, and hence to elaborate his country's and people's position so as not to restrict oneself to only following the event.

When the event took place Arab rulers and the rulers of countries whose religion of their people is Islam, rushed to condemn the event. The Westerners rushed within hours to make statements and adopt resolutions, some of which are dangerous ones, in solidarity with America and against terrorism.

Even before being sure, western governments decided to join their forces to the America even if that meant declaring war on the party that will be proved to have been involved in what happened.

It is only normal to say that by the explanation of the present situation, as it has been said or by comparison to the action previously taken by America against specific countries, it could be enough for some of the executors of the operation to have come from a country named by America or said to have instigated the operation, for the American military retaliation on what they call an aggression. We don't know if they would do the same thing whether any of the planners and executors of the operation were found, to have lived or held the nationality of a Western country or whether the intention and the designs are already made against an Islamic party.

It is most probable from the beating of media war drums that America and some Western governments are targeting a party who won't be but Muslim.

The event that took place in America is an extraordinary event. It is not a simple one. According to figures announced by official American sources or by what has been spread by the media, the number of victims is great. Nobody has any doubts, or denies that America and the West have the capabilities to mobilize force and use it, to inflict destruction on others on the basis of simple doubts or even whimsically, and can send their American missiles and the NATO fighters to where ever they want to destroy and harm whoever America decides to harm in a fit of anger, by greed, or by being pushed by Zionism.

Many countries of the world have suffered from America's technological might, and many peoples do recognize that America had killed thousands or even millions of human beings in their countries.

The event that took place in America was an extraordinary one. It is not a simple event.

It is the first time that someone crosses to America to unleash the fire of his anger inside it, as indicated by what was said by the media, on the hypothesis that the executors of this act came from abroad.

Since this event is unprecedented, is it wise to deal with it by precedent methods that can be used by whoever has the technical and scientific capacities of America and the West?

If the target and the aim is one or more Islamic countries, as it has been said by the media and the intelligence services of some Western countries, this would only fall in the same direction that America and the West have always taken by targeting their fire on wherever they want to experiment a new weapon on.

We ask again: America's targeting the fire of its weapons on specific targets, and harming it or destroying it with the support of Western governments and of a fabricated story would it solve the problem? Would this bring security to America and the world? Or Isn't the use by America and some Western governments of their fire against others in the world including, or in the forefront of whom the Arabs and the Muslims, is one of the most important reasons of the lack of stability in the world at the present time?

Isn't the evil inflicted on America in the act of September 11, 2001, and nothing else is a result of this and other acts? This is the main question and this is what the American administration along with of the Western governments or the Western public opinion should answer in the first place with serenity and responsibility, without emotional reaction and without the use of the same old methods that America used against the world.

On September 12, 2001, we said that no one crossed the Atlantic to America carrying weapons before this event, except the Westerners who established the United States of America. America is the one who crossed the Atlantic carrying arms of destruction and death against the world. Here we want to ask a question: wasn't the use of American weapons, including the nuclear weapon against Japan, enough before September 11, 2001, for America to prepare to use it in a heavier and a stronger way? Or isn't using it in an irresponsible way, and without justification as does any oppressive force in the world, is what made America the most hated country in the world, starting from the Third World, to the Medium World and passing to the civilized world, as is the world divided by the West and America?

The national security of America and the security of the world could be attained if the American leaders and those who beat the drums for them among the rulers of the present time in the West or outside the West become rational, if America disengages itself from its evil alliance with Zionism, which has been scheming to exploit the world and plunge it in blood and darkness, by using America and some Western countries.

What the American peoples need mostly is someone who tells them the truth, courageously and honestly as it is. They don't need fanfares and cheerleaders, if they want to take a lesson from the event so as to reach a real awakening, in spite of the enormity of the event that hit America. But the world, including the rulers of America, should say all this to the American peoples, so as to have the courage to tell the truth and act according to what is right and not what to is wrong and unjust, to undertake their responsibilities in fairness and justice, and by recourse to reason, passion, according to the spirit of chance and capability.

In addition, we say to the American peoples, what happened on September 11, 2001 should be compared to what their government and their armies are doing in the world, for example, the international agencies have stated that more than one million and a half Iraqis have died because of the blockade imposed by America and some Western countries, in addition to the tens of thousands who died or are injured in the military action perpetrated by America along with those who allied with it against Iraq. Hundreds of bridges, churches, mosques, colleges, schools, factories, palaces, hotels, and thousands of private houses were destroyed or damaged by the American and Western bombardment, which is ongoing even today against Iraq. If you replay the images of the footage taken by the western media itself of this destruction, you will see that they are not different from the images of the two buildings hit by the Boing airplanes, if not more atrocious, especially when they are mixed with the remains of men, women, and children. There is, however, one difference, namely that those who direct their missiles and bombs to the targets, whether Americans or from another Western country, are mostly targeting by remote controls, that is why they do so as if they were playing an amusing game. As for those who acted on September 11, 2001, they did it from a close range, and with, I imagine, giving their lives willingly, with an irrevocable determination.

For this reason also, the Americans, and the world with them, should understand the argument that made those people give their lives in sacrifi, and what they sacrificed themselves for, in that way.

When one million and a half Iraqi human beings die, according to Western documents, from a population of twenty five million, because of the American blockade and aggression, it means that Iraq has lost about one twentieth of its population. And just as your beautiful skyscrapers were destroyed and caused your grief, beautiful buildings and precious homes crumbled over their owners in Lebanon, Palestine and Iraq by American weapons used by the Zionists. In only one place, which was a civilian shelter, which is the Ameriyah Shelter, more than four hundred human beings, children, young and old men and women, died in Iraq by American bombs.

In the same day, the 11th of September, one of their aggressive military airplanes was shot down over Iraq. And on the same day of the event in America on 11th September, and American jet fighter was perpetration aggression against Iraq and was shot down.

As for what is going on in Palestine, if Zionist let you see on your TVs the bodies of children, women and men who are daily killed by American weapons, and with American backing to the Zionist entity, the pain you are feeling would be appeased.

Americans should feel the pain they have inflicted on other peoples of the world, so as when they suffer, they will find the right solution and the right path.

All that has been inflicted on the Arabs and Muslims by America and the West, didn't push Muslims to become racists and harass the Westerners who walk in the streets of Baghdad, Damascus, Tunis, Cairo and other Arab capitals, even when the Westerners, and especially Americans insulted the holy sites of Muslim and Arabs by what is almost an occupation of Saudi Arabia in order to launch their evil fires against Baghdad, and when the American carriers roam the Arab Gulf, and their fighters daily roam the sky to throw tons of bombs and missiles over Iraq, so that about two hundred thousand tons of bombs have been used against Iraq, in addition to using depleted uranium! All these are facts that are very well known not only to Arabs and Muslims, but to the whole world also. But because of only one incident that happened in America in one day, and upon an unconfirmed accusations so far, Arabs and Muslims, including some who hold the American citizenship, are being harassed openly and publicly in America and some Western countries. Some western countries are preparing themselves to participate in an American military action, against an Islamic country as the indications point out. In this case, who is being fanatic?

Isn't this solidarity, and this in-advance approval by some Western leaders, of a military aggression against an Islamic country, the most flagrant form of the new Crusades, fanaticism. It reminds Arabs and Muslims of those Crusade war launched by the West and NATO against Iraq?

Finally, if you, rulers respect and cherish the blood of your peoples, why do you find it easy to shed the blood of others including the blood of Arabs and Muslims? If you respect your values, why don't you respect the values of Arabs and Muslims?

America needs wisdom, not power. It has used power, along with the West, to its extreme extent, only to find out latter that it doesn't achieve what they wanted. Will the rulers of America try wisdom just for once so that their people can live in security and stability?

"In the name of God, Most Gracious, Most merciful"

"Invite all to the way of thy Lord with the wisdom and beautiful preaching, and argue with them in ways that are best and most gracious, for the lord knows best who have strayed from His path and who receive guidance."

Second Open Letter From President Saddam Hussein to the Peoples of the United States, Western Peoples and their Goverments, September 18, 2001

In the name of God, the most Compassionate, the most Merciful.

Once again, we make a return to comment on the incidence that took place in America on September 11, not for its significance as such, but for the implications surrounding it and its ramifications in terms of results on the level of the world of which we are part or rather a special case as a nation known as it is with the basis and uniqueness of its faith.

On previous occasions, we have already said that the United States needs to try wisdom after it has tried force over the last fifty years or even more. We still see that this is the most important thing the world must advise the US about if there is anybody who wants to say something or adopt an attitude towards this incidence, and who is concerned about world peace and stability. This is the case if the US and the world are convinced with the dictum and the verdict, namely that what has happened came to America from without, not within.

It is among the indisputables in the law or general norms, in dealings, in social life, and even political life, that any charge should be based on evidence if the one who makes the accusation is keen to convince others or has respect to that who listens to the accusation or is concerned with it as part of the minimal obligation of his duty. But the US has made the charge before verification, even before possessing the minimum evidence about such a charge. It has even not availed itself the opportunity to verify things, first and foremost. It started a drive of incitement and threat, or said something irresponsible by broadening the base of charges to include states, circles and individuals.

American officials set about making charges or giving the guided media, the Zionist media and its symbols within the authority and outside it a free hand in order to prepare the public mind for the charge. What does this mean?

In a nutshell, it means that the US gives no heed to the law or rely on it. It has no concern for the counter viewpoint in line with its dangerous policy towards this issue or others. That is why we find that it takes no pain to secure evidence. Therefore, it needs no evidence to pass its verdict. It is content with saying something, passing verdicts, whether people other than the American officials are convinced or not. This means, in keeping with the policy it has pursued since 1990, that it has no regard to the viewpoint of the peoples and governments in the world in it entirety. It gives it no weight or heed despite the fact that it claims to be the democratic state (number one) in the world. The basic meaning of democracy even by the standards of its initial emergence in the Western world, that facts should lay bare before the people so that the people would assume their responsibility with full awareness. Our description of the US attitude vis-à-vis this incidence is a practical description. It means that American officials do not respect even their own people's viewpoint, let alone the world's. In this conduct, the American officials behave as though they are deluding the peoples, beating up the misleading media drums to do the job of mobilizing them against enemy or enemies against whom no evidence about their accountability for the action they are accused of has been furnished. All the officials there seek to achieve is to foment the hostility of the peoples of the US against whoever they assumed to be an enemy before the incidence has occurred. The tax-payer would be in a position where he is prepared to accept the blackmail trap arms manufacturers have laid for him in addition to the wrangled interests on the level of senior military and civil officials in the US.

One might argue that political verdicts do not always emanate from the same bases, procedures or courses adopted by the judiciary or criminal courts. Rather, precedents and back-grounds could suffice to arrive at a conclusion which may prove right. Even if, for the sake of argument, we go along this notion, just to keep the debate uninterrupted, we say that this could be true about the media and statements which are of media and propaganda nature, even political statements. In this instance, the error could not be necessarily fatal.

But is this permissible in war?

Once more, we say that war is not an ordinary case. Neither is it procedural in the life of nations and peoples. It is a case of unavoidable exception. Evidence based on conclusion is not enough, even if it is solid to make a charge against a given party or several parties, a state or several states to the extent that the one who makes the charge declares war at the party or parties against which charges were made and bears the responsibility of whatever harm might be sustained by his own people and the others including death, the destruction of possessions and the ensuing serious repercussions. It was only the US administration that has made the charge against a certain religion, not just a given nationality.

Let us also accept the interventions of those who contend that the US has not said this, through its senior officials and within this limitation. In fact, some officials have denied that their policy is one of making the charge against a given religion. However, we believe that the lack of evidence to make a charge, the disrespect to the golden sound rule of proper accusation which leads to the declaration of war and restricts the charge to a certain nation, states, designations and individuals, can only be understood as a premeditated charge without evidence that the action was carried out by Moslems. This is complemented by free reins for the media to float it, to prepare the public opinion to accept it or to be tuned to it so that anything opposed to it would sound like a discord.

Below is the list:

Afghanistan. Usama bin Laden...the Islamic Qa'ida (base) party or organization...Syria.   Yemen...Algeria.   Iraq...Lebanon...Palestine. The list may be curtailed or enlarged according to the pretexts of the policy of power, which has found its opportunity or the power that is looking for its opportunity to declare war. Whether the items of the list are increased or cut down, would all this mean anything but the accusation of Moslems, including, or rather in the forefront of whom Arabs? Why should this cross the minds of US officials unless they have basically assumed themselves and their policy to be enemies of Arabs and Moslems?

Could this charge mean anything other than the desire to settle old scores, all based on the assumption that their foreign policies are incompatible with the American policy, or they do not give in to the US-Zionist policy vis-à-vis the world and Palestine?

Consider statements by the US officials who say the war would be long because it is aimed at several states. Notice the blackmail or better, the terrorism they mean and which was designed to include several states and parties on a list that could be longer or shorter in accordance with a policy of sheer terrorism and blackmail, first and foremost, the illusion that Arabs and Moslems and the people of Palestine would leave the arena for the aggression of the Zionist entity and its vile imperialism.

These charges which were made without consideration and in an instantaneous way mean that the mentality of the US administration has been pre-loaded, prior to the incidence, even if we apply the norms of today and not the norms of the law. It has made assumption tantamount to conclusive verdict, namely that Islam, with Arabs in the lead of Moslems are enemies of the US. More precisely, the US on the level of its rulers has taken it as a final verdict that it is the enemy of Arabs and Moslems. In so doing, they have stored the final verdict in their minds. On this basis, they built their preparation in advance. On this basis too, they prepared (the mind) of the computer, which was programmed on this assumption, which has taken the form of a conclusive verdict. This reminds us of the free reins given to political writers, the so-called thinkers, inclupast heads of state and ministers who the Zionist policy wanted, over the last ten or fifteen years to assume that faith based on the religion of Islam with the ensuing implication is the new enemy of the US and the West and it is the backdrop against which American rulers act, with the participation of some Western rulers who came under the pressure and interpretations of Zionist thought and scheming.

Obviously, this assumption is no longer a pure assumption for the purpose of scrutiny testing and examination. It has become part and parcel of conclusive verdicts. That is why the verdict was instantaneous, without consideration or waiting for the evidence to have a basis, evidence on which the pre-supposition is based in order to be a conclusive one. The charge has not only been made against all governments in Islamic or Arab states but also against all Islamic peoples, including the Arab nation and to all designations, parties, states and governments whose policies do not please the US, whose policies and positions are not palatable to the US in particular or because they call for the liberation of

Palestine and a halt to the US aggression on Iraq, and adherence to their independence and their nations' heritage.

Any one who is surprised by this practical conclusion, allowing courteous words to be said on the margin of verdicts to replace it, has to contemplate our verdict:

The US has declared it is at war. It is gearing up for war since the early moments in the wake of the incidence, as though it were the opportunity those concerned have been waiting for. It has allocated the necessary funds for the war, or part of them. Have you ever heard or read in the near on far history, of a state declaring war before even defining who its enemy is? The opportunity to declare the state of war came with the incidence that befell it. It is not yet known whether it was carried out by a foreign enemy or from inside. Thus, the war declared by America would cease to be a reason for the incidence. Rather, it is the incidence that has availed the opportunity to launch the war, which has not been a result of the incidence under any circumstances!

One might contend it is the nature of the incidence, the scale of pain the American officials felt as a result of what their peoples suffered, the embarrassment they felt due to the sufferings that hit the people there, that prompted American rulers to rush to declare war. The suffering of the people is not caused by the incidence alone, but by the failure of the authorities concerned which have been preoccupied by hatching conspiracies abroad, assassination and sabotage operations against world states and freedom-loving people. They rushed to declare war and name the parties so that they would leave no option but to launch the war. Once again, we say, could this be a reason and ground to facilitate the charge and the subsequent resolutions, why should not it be a ground for others as well?

If the fall in the whirlwind of rage, not the pre-meditated planning, results into war resolutions on their senior level inside the US, why should not you expect someone to direct his fire to it under the pressure of similar considerations or danger?

Once again we say that the US administration and those in the West who allied themselves with it against Arabs and Moslems, now and in the past, or rather against the world, in all the arenas that witnessed the scourges of the alliance, are in need to take recourse to wisdom after they have had power at their disposal and deployed it to such an extent that it ceased to frighten those who experienced it. Dignity, the sovereignty of the homeland and the freedom of the sincere man is a sacred case, along with other sacred things which real Moslems uphold, including, Arabs who are in the lead.

If this is the practical description of the pre-mediated intentions that decided war against Arabs and Moslems, while the party that took the decision waits for a cover to declare a war, and may launch it against those whom it has been biding time, could there be anyone who could avert it other than God, the Almighty? Anyone other than the will of the peoples, when they become fully aware, after they know and fear God, after they have believed in Him.

"For us Allah sufficeth, and He is the best disposer of affairs". (Holly Quran)

Once again we say that the peoples do not believe any more the slogans of the United States, accept those whom it intends evil against. Even when it says it is against terrorism, the United States doesn't apply this to the World, and according to the International Law. But according to its will to impose what it wants on the World and refuse what it thinks might be harmful to it only, and export the other kinds of it to the World. To certify this, could the United States tell its peoples how many organizations working against their own countries are existing in the United States? And how many of those, the term terrorism could be applied to if one standard is used and not the double standards? And how many are those it finances overtly and covertly? How many are those accused with killing and theft in other countries are now in the United States? If the United States presents such inventory to its peoples and to the World, and initiated implementing one standard and one norm on its agents and those it calls friends. And if it starts the same storm against the killers in the Zionist entity responsible of killing Palestinians in occupied Palestine and in Tunis and Lebanon. And if it charges its own secret services with what they committed of special actions and assassinations they brag to publish in the form of stories. Only then one can believe the new American slogans that America is trying to make them believe. Only then it becomes legitimate to ask the World to do what it believes is useful for its security and the security of the World.

It is a chance to air an opinion whose time has come. It is also addressed to the peoples of the US and the Western people in general. Zionism has been planning for the domination of the world since its well-known conference it convened in Basle in 1897. Ever since, it has been working in this direction. It has scored successes you can feel by controlling finance, media and commerce centres in your countries and whoever rules in your name, here and there, in decision-making centres. But its domination is not yet fulfilled to have its will absolute and final. This could only be feasible when two heavenly faiths upheld by the biggest bloc in the world are thrown into conflict. Otherwise, Zionism would be denied the accomplishment of all its ambitions. The masterminds of Zionism are, therefore, working for a clash between Christianity and Islam on the assumption that this, and only this, could secure the chance to dominate the world, when new opportunities open up for their domination. Could there be any better situation than that when the stealing dog finds his household pre-occupied by a grief so that it could win the thing it has set its eye on, the thing that whetted its mouth? Would the sensible men in the West be aware of that? Or would Zionism outsmart them to attain its aims?

A Third Open Letter from President Saddam Hussein to the Peoples of the United States, Western Peoples and Governments, October 29, 2001

In the name of God the Merciful, The Compassionate

Once again we address a letter to all the peoples and governments of the West, including the United State.

Peace be upon those who expect a greeting of peace from us, or upon those who answer it by saying: and peace be upon you too (wa Alaikum Asalam).

The world focused its full attention on the analysis and follow up of the events of last September, but those who made an in-depth analysis may have not been the majority of the people. Nevertheless, it seems to us that they have, now, increased in number. The number of officials in power who are looking into the depth of what happened, its motives or reasons, and its results and effects, has also increased. Their number and way of conduct, at the time of the event, was deplorable for those who are not aware that not everyone is capable of a deep contemplation of major events or complex circumstances, just as not many people are capable of dreaming of what is better.

Now that the emotions have relatively calmed down in the heart and spirit of those who applauded the event, or those who condemned it, I say that, the role of leaders should be played, with their people's support, on the basis of the description and the role of their responsibilities. One of the most important qualities of any leader is saving other from death not by marking the dark ditches on the road, but also by preventing those who do not see the marks from falling into the abyss. Then comes the quality of exaltation, or ascendancy of the people he is in charge of, along with their potential thought and action. The danger that may threaten any people or nation, does not call upon the people in charge to lead the way against this danger only, but also to analyze its reasons in view of abating them, or treating those reasons radically, to eliminate them so that they would never surge again.

I am sorry to say that the general approach in this direction is still weak, so far. Western governments are the first in this phenomena of weakness. Some voices have risen on the part of some peoples, journalists, writers, and, in a very restricted way, the voices of those who are preparing themselves, in the shadow, to replace the rulers there. Nevertheless, the latter are still hesitant voices that deal with the situation in the light of the balance of interests of the posts they expect to occupy, and of the influence of the centers of power. As for the United States, the hope in the awareness of its people is greater than it is in its Administrations, if the people could see the facts as they are, unless these Administrations are set free from the conclusive influence of Zionism, and other centers of influence which serve their own interests that are associated with their well-known goals.

The events of September 11, and the following reaction of people in rage, or those who took advantage of the situation, including waging the aggression on Afghanistan on the basis of suspicions, and the accompanying insinuations and statements by the media or by American, and non-American leaders, have shown that this vast world can be set on fire by a spark coming from the West, even if that spark comes all the way from across the Atlantic. Naturally, setting something on fire is easier than extinguishing it, and because deeds of virtue exalt the soul and the being, while evil deeds downgrade them, the latter become easier to commit for those who are tempted to do so.

On the basis of this realistic image, the entire world needs to be saved from the deep abyss it is being push into by the US, and the likes of the US, whether they are states, individuals, or organizations. In fact, now that we know the limits of how American rulers conduct themselves in crisis, the US itself needs to be saved by the world while it is saving itself. Otherwise, the world will be pulled down by the weight of the US while falling down to the bottom of a deep pit from which it will not be able to come out until that pit is filled with blood and tragedies, not to mention those who will suffocate because they cannot swim.

As we said before to those who launched aggressions on us, including the US, in and before Um-Almarik (the mother of the battles), the world, like Iraq and its Arab nation, needs steadfastness to face the aggression, make it miss its targets. It must not allow the US to be victorious. The victory of the US and its allies over Iraq would conceal the opposing attitude and analysis, and would not allow it to emerge again for a long time. In fact, the US is in no need for additional vanity and arrogance, but if it ever defeated Iraq, God forbid, it would acquire an additional vanity that would push it to a higher level of vanity, which would bring it closer to not farther from the abyss.

Yes, vanity needs to be confronted, and the oppressor needs to be confronted, just as those who find it easy to commit evil deeds and throw embers at people, need to be confronted. On the basis of what we said about Iraq while confronting aggressions, the world now needs to abort the US aggressive schemes, including its aggression on the Afghan people, which must stop.

Again we say that when someone feels that he is unjustly treated, and no one is repulsing or stopping the injustice inflicted on him, he personally seeks ways and means for lifting that justice. Of course, not everyone is capable of finding the best way for lifting the injustice inflicted on him. People resort to what they think is the best way according to their own ideas, and they are not all capable of reaching out for what is beyond what is available to arrive to the best idea or means.

To find the best way, after having found their way to God and His rights, those who are inflicted by injustice need not to be isolated from their natural milieu, or be ignored deliberately, or as a result of mis-appreciation, by the officials in this milieu. They should, rather, be reassured and helped to save themselves, and their surroundings. It is only normal to say that punishment is a necessity in our world, because what is a necessity in the other world must also be necessary in our world on Earth. But, the punishment in the other world is fair and just, and the prophets and messengers of God (peace be upon them all) conducted punishment and called for it in justice, and not on the basis of suspicions and whims. Hence, any punishment conducted by man must be just and convincing. I think, that you, often criticize those whom you criticize in order to weaken them, by saying that they use emergency laws, and what emergency laws, by western standards, cannot be a general rule. But now, unlike what you used to say about those whom you accuse of being dictators and despots, we see dozens of emergency laws and measures adopted by the governments of the West, with the US in the forefront, after facing one painful event.

Do you know how many painful events, larger and more dangerous than that of September 11 in US, were inflicted upon countries and peoples whom you used to accuse of being non-democratic?! This fact alone, is an example that should be pondered upon by the governments and peoples of the West, but it is not our main subject here.

Once again, we say that, injustice and the pressure that results from it on people lead to explosions. As explosions are not always organized, it is to be expected that they may harm those who make them and others. The events of September 11, should be seen on this basis, and on the basis of imbalanced reactions, on the part of governments accused of being democratic, if the Americans are sure that these were carried out by people from abroad.

To concentrate not on what is important, but rather on what is the most important, we say again that after having seen that the flames of any fire can expand to cover all the world, it first and foremost, needs justice based on fairness. The best and most sublime expression of this is in what we have learned from what God the Al Mighty ordered to be, or not to be. If we disagree in the essence of this, then our criteria should be, that we should not prevent others from getting or enjoying what we want for ourselves, and that we should not adopt double standards, by giving others what we do not want or refuse for ourselves. Everybody must be aware that no one who has a fortune can be safe in the middle of a society of hungry people. His problem would be greater if he had made his fortune by exploiting those hungry people, and at their expense. The second Caliph in the state of Islam, Omar Ibin Alkhatab (God be pleased with him) ordered the suspension of the punishment of cutting the hand of a thief in the year of Remada (drought) despite the fact that this punishment in clearly stipulated in the Holy Quran. He did so, because he was aware, by his sense of a believer, the correct standards of Faith may be shaken when a man or his family are hungry, and also because he believed that hunger is more aggressive than the act of stealing, and that saving a man's life was more important than saving somebody's property. Hence, he froze a holy rule (Sharia). Have the people of our present time learned this lesson, so that they can live in peace and security? Or do the parties concerned think that the security they want for themselves, will be achieved by amplifying the killing, intimidation, and starvation of others?!

We have heard in the news, recently, that American officials think that the source of anthrax is probably the US itself. Is this conclusion or information just a tactic to divert the attention of those who were terrorized to hear that Bin Laden is the source of anthrax, and to hear insinuations to other accusations, that many Americans think that they should not persist in harming the people he cares for, because that would push him to a stronger reaction in this way or by other means? Or have they done this to divert attention from the incompetence of American official bodies in the events of September 11, and they find now that they have achieved their goal and consequently, the act and the actors should be buried?!

Anyhow, this and other things show that weapons of mass destruction become a burden on their owners and on humanity, if they were not absolutely necessary for self-defense and defending their countries.

Hence, instead of getting themselves and the world busy with the so-called anti-missiles shield so that they drain their budget, and the budgets of other nations, as well as the pockets of American tax-payers, they should be busy in eliminating the weapons of mass destruction in the US first, and then or at the same time, in other parts of the world. It goes without saying, that the West, including the US, are the ones who first built the weapons of mass destruction i.e. nuclear, biological, and chemical weapons. It was the West, and the US in the first place, who used these weapons. The events of September, and the what Americans themselves said that the anthrax came from the US, clearly show the importance of world co-operation, on the basis of a binding agreement to get rid of the burden and the threat of the weapons of mass destruction, as a first step that might stimulate other steps, if injustice and aggression contracted. The utmost threat to humanity, and to the peoples of the US, is the American weapons of mass destruction, along with the similar weapons of the Zionist entity, and along or after it, the similar weapons of other countries.

As the US is across the Atlantic, it is the first country to be asked to make such an initiative in order to confirm its credibility. And because the Zionist entity usurps and occupies Arab territories, and holy places, oppresses the Arabs and injures their human feelings, and as blunders are expected from it, and the reaction of the oppressed people is to be expected, it becomes necessary to disarm the Zionist entity of these weapons.

At that moment, and when the US is really willing to disarm itself of these weapons, we do not think that anyone of a sound mind would stay out of the framework of such a practical plan.

It is then, that the US will adopt a balanced attitude toward the world, and will find the path of wisdom. The world will deal with it in respect and love, when they see love and respect in Americans relations with them. The world, including US, will live in peace, and not on the brink of an abyss. The surveillance of the prevailing security, will be based on a sort of real solidarity: the solidarity of brave and just men, and not the solidarity based on intimidation and fear of the powerful, or which serves interests or creates opportunities.

I pray to God the Al-Mighty that I have conveyed the message, and let God be my witness. God is the greatest. God is the greatest.

Saddam Hussein

Shabban 13, 1422 H.
October 29, 2001.

A Letter From Saddam Hussein
to an American Citizen,
October 18, 2001

From: Saddam Hussein To: Christopher J. Love

In the name of God, the Merciful, the Compassionate.

Dear brother in the family of mankind!

I read your e-mail message of October 2nd carefully and I have well pondered over your emotions regarding the victims of the two towers.

All I can say is presenting my condolences to you, and to reiterate the Muslims linguistic formula on occasion, like this: (God has created us, and to him we return. May God give you long life)

In a letter of reply like this, there may be no room to say all I want, not to acquaint you with Saddam Hussein's and his comrades in the leadership way of thinking, or of how Iraqis think through them, and of the kind of principles they believe in.

Nevertheless, as you have come to me to know about things, as I understood from your message: the way my people, the Arabs and Muslims, for whom the Arabs are a model, think. You wanted an answer to these questions by addressing yourself to an official in the leadership of this people, and this religion, as well as to someone from the region, you call the Middle-East.

I may give you an explanation to what happened to the two towers, and made America mourn, and inflicted pain and sorrow on others, because such an event has been inflicted on other people in the past, including Arabs and Muslims, in many cases.

I began this letter, by addressing you by the word "brother", although you are neither Iraqi or Arab, nor a Muslim, as can be seen by your name.

Christopher, do you know why I called you brother? Because I never forget, that all mankind come from Adam and Eve. They are all brothers, although they later became different nations and adherent to different religions. Hence, to our understanding, we are one family within the peoples of our earth.

In this family, there is vice and virtue, good and bad people. As long as a man safeguards his rights and duties, within himself, and with humanity, avoids transgressing other peoples' rights, greed, and harming others, and tries to be useful to others, only if they ask for his help, he becomes their brother. But, when any member of this family of mankind oppresses, exploits, unjustly wages wars on them, or lies and deceives others, he would be acting like a devil in the form of man.

We, Arabs, have learned this, brother Christopher, before any nation on earth. We have taught it to you, and to all the adherents of divine religions in the Universe, because God the Almighty, had created Adam and Eve on our land. There is no other chronicle or religion, that pretends, or can prove the contrary. Abraham, the friend of God and the father of all prophets, is one of us, as are all the other prophets. Whenever, God made a revelation, the Arabs were the people to undertake the mission of spreading it to other non Arab nations, after believing in it themselves. Again, I say that this the fundamental basis of the humanitarian viewpoint of, not only Saddam Hussein and the Iraqi people with him, but also of all Arabs, in all their great homeland, which was divided by British and French colonialism, and which the

US is trying to halt its people's unity, and forbid them from enjoying their rights which God bestowed on them on their proper land.

Once again I say, that the basic general rule is that, he who wants to avoid the harm of others, must not harm them. He who wants to enjoy the fruits of his crops must not damage the crops of others. In Iraq, and in the Arab rural regions, and that could be true in different degrees, all over the world, people would fight each other, and some of them maybe killed, but no one ever burns the crops of others. If a criminal ever did so, he would be considered an outcast, and his blood would be shed. Why is such an act so severely judged, although, in comparison, the killing of a man is much more a serious act than the burning of crops? This customary law in the Iraqi countryside, and maybe in the Arab and world also, is based on two reasons: First: a man, can think, hide, and confront others, while crops cannot run, hide, or draw a gun on who wants to harm them. Second: a man cannot live without crops, and for this reason, burning his crops is equal to depriving him from his right to live, and also, because more than one family may have a share in these crops. The damage would be inflicted, not only on the share of the person who is meant to be harmed. It would include the shares of the entire family: women, children, old people, or even young men, who can carry weapons. It is for this reason, that our religion prohibits the killing of woman, children and old men, as well as the uprooting of trees, when a war is fought, by necessity, between two armies.

Do you know, brother Christopher, that your Domini-station, in its war against the people of Iraq, has been burning not only the cereals in silos, but even the harvest by throwing flares in order to make Iraqi people starve?

Do you know what does this mean? It means collective death. Your successive administrations have killed one billion and a half Iraqis in eleven years as a result of the blockade it has imposed on Iraq, according to statistics published international organizations, including American humanitarian organization. You can ask them for details, by Internet.

Food is important and holy to people, because it is related to man's right to live. In the same way medicine has the same sanctity. This is something we have learned from our history and civilization which are thousands of years old, Hence I remind you of the Crusades in 1096–1291 by which the western aggressors came to occupy the land of Arabs, under the pretext of saving Al-Quds from the infidel Muslims as confirmed by documents issued by the west itself. Notice the motto, dear Christopher: "Saving Al-Quads from the infidel Muslims"! So, the Muslims are infidels, not in the eyes of the church, but in the eyes of the Western leaders who mobilized the nations of the West to come as invaders to the holy land of Al-Quads, which is the land on which landed Prophet Mohammed "Peace be upon him" in his divine nocturnal journey.

An individual person in a nation, may be fanatic because of a wrong reasoning, or awareness, but could leaders be so too?

You may say that this is something that happened a very long time ago. But what made me mention it in my letter to you, is what I saw, and heard of some leaders, not ordinary Western citizens. It seems that as if those leaders have recalled all this inventory of fanaticism and hatred of the times of the Crusades, in which the Western leaders considered the Arabs, who are the people of the country and the owners of the land, as infidels who must be expelled from their land by force.

They have, now, planted the Zionist entity in our land to replace that hatred. They have revived the memory of the old Crusades wars by a new war of Crusades, called for by the highest ranking rulers in your country, and in other countries of the west.

Isn't it a paradox, and double standards, to accuse a citizen of fanaticism, to denounce his fanatic attitude and than to mobilize armies against him, and against the country in which he is living, on the basis of nothing but suspicions, while waging an outrageous campaign of hatred and fanaticism to the maximum, which even includes calling for, and the recalling the old Crusades wars against Arab and Muslims, as we mentioned?

Nevertheless it is well-known, that when the Arabs and Muslims leader Saddling Al-Ayoubi, was told that the leader of Crusades, Richard, who was called the (Heart of Lion), was ill, he sent him a doctor, and that when his horse was killed in a battle, he refused to fight anyone before mounting another horse.

But do you know that your administration has, one way or the other, deprived the people of Iraq from food and medicine?

Do you know the meaning of the death of one million and a half human beings, in addition to those who are killed by bombs inadmissible?

Maybe, you and the majority of the peoples of America, do not know that American bombardment, and death harvest caused by fighter jets, and missiles, are ongoing in Iraq for the last eleven years, and have not stopped until the moment of writing this letter? Do you know why you don't know?! Because the media in your country which is controlled by Zionism, do not want you to known. And because your administration, which says that it is necessary for the peoples of the world to know, does not want you to know. You should ask your administration, why doesn't it speak to you about facts? Why doesn't present you any information except its devilish fancies?

As for me, I can tell you why Zionism doesn't want you to know the harm inflicted on the people of Iraq. The Zionist and the American administration believe that it is necessary that Iraqis die. The Jewish

Alberta, the former US Secretary of State, spoke in this way, or in a similar case, when she said that the objectives of the US foreign policy, justify the death of Iraqi children. The reason is that the Iraqis refused the Zionist usurpation of Arab and Palestinian territories. They refuse to accept the crimes of occupying Palestine, the Golan, and the Lebanese territories, and refuse do accept the Zionists confiscation of the holy places of the believers in God, including Muslims there.

Hence, whenever Zionism has the upper hand over high ranking officials in America, it pushes the administration toward a confrontation with the Arabs, and reinforces Zionist entity, at the expense of Arab and Palestinian rights.

By the way, please ask for the videotapes to see how the Jews, in the occupied territories, kill old men, children and women, in front of the cameras. Do you know that all these crimes have been perpetrated since 1935 by using Western weapons, and in fact, American weapons in particular, weapons that cost billions of dollars, the administration takes from American tax-payers to be granted as an aid to the Zionist entity?

So, the Arabs and Muslims did not cross the Atlantic, as invaders or aggressors. They did not colonize America. It is America that brought them all kinds of sufferings. If any of your rulers says something different, please discuss it with them. For example, if they say that they crossed the Atlantic to make sure that you get your oil supplies, tell them that oil is guaranteed by mutual interests and non-aggression, not by aggressions, killing, violating other people's rights, and destroying all sanctities.

If your rules say that, they crossed the Atlantic in the past to fight Communism so that it does not invade the West, tell them that the ex-Soviet Union has fallen apart, as has the Warsaw Pact, although I personally don't accept the contradiction between the call for the freedom of thinking, and saying that the Western way of thinking is more vital and modern, as the intellectuals and leaders of the West say, and between fearing Communism.

Do you know, brother Christopher, that the NATO, which was created under the pretext of confronting Communism, still exists, and was even enlarged after the collapse of the Warsaw Pact. Decisions of death are taken in its name, against some peoples of the world sometimes, as was the case against Yugoslavia, because it is an independent, and Slovak country, and because the majority of its people are Orthodox, not because their oppression of Muslims in Bosnia, as was claimed, to fool the Muslims, and falsely win their support in international forums?

If we go on, we can give thousands of examples on the blind fanaticism exported by the West to the world with American participation during the last 50 years. But I don't want to burden you. I only want to tell you that the people of Iraq are against all kinds of fanaticism, whether based on religion, nationality or race. They are against the use of fanaticism as a cover for harming people whom God does not accept to harm. They call for love between the peoples and nations of the world. Nevertheless, we do not believe in love on one side only.

Iraq has been harmed severely by the fanaticism of others, including America. It was also severely harmed by terrorism. Maybe you don't know that many the members of our leadership were victims of terrorism and terrorists. Some of them escaped death, by the will of God, after being injured or missed by the terrorists, in addition to the pain inflicted to our people.

Do you know brother, that your administration's reaction to that, was one of encouraging it and rejoicing? Do you know that your administration has been encouraging terrorism against us for the past eleven years, calling to overthrow us by force, allocating special funds to do so, and boasting about not fearing God, as it publicly announces that on TV screens, because Iraq does not have the same destructive force and armament of America? The Palestinians, whose right to resist the occupation forces are guaranteed by the international law, promulgated by America and the other big powers, are considered terrorists because they resist the Zionist occupation of their territories, and holy places.

Tell me, brother, if the Vatican is occupied by Arabs, or non-Arab Muslims, wouldn't its people fight the occupying forces? Wouldn't the English people fight for the Westminster cathedral? Or wouldn't the French people, defend Notredame? I say they must fight for them! Why, then, are your armies occupying Mecca and the land of our Prophet? Why are you occupying the regional waters in the Arab Gulf, in addition to territories in its countries? Why is your ally, the Zionist entity, occupying our holy places, and territories, in Palestine, by using your arms, and financial, political, media, and moral support? And, why are your administration killing people, including children in Iraq, Afghanistan, and in Palestine now, just as it did, before that, in Lebanon, Sudan, Somalia and Libya, and the list of Arabs and Muslims to be killed is long?

I know that Arabs are far from being fanatic. Do you know why? Because, God, the Almighty, assigned them with the mission of delivering the messages of all religions to humanity, and not to Arabs alone. They have fulfilled their mission, so that all Christians are now indebted to Arabs for guiding them to Faith, which God wanted them to have when, He made it possible for them to reach you, or for you to reach them, so that you know what they believe in, and be affected by it.

I know that Arabs, in general, do not adopt fanatic stances against any people for religious reasons. But, can anyone guarantee that one fanaticism does not create another? Can anyone guarantee that the death toll and killing, inflicted upon Arabs and Muslims by the American armies, would not lead to a counter-reaction, whether that reaction is well guided, or is a random one, that pleases no one except those who carry it out?

These words are general rules and principles, although I still do not know who is behind what happened to the towers on September 11, 2001. Your government did not help me, or anyone else, by showing, or communicating the information it possesses, so that we can elaborate an opinion, if it needed to know the opinion of those whose people it daily attacks with bombs, starves to death, and deprives from the right to live, construct, and deploy their creativity.

Our law, which is borne of our religion and heritage, and of our reasoning which is thousands of years deep, stipulates: "the Plaintiff should present evidence and the defendant should take an oath." But the plaintiff, which is your administration did not present any evidence so far. Nevertheless, it accused the people it accused, without showing us, or anyone else, any evidence, except for Blair and the ruler of Palestine, as they both said. The people accused have not pleaded guilty.

Anyhow, I don't think that your administration deserves the condolences of Iraqis, except if it presents its condolences to the Iraqi people for the one million and a half Iraqis it killed, and apologists them, for the crimes it committed against them. As for the American people, we have sent them our condolences through Mr. Tared Assize's letter to the Voices in the Wilderness Organization and Mr. Ramsi Clark, the former Attorney General, on Sept. 18,2001.

Dear brother,

He who does not want his harvest to be burned must not set fine to the harvest of others. He, who wants to live in security, should accept the right of others to live in security, and he who is irritated, or raged by an aggression, should not aggress others. He who cherishes the lives of his people, should remember that God created all people equal at birth, in death, and in their human values, that's why he should remember that the lives of others are also cherished by their people. He who strikes people with remote control missiles should expect, that there would be someone to seek revenge, for his dignity and the dignity of his people, and consequently does something harmful, or fatal, by stabbing a dagger in his body, or taking his life by a sword.

He who sees himself as a man, who revenges his dignity, should not deprive other men from their dignity, and he who calls for the respect of his people, men and women, should respect the people of other nations.

He who remembers God, must not ignore or forget, that God the Almighty, is capable of everything, and of providing the weak with what makes those who underestimate them, make heed of their rights and respect them.

In any case, the security of humanity is, in our view, a responsibility on the shoulders of all good people. Any irresponsible action on the part of superpowers may give way to a counter irresponsible action by the people, even if the smaller nations do not take such a course of action.

Finally there is something in your letter that you asked to be corrected, if it was wrong about the ex President Bush, is giving us reason to believe that he was our ally in the issue of Kuwait, but he was forced to abide with the United-Nations…. The Fact, Mr. Christopher, is that, it was President Bush who adopted the logic of war, right from the first day of those events. He refused solving the problem politically, and entering into a dialogue with us. The resolutions of the United Nations were, in fact, adopted under pressure from Bush and his administration. He then waged the war against Iraq, in a way that had nothing to do with the issue of Kuwait. His objective was to destroy all Iraq, and to deprive its people of the edifice they built, in several decades, and not merely getting the Iraqi armed forces out of Kuwait. He did that in 1991, and he later committed similar things, and he and his administration, are still doing so under different pretexts and justifications.

Wishing that you will have the opportunity to see the fact as they are, and not as your administration present them,

Yours truly
Saddam Hussein

Baghdad, Shabban 2,1422 H.
Oct. 18, 2001

President Saddam Hussein Address Call to the Brother Arabs: Regimes, Goverments and People/December 15, 2001

In the name of Allah, the Merciful, be Compassionate

Your majesties, highnesses, and excellencies!

Brother Arabs, regimes, governments and people!

Peace be upon you!

I address you this time in the name of the leadership and people of Iraq directly. It is a brotherly call addressed to you after the flood has reached its climax and after the destruction, terror, murder and sacrilege practised by the aggressive, terrorist and criminal Zionist entity, together with its tyrannical ally, the US, have come to a head against our brothers and our faithful struggling people in plundered Palestine. If evil achieves its objectives there, Allah forbid, its gluttony for more will increase and it will afflict our people and other parts of our wide homeland too, in addition to the suffering that has been and is still being inflicted upon the people of Palestine.

Therefore, brothers, I address this message to you as a specific call for the sake of Palestine and, through Palestine and its Holy Quds, for the sake of us all and, through our nation, for the sake of all humanity, which is afflicted with the tyranny of the evil American-Zionist alliance.

Brothers!

When we address this call to you, we do not set out of imagination but out of a deep faith in, and a full understanding of the heritage of our nation and its glorious history. This history reveals that our nation, even under the most complicated and the hardest circumstances, has always found its way when its potential and resolution have been mobilized. No matter how heavy misfortunes weigh on our nation, or how dark the veils of night hang down on it, it has been able, when following the right path, to light candles on both sides of the road to guide it towards its choice and its objectives.

We, brothers, seek for Allah's reward and seek for honour in this life and the next. We seek for them with you and through our gathering and our joint action, and not apart from you, unless we find ourselves compelled to act, each according to the stand, which suits his viewpoint and belief. Therefore, and although we are aware of the circumstances involving the bearers of official titles in the nation and their capabilities, we have a great hope in you, brothers, to mobilize resolution so that we win jointly and not individually, Allah's favour and the favour of our nation and humanity at large. If any of us, within the boundaries of his country and on the basis of the peculiarity of his sphere and his capability, sees that the troubles he has are a burden too heavy for him to carry, it is with solidarity, joint force and joint action that these troubles and others become lighter in weight. Group resolution, or the resolution generated by the sense of solidarity or joint action, will make them easier to carry and will make the shoulders stronger and more capable of endurance and steadfastness. That is because Allah's Hand is with the group that has faith in Him and that trusts in Him, glorified be His name. Whoever supports right against wrong will receive Allah's support in this life and His honour and best reward in the next.

We do not want to burden you, brothers, with the details and remind you of what is happening to our faithful people who are being afflicted with the evil of the US-supported Zionists. What is happening to our people and our brothers there is clear enough even if we only see it on television.

Arabs!

Many of those who held titles of responsibility amongst us and, per-haps, many in certain circles among the Arab nation used to blame the Palestinians. They claimed that the Palestinians did not resist the Zion-ist occupation, as they should have from the year 1930 to the defeat of some Arab regimes in the year 1948 and afterwards.

But what can any just and indubitable person say now about the stand of the heroic people of Palestine, men and women, children, youths and old men?

The stand of the heroic people of Palestine, who are now facing alone the alliance and conspiracy of Zionism and Imperialism, which were originally designed for the whole nation, is set against the stand near-ing impotency on the Arab side. In all cases, the reason for this impo-tency is not the weakness of the potential of the nation or the will of the people. It is, rather, the weakness of the will of the decision makers or their unwillingness to shoulder their responsibility with the honour, the patriotism and the life buoy to carry all to the shore of safety. It is painful to see how they have abandoned the simplest rights and princi-ples of pan-Arabism and the meanings of faith entrusted to our titles and the titles of others by the heritage of our immortal nation. They have abandoned all the meanings which make our nation one nation, called up by the Merciful and the Compassionate to be the ideal for

those who believe in Allah, the One and only One, and the beacon of
faith and virtue to overcome wrong and to champion right.

Arabs!

We are all called upon to remember and never forget our duties
towards Allah, towards our nation, towards our people and even
towards humanity. We can do this through a stand of honour,
achieved in any form that raises it above the state of deterioration and
impotency through which our nation passes now, and above the state
of only watching our struggling heroic Palestinian people while they
face murder and destruction daily. We all perhaps remember the
results of the abandonment and treason, which happened in 1948, and
must keep in mind what may happen if things go on now the way they
did then.

It is required of us, brothers, to say—in one voice, with a faithful and
sure heart and in a stand whose lines are free of weakness that may
cause anyone who harbours it to stray out of the frame of the minimum of his faithful patriotic, national and human responsibility—that
the US is an aggressive and a terrorist power and that the Zionist entity
is not only a usurper of the land of Palestine and the lands of the Arabs
and their legitimate rights in sovereignty and security, but it has also
become an open, evil, destructive and terrorist centre against the people of Palestine and against our nation as a whole. Our side should give
up the policy of servility, covering up, weakness and flattery at the
expense of right and should say openly that the US encourages the
Zionist entity to survive at the expense of the Arabs and to kill Arabs
and believers, that the objectives of the US and those of the Zionist
entity are the same, that their wicked behaviour is one, that their aim is
to humiliate and destroy the nation and that the events of September
11 are nothing but a cover they used to pursue that wicked plan in
humiliating and destroying the nation. We have to postpone all our
differences and concentrate on taking an honourable stand before

Allah, history and the people, testifying that we, governments and people, have taken that stand jointly and with full solidarity. This is the only way through which we may regain the respect of the world, now that the world and its representative assemblies have started to slight the Arabs, their potential and their stand. Some, perhaps, scorn the Arabs for their weakness. Foremost, of those who behave in this manner towards the Arabs are the US and its ally, the Zionist entity.

Brother Arabs!

We should only remember the causes and reasons for our unity in this difficult crisis. We should try to forget or postpone all that may lead to our division, which is desired by our enemy under all titles and names. We should reject any plan to divide the potentials, stands and titles of the leadership of the people of Palestine and their heroic groups according to the wicked tactics of Zionism, supported by the US and some western governments, which aim at weakening the people of Palestine and their will for struggle.

He who is not urged by the fervour of the blood ties and principles should be urged by the imminent danger in order to take part in the joint action.

He whose position does not help him to remember the great objectives of our nation and its great role inspreading faith should remember that the destiny of the Arabs, and the nation we are now responsible for before Allah, will be achieved only through our unity and not through our division and quarrels.

Iraq is ready, people, regime and leadership, to shoulder its responsibility so that we may reach a stand which will please Allah and our nation so that history may record later on all that give glory to our grandchildren, after our children, with a stand of honour after we respond to the call of the believing mind, the pure conscience, the faithful heart and the free and honourable aspiration. Allah will protect all those who believes and trust in Him, glorified be His name.

Brothers!

Under certain circumstances, those who are in positions of responsibility, whether they hold titles of power or other titles among the people, are faced with options all of which are difficult. But in emergency cases, like the one we are in now, any decision or option becomes encompassed by dangers and possibilities which may be undesired at the starting point. Since difficult emergency cases do not all come in form of a premeditated option, they must be faced with options and decisions just as difficult.

If wisdom requires that silence or political tactics are resorted to, in circumstances of easy and comfortable options, especially in peace time, options and decisions to face a circumstance of war, aggression and rising evil imposed by others on our nation and people, require other measures. They require that they be subjected to the balance of a deep and comprehensive vision to adopt measures that will ward off evil, reject wrong and support right with the least possible losses and with a stand that will please Allah, fortify the nation, secure its future by leaving the doors of future open without obstacles. It is an ordeal and a trial, brothers. So, let us face both of them with the help of the Almighty, glorified be His name, and the support of our nation and its great potential, after trusting in the Omnipotent Allah, exalted by His Omnipotence.

We find that supporting our people in Palestine in their hard ordeal is virtually a binding necessity. We find that what each of us has so far offered to them is not only less than what our duty requires but also less than what we are capable of offering, if we will it so.

Our collective determination will be in a better position if our minds are set on their objectives firmly.

This will happen, if we want it to happen, when we call each other for an urgent meeting on the summit level without waiting for an additional time to discuss the aggression against the people of Palestine solely.

Whoever says that it is possible to do so in March next, will be like one who gives hope for a person standing on live coals that he will fetch him a fire extinguisher several months later.

The Arabs used to call for meetings on the summit level within short intervals of time for affairs not more dangerous than what is happening in Palestine now.

Let us call each other for this meeting with pure hearts and with minds desirous to be cleansed.

Let us make the strength and the capability of each of us a strength and a capability for him who needs to increase his, or who lacks anyone of them.

Let us make our joint capability, which interact in the light of a programme to ward off aggression and evil against our nation as a whole, the capability in whose light we act and which we develop after we trust in Allah and call upon Him to be our witness.

Let the meeting place be the Honourable Ka'ba or any Arab capital whose location secures the presence of all of us.

Calling our brothers to this meeting does not cancel the next meeting. It is not a substitute for it either. It is a call for an emergency meeting in a circumstance of real emergency in all standards and considerations.

Allah is the greatest!

Allah is the greatest!

Allah is the greatest!

Saddam Hussein
Ramadhan 30, 1422 H.
December 15, 2001 A.D.

President Saddam Hussein's Address on the 81st Anniversary of the Establishment of Iraqi Army On January 6,1921 in 6/1/2002

In the Name of Allah, the Merciful, the Compassionate

Great People!

Brothers, men of sublime values and loyal stand, men of our valiant armed forces!

Arabs, sons of our glorious nation!

Another year has passed to be added to the credit of your army, the proud, faithful and striving army of Iraq, which is now standing its glorious test. It is the army of the nation of faith, virtue, zeal, chivalry and divine messages, the army of the Arabs, the army of Al-Qadissya and the Grand Battle, the Mother of all Battles, the army of the national and Pan-Arab faithful tasks, and the army of Palestine.

Another year is opening its pages for those whom we are talking about, those who are supported by the vast credit of values, sacrifices and preparedness to achieve everything that promotes the nation and the people, and protects land and honour, dignity of the homeland, conscience of history and good repute of men and women.

This is the vow of these men, and it is the vow of all of us. It is the call of history and the aspiration of the future generations for whatever honours and does not shame them before themselves and before the Almighty and Omnipotent Allah in the first place.

It is the vow for which our righteous martyrs and the heroes of the Arab nation everywhere have sacrificed themselves, marching on its path with steadfastness, unshaken by any wind, even it were a fierce icy gale. On the path of this vow there is no place for a sense of loneliness which may enter the soul and play the game of the devil with it to confuse the hearts and minds and shake, in them, the solidity of faith and the firmness of stand by whatever is right and the readiness to combat whatever is wrong until one of the two fair rewards is won: victory or martyrdom. Victory means the victory in life decreed by Allah for the believers, and martyrdom means the martyrdom of those who live with their Lord and are provided by Him. It is the victory which honours the living, gladdens the souls of the martyrs and is blessed by the Merciful, the Compassionate Allah. The obstacles facing the march will be nothing but lessons that deepen faith and determination, increase resolution, and, with these, enlarge horizons for optimism and confidence in success.

In the light of what has been said and what it signifies, the vow is made to the new Christian year and to the Sixth Day of January in it, as it was made in the past Islamic and Christian years, by the army of July, by the people of this army and its leadership. The army of July vows that it will be united in one state, one spirit and one destiny with the people, the principles of the nation, the fragrance of history and the legitimate aspirations for the future. In this unified state, the army will not compete with the people or with the ardent sons of the nation or with the armies of the Arabs except for what is higher in values, firmer in stand, deeper in connection and loftier in prestige.

It is a new year and a new additional vow, made before the people and before the nation. It is a vow of renewed resolution rising in capability and significance, a genuine chivalrous stand of faith, severed neither from the vow of the starting point nor from the great hopes growing out of the march, the performance and the trust before the people. It is an honest chivalrous stand, faithful in its ardour, trusting in the One and Only in its ascent towards glory, virtue, right and justice. It fills with anger the hearts of those whose protector is the Devil, and fills with joy the hearts of the believers and the heart of every honest person who keeps a vow and fulfils a promise. It makes the martyrs glad.

Blessed be the martyrs!

Blessed be the martyrs!

Brothers, Arabs, Friends!

Whenever an occasion makes it necessary that I speak about the Iraqis or about the army, whose attributes I have summed up in this and in other speeches, I feel embarrassed. It is not because I cannot say or write what should be said or written about them, but because I fear that I may not recall all that they deserve to be recalled about them and, thus, give them only part of their due in the light of what my soul likes to say about them and what does justice to their history. I am afraid that some narrow-minded people may interpret what I say as merely panegyric of a state which the speaker is part of.

Although I hate hesitation, the feeling of embarrassment in this regard adds conviction to certitude and places those who are just before a historical responsibility to tell the truth and do justice to the truthful. In that case, I find myself facing an embarrassment of another type and a query from another perspective. Is it possible, I wonder that an occasion like this one can contain a serious portion of what should be said under the circumstances of this hateful embargo? Can it contain what should be said, besides, about the sweet patience of the people in a battle which, in the Mother of all Battles alone, has been going on for eleven years? If the pen is capable of writing, and if he who delivers the speech is prepared for it, can all that is known about the struggle and patience of this army be said when we find that its support and depth are the great people of Iraq? I turn to myself again and say: the foundation of whatever is said should be truth and honesty. It is not necessary that we say now, and on this occasion, all that should be said or all that we know, to do justice to this striving and valiant army. In whatever we say, or do not say, on this or on any other occasion, we will content ourselves by saying that our army and our people, united in one state as they are, live in our conscience. They both share in the position of sight in our eyes and permeate through our soul in every action we take and every meditation we make. Nothing is given preference in our soul over them and over our glorious nation but that given to the Great Omnipotent Allah. He, glorified be His Name, is our Protector, and it is He Who has decreed for us the firm stand we, our people and our army take towards what we stand firmly upon.

Brothers!

You all know the fundamentals of the glorious record of the army of July, the army of Al-Qadissiya and the Mother of all Battles. You know how it has never let you down, but rather it has upheld you in action and in stand. Its action has been a genuine part of the significance of your Standard, the Standard of Allahu-Akbar (Allah is the greatest). It has upheld the faithful Arab military after recalling its values. It has ascended to where it should ascend through the high sense of responsibility it has maintained towards the Arab military, towards the nation and towards the homeland.

You well knew how your army was during the past years and throughout the turning points in its history. It was an everlasting record of bravery, chivalry, zeal and striving based upon its great faith, its vow and its manly stand. And as it did in the past, it keeps now its vow before Allah that it will maintain the same spirit and will rise towards what is even better, trusting in Him, glorified be His Name, believing in the role of the people and the nation and their rights. It will remain loyal to the interests of the people, jealous of the sovereignty and dignity of the homeland and truthful to the vow it has made to maintain the aspirations and the rights of the nation, wherever it finds the way to do so, or wherever Allah seizes an opportunity of honour and a role for it to safeguard these aspirations and rights.

And Allah is the greatest!

You have told the invaders and the covetous, in the thick of all battles, that the homeland and the nation are held as a trust by you, the manly men of self-respect, ardent zeal and faith.

Together with you, the people have told them, with the greatest preparedness and conviction, that every Iraqi born to a glorious mother is, after trusting in Allah, a trustworthy and dependable project for the army of the peoand the nation.

And as Iraq is a trust held by you, your nation and its great homeland are also a trust whenever a caller for jihad calls upon you to defend land, honour, sanctities and sanctuaries.

And as your debased enemies failed in the past, so will any aggressor, if he lets himself be seduced into committing an evil act against your trust. He will be shamed by Allah and will be thwarted in his base aims. Then, only the foreheads of your tyrannical enemies will become dark, while the lustrous foreheads will be found wherever you gather together with all the virtuous, self-respecting and striving sons of your nation. This will happen because Allah supports your nation and your people as long as they obey Him, glorified be His Name, and pray to Him to keep faith and faithful chivalry in your hearts and to shame the unbelievers.

A salute to all Muslim mujahideen who have followed the faithful examples of Islam and Arabism!

A salute to them wherever they are, giving away soul and substance in sacrifice for the great values of faith and virtue, and facing oppression, falsehood and tyranny to defend right and seek for fairness and justice!

A salute to all the chivalrous heroes of humanity as they face injustice and tyranny. From the leadership and the free, striving and loyal people of Iraq we extend to them the best of regards, love and solidarity!

A salute to the chivalrous heroes of Arabism and faith!

A salute to the sisters of the glorious Iraqi women among the heroic people of Palestine!

A salute to the brave men who are loyal to the vow and promise they have made before Allah, the people and the nation!

A kiss from us on the foreheads of all the elderly people, the young boys and girls and the children who face Zionism and its ally, the US, and who combat aggression with soul and substance in order to uphold truth and crush falsehood.

It is not out of weakness on our part or on the part of the free, striving and loyal people of Iraq to say to them: We are with you, though without having our swords with them, or without advancing one step forward wherever some fall one step behind. But it is the circumstances and the barriers of politics and geography, which you know, that impose this situation, until Allah gives permission to bring about a situation different from this one.

A curse upon everything that is negative in the circumstances!

May every year bring prosperity to the army of Iraq, which is the army of faithful Arabism and the army of Palestine!

May every year bring prosperity to all!

Blessed be the martyrs!

Blessed be the martyrs!

Long live our glorious nation!

Long live Palestine, free and Arab from the river to the sea and from the sea to the river!

May disgrace and curses fall upon Zionism and its damned and detestable entity and upon its evil allies!

Long live Iraq!

Long live the army of Iraq!

And Allah is the greatest!

Allah is the greatest!

President Saddam Hussein: Iraq Decide Completely Stopping Oil Exporting In April 8, 2002

In the Name of God, Most gracious, Most Merciful

Our Lord! Let not our hearts deviate now after thou hast guided us, but grant mercy, from thine own presence, for Thou art the Grantor of bounties without measure. (The holy Quran III, 8)

Great Iraqi people!

Heroic people of glory, faith, jihad, sacrifices, and bravery!

Great Arab nation everywhere!

Arab Mujahidins!

Courageous, heroic, Mujahidins, men and women of the people of Palestine!

Alsalamualikum,

Our Arab nation's capabilities and stand to the point of mocking at these capabilities. They are even using part of them against the best of the Arab nation, after having tamed those whom they have made accept the weakness and humility of themselves.

What is going on against our oppressed people in Palestine provokes every free and faithful spirit. The killing, destruction, and humiliation this is ongoing in Palestine, are basically carried out against the Arab and Islamic nation, and not against the heroic and glorious Palestinians, who are facing the Zionist enemy and its aggressive forces with stones and simple weapons using their chest which are full of faith for amunition. While they do so, they are fully optimistic that the future is for the Palestinians and the Arab nation, not for the usurping Zionist entity nor for the American Administrations which are the enemy of the peoples and nations.

Dear Brothers!

The Zionist aggression, which is killing publicly in front of TV cameras our brothers and sisters, and our people in Palestine, is perpetrated by a common arrangement between the Zionist entity and the American Administration. The objective is not only to occupy Palestinian and Arab territories as happened in 1948 and 1967, but also to break the Palestinian and Arab will, and force them to surrender in humility to the Zionist American alliance.

Whereas destiny draws for its people what they deserve of honour and virtue and makes them a reference point before God, their nation, and history, proportionally with what their capability, faith and action draw for them when they face difficulties to pass the difficult test of overcoming the obstacles on the road in a way that pleases God and the nation.

Whereas Americans and those who back them have become deaf to the savage massacres perpetrated by the Zionist entity against our people in Palestine, with their complicity.

Whereas when any of the elements of wealth is not used to hold faith and honour high, and to defend their values, it becomes aburden and weakness.

Whereas the enemies of the nation and humanity do not understand but a practical language, and the reactions that undermine their interests and affect them in a way that exasperates their evil indinations and hostility to the Arab nation including the Palestinian people.

Whereas the Arab and Islamic peoples, and even all the honest people in the world, have expressed their opinion and made clear where they stand by all these demonstrations and other means of protesting against the enemy. They have shown their solidarity with the Palestinian people, Arab officials who have spoken have said what they are capable of saying or willing to say.

But the enemy was not deterred and did not put an end to its cowardly attacks, along with its American ally, against the unarmed and mujahid people of Palestine who do not have but the force of their faith and their noble leadership.

Whereas we are one nation with a common destiny, and a common security...and whereas the killing of any believer, or the bloodshed in Ramala, Bethlehem, Gaza Jenin, or Al-Quds, is like shedding blood, God forbid, in any other Arab city, or in Baghdad, Mossul, south, Karbela, Salah-al-din, Arbil, or any other Iraqi City of village.

The Revolution Command Council, the Iraqi leadership of the Ba'th Arab Socialist Party, and the Cabinet in their meeting on 8 April 2002 declare, in the name of the faithful, honest, mujahid, noble, Iraqi people: completely stopping oil exporting starting from this afternoon April 8, through the pipelines going to the Turkish port on the Mediterranean, and our ports in Bassra for a period of the thirty days after which we will further decide, or until the Zionist entity's armed forces have unconditionally withdrawn from the Palestinian territories they have occupied and have shown respect for the will of the Palestinian people and the Arab nation to sovereignty, security, dignity and life.

This decision is basically taken against the Zionist entity, and the American aggressive policy, and not against anyone else. It is not meant to harm anyone but those who have decided to harm the Arab nation, including the Palestinian people, which harms every noble believer in humanity. By this decision we mean to ring the alarm bell and voice of the faithful nation by word and action that remind those who have for gotten that God is great.

Let the debased be despised!

God is great, glory to the Almighty!

We hope that our Arab and Muslim brothers, and even all believers, will encourage and bless this step, and will reinforce it by similar steps by the oil producers, or other steps by the others, each one in light of his opportunity to effectively plea. God, and the people, to enhance the elements of force in oneself and in the nation.

God is great!

Let the debased be despised.

President Saddam Hussein addresses Arab Leaders in April 22, 2002

In the name of God, Most Gracious, Most merciful,

Dear Arab brothers!

Kings, Presidents, Emirs and officials!

And through you, to our dear Arab people everywhere!

Assalamu Alaykum-Peace be upon you!

Once again, I bring forward to you my viewpoints and suggestions. I may be exasperating but my only excuse to you, after God, is that I am seeking what might please God and what might give us glory before our people and history. And make us gain true respect of nations and peoples of the world. At a time when our Palestinian brothers are being killed, our sacred places violated, our wealth being ransacked, or about to, on a large scale, if we will not agree upon a plan of action with the help of God, to summon our will and faith.

I don't think that we might disagree that the will of our people in all our countries is at a high level, thanks to God. This will was clearly seen throughout the current crisis by everybody, whether officials decision makers, or every single citizen.

Dear brothers!

Similar conditions have put our nation in a difficult dilemma in past times, our glorious nation had always proved to be equal to the challenge, and faced it in the name of God, and proved itself and gained victory over those who wanted to humiliate it, usurp its right in life in general, or its right to chose its way and aims that do not harm the principles of humanity at large, and its right to recover its rights from usurpers, so as to lead a free and decent life, after making due sacrifices by a unified and organized action that leads the nation to achieve certain aims on the basic of the good intentions and collective will of joint action. But when the nation ignores this and does not see the suitable moment for the right action, its fate will be not only humiliation but also a lot of bloodshed of its people. It will furthermore loose respect and will no longer be able to mount to higher milestones that may make it be effective in life, and will not be able to protect its wealth, and values.

There is no doubt now that we are all facing, as leaders or peoples of the of the countries of our one Arab nation, such choice, I think that if anyone of us deeply thinks of his surroundings, he will find himself before this choice.

I must now ask you, dear brothers and myself: shall we choose the right aims and methods, and succeed in distributing duties among us in a spirit of collective and brotherly leadership as faithful sons of our nation. Or shall we miss the chance and leave the initiative in the hand of the enemies of our nation, who are the enemies of God and humanity, and the allies of Satan? Then each and everyone of us will live in disgrace before God, himself, his nation and this generation of which we must be proud for having demonstrated the highest level of awareness, faith and readiness to make sacrifices, in a way that no one can miss or recognize.

What I wish for you and for myself, dear brothers, is that we make our choice without hesitation, get together and not separate, work and not be lazy, and prepare ourselves together for the way we choose and not to allow our enemy and his evil choices to succeed and defeat us, after subjecting us to bitter fait-accompli that no one could accept, since we all by the grace of God, will work to please God and our nation, and to defeat evil and evil doers.

Brothers!

Our history, like the history of other nations and peoples, tells us that one of the most important weak points in which the vicious enemy finds a breach by which he can kill that nation, is the separation between the ruler and his people, or the separation or disagreement between rulers in the same nation and people, so that each acts on his own.

Hence, the greedy foreign enemies would resort to enhance and create fear to trouble and make conspiracies by frightening the ruler from his own people and from any way they have chosen which he cannot decide to accept. They make every ruler afraid from other rulers, or they make him believe that he is their preferred ruler in his nation.

Most of you are military men, or at least have a certain knowledge and experience in this domain, this is why I say: just as armies try in the battlefield to separate the infantry from the armored forces are the frontline forces from the others in order to weaken their performance and effect and consequently easily defeat them, in a similar manner, those who want to exploit us, resort to making the rulers afraid of their people, or making them seem weak in the eyes of their people in order to weaken both sides or anyone of them. The weakness of anyone of them would result into the weakness of both of them.

Furthermore, the enemy, tries to make anyone of us as regimes or individuals, according to our responsibilities, believe that this or that act, this collective Arab action or that, and this idea and suggestion or that, in fact serve the interests of this or that party alone, or distinguishes this or that ruler or leader at the expense of the others. The same plots and schemes are made by the enemy within the same people in our countries or at the level of the entire nation, using the same methods for the same purposes, by suggesting to this or that political party or trade union and federation when they try to organize a joint work, that this or that joint action or decision would only be in the benefit of this or that side, at the expense of this or that organization.

This would discourage and weaken their common will for collective action.

Moreover, the importance of the greedy enemy has reached such a point, in preparing the psychological, political and intellectual arena to further weaken the nation and achieve his aims by division or at least by the absence of the unity of opinion, aims, stands and necessary action. The enemy, is furthermore, exploiting the fact that our nation consist of more than twenty countries, to say or make believe that this or that idea, opinion, suggestion, plan or goal is only meant to serve this or that Arab country at that expense of this or that country. In order to enhance doubts, fears or the unoriginal tendency of whose hearts and minds may weakly respond to the values and principles of our being one nation, or might misinterpret or not see the real motives of this or that foreigner who wants to exploits us.

Moreover, the enemy is encouraging and creating feelings of jealousy and envy among our nation of even the natural resources in some of our countries. In order to diminish the feeling that any natural resource or wealth, or the number of the population, are in fact, elements of strength for the entire Arab nation, and not a negative factor, that must used in favor of the nation not against it.

In addition to that, the foreigners are encouraging some people that the steadfastness of any Arab country, regime or ruler, or even of any mujahid who stands against his greed, is a stand that would lead to weakening the others, rather than strengthening and encouraging them to face the enemy. The enemy is even presenting weakness as an equivalent of wisdom and reason, and presenting the capabilities to stop his vicious needs as an equivalent of foolishness and impatience. He is even endeavoring and hoping to transfer the conflict between the rulers on the one hand and the people on the other, to something that would prevent the rulers from undertaking their basic duty of principles. Instead of mobilization of everybody: rulers and people, the leadership and the citizens trench: the trench of justice and faith so as to defend their nation's rights, morals and its noble principles.

Dear brothers, we are the people of one nation, and this is a great honor for which we must thank God. But, at the same time, this identity represents a great responsibility, if we carry it on with honor and enthusiasm; but it would become a heavy burden if we fall in contradiction with it or if we parted from it in mind and in action. I do not think that the deprave himself belonging to the nation of the Glorious Qura'an, historical glories, the cradle of Heavenly religio, Prophets and Messengers, and the land of the banner and the sword of justice that had honored our nation and humanity at large.

Brothers, the people, every country of our nation, have said their word about what is going on around them, and about what they want in a clear and strong way by various activities in all parts of our nation from the Atlantic Ocean to the Arab Gulf. What we all saw is enough to make us have a clear idea of what the people want, if anyone of us wanted to make up his mind and express his opinion...

Here, I may help you, or help myself, by answering the question: is it the people who draw the policy of a state, or is it, rather, the officials in power or the leaders who draw this policy? I say: policies are drawn by the official in charge of the state, and particularly, by the leadership. But, no official should decide anything away from his people's conscience, interests, and dignity, or even from their opinion and wishes in circumstances like this. Regardless of the accuracy of the people's opinion and wishes in the details of this or that matter, such a stand by the ruler as part of his people is better for him. It is more honorable than standing against his people, or not providing them with the minimum of what they want and call for. Any decision taken unilaterally by the ruler contradicting his people's opinion, would place the concerned ruler or leader at a distance from the people even if his decision is at the first glance and technically and politically better than the people's opinion. The ruler would be considered as a forfeiter because his decision will lead to forfeiting his people's stand by him in crucial situations. Hence the ruler will be weakened and miss the chance of reform.

Brothers!

The foreigner is trying to intimidate us, or to make some of us afraid of own people by saying to him that your rule or chair, or even your life is at stake if you do not follow my will. Consequently, we should all have faith and say that, God willing, we are not afraid of our people but rather we count on them. It is in fact by our people, and God's help, that we make anyone who wants to harm or exploit us a afraid of us. We will, thus, find our people hailing, loving, and proud of us, in addition to the Almighty's mercy and blessings, which put us, and all believers, in highest levels and happiness.

When the foreigner tries to incite contention among us, we must tell him that the force and capabilities of any of our countries is the force and capabilities of us all, just as any weakness weakens us all.

After all this introduction, which I hope was not wearisome, you may ask: what do you suggest then? What I suggest is what I hear or deduce from your statements, and your saying, or the saying of many of you, including the writer of present letter, that: lets not speak or describe our nation's weakness, or why or how, because to publicly talk about that at a time like this particularly when the distinction of our nation, its good attributes, and the elements of its force and capabilities are not seen, would seem like an attempt to disown one's responsibility to exalt the nation by bringing together and to attend to its points of weakness. We should all, call for, and work on strengthening any points of weakness in the nation, and using the elements of strength in it collectively and systematically. The roles and attitudes should be distributed on us according to what every one of us can best do. Or communication and diagnosis of the our points of strength and weakness should not be carried out in an academically theoretical way, nor in a neutral manner between what is just and unjust, or in an isolationist spirit under the influence or illusion of weakness, hoping that the wrongdoers would exempt this country or that, or this regime or that or even this ruler or that, from their conspiracies and harm. No one of us should be under the delusion of a strength that enables him to do without the efforts and force of fellow brothers, except after trying and reaching, God forbid, a point of despair. Together we make a force of faith and loyalty that renders glory on us, protects our land and rights, and recovers what is usurped from it with the help of God the Almighty.

No one should make the mistake of thinking that if he is isolated from the other, he would be able by his force alone, protect his rights, and recover what my be usurped of it, because if weakness and the foreigner's greed prevailed, no one could escape them even, God forbid, at the price of himself, his people, and God's mercy. The other should gently but clearly remind whoever of us who forgets that we are one nation, and that the usurpers and those who want to exploit us scheming against us as a one nation. We should consider the different names of our countries, political systems, and history as a source of a strong action in favor of our nation, its higher interests, and national security. They should not be considered a burden and a rejected weight on us. The conditions prevailing in the world toady are not the same conditions in which our people in their countries fought to free themselves of the old colonialism. Nevertheless, even in those condition was their any country, big or small, that did not take force from the very name of the Arab nation, and remind its people the fact that they belong to this nation? Is their anyone who has not turned to the nation's potential, in part or in whole, against the foreign occupation forces, for liberation, or in the wars against them?

In any case if we can not encourage, we should not in inconvenienced by the initiative of the people in what they believe would harm our enemy. For example, trade and professional unions and federations can do much to harm the enemy including calling for a strike of the workers of oil exporting ports or oil tankers with contracts with the country meant to be harmed, the loading and unloading workers of cargo ships of a certain country, the staff and workers of railways, ports, airports, external communication, etc. We can continue to give such examples, as you know. In fact, trade unions and federations used to do something of that, but now they have become used to weighting their words and sentences by the balance of their ministries of foreign affairs, or something less than that.

The presence of a stronger opinion, that is expressed in a direct way in a different style and language of that of the concerned diplomats, is useful to the governments and their polices in a conflict like this. Such an opinion would do them harm, if they wanted, because attenuating the language of demanding, and the action to the necessities of circumstantial situation as viewed by the diplomats, on all official and nonofficial levels, is harmful to our countries in this and other battles.

When diplomacy fails, other means and capabilities begin their role of action, which may last. Means as a result of habit and the inadequate relation with the source of decisions and of guiding it as if it is disabled and cannot quickly resurge in spirit, will, strength and means.

Zionism, the American administrations, and who has or will become their allies, have prepared themselves to confront the Arab nation, including Palestine as one nation. So it is our duty, by the rule of our doctrine, to avoid saying by the rule Sharia and authenticity, to prepare ourselves on this basis, which is the real thing in us, and is the rule of history and destiny. It is not anybody's invention, or a mere wish of someone, when evil and devil are with themselves, we are bond by duty to be with ourselves with the guidance of God the merciful. Here, I would like to recall that some Arab brothers said recently that (Zionism has had the upper hand over the American administrations). Zionism has the upper hand over the American administrations to use them against us, and it becomes one and the same with us, against our nation, as we have repeatedly said, to facilitate the realization of the Zionists' covetous schemes in our Arab nation. Therefore, it is our duty to be with ourselves, to mobilize our utmost force and sin all fields, and not to hope for anything good for our nation and Arab security from the US. For the American administration will walk as they walk now up to their knees in Arab and Muslim blood. We must all believe that no one can defeat our nation by injustice since it is justly on its own land. Our nation would only be defeated if it abandons its distinctive attributes, and duties, and if the guides in it go to sleep.

Our people is awake, dear brothers, so it is our patriotic, national, moral, Arab, faithful, and constitutional duty that is calling us in our capacity of rulers not to go to sleep, nor to be inadvertent or weaken. Anyone who does not follow this in his attitude with his nation, will lose himself, and lose his way, after losing the compass that leads him to it. Even when the people find that they have to change anyone of us if they get angry, it would be a loss had he taken the right path. And I do not think that anyone of us, including the writer of this letter, would choose this fate or accept it for himself.

The strength of the nation is a living part of it capability of defending its national security from any threats. The wealth of the nation is part of its strength and effective means. Other nations have used it throughout history, and they may have even used what is contradictory to the law they put in the UN documents, as did the US in particular with cereal contracts. You probably remember its policy against Egypt, how it cancelled the cereal contract which it had signed with Iraq in Feb. 1990, and how it used this against the ex Soviet Union and is using it against Russia now. You may also know that the US with the support of the UK has hindered medicine contracts for the Iraqi people despite the fact that their prices have already been paid before August 1990. They have stopped all the other means of life from the Iraqi people to kill them and decrease the number of the population. The US and UK do all these things although their national security are not threatened by our countries, if it is security for themselves and for the world that they wants, with respecting other peoples, their land, national and Arab choices, their choice of their doctrine, beliefs and values.

Not to seem to be ignoring the comments made by some of my brothers in oil producing countries, epically that oil is not a weapon...it is not a cannon, a tank, or a jet fighter. I say: Yes, oil is not a tank, a jet fighter or a cannon, but it can be used as a weapon, when the muzzles of the cannons, tanks and jet fighters are not working, or are not meant to be used. As for saying: we can not, or we are not ready to use the weapon for those who have weapons, and that oil is not a cannon, a tank or a jet fighter for those who have oil, then what would, and by what can we confront those who want to exploit us, the aggressors, and the usurpers?

On this occasion, I would like remind my brothers of some their fathers and grandfathers' values when they confronted any aggression.

Every man would go out to face the enemy even if the battle was at its fiercest stage, or if the aggressor had launched the attack with rifles, cannons, and jet fighters. It would be disgraceful for any man not to go out to the battlefield even if he had nothing but an axe, a dagger, or club, otherwise the law of (who does not have a weapon equal to the weapon of the aggressor or the usurper, must surrender to those who better weapons) would be applied.

If anyone was late or stayed behind, he would be called names that I do not think that anyone of us would accept for himself. He would even be forbidden to sit on the chairs of men in gatherings and meetings and no one would serve him coffee. The history of our nation is full of such examples, whether in the wars and struggle for independence or in the annals of conflicts between fighting tribes.

Now, haven't the Palestinians faced the bombs, jet fighters, cannons, missiles and rifles? What would be said of the attitude of Palestinians had they not confronted the aggressors in this way?

Haven't the Zionists used even water and food when they besieged the Palestinians, especially in heroic Jenin? Did they use water and food as a weapon in the battle against those heroes?

The history of the wars between polytheists and the Muslims under the leadership of the Prophet(God Pray on Him) is full of such lessons. When the conflict begins each party tries to overcome the will of the other, or to subject it to his own will. Hence, the one who is defending his will from being subjected, and his sanctities and land from being violated and humiliated, must use his weapons in harmonized succession, each in its own field, so as he can defeat the will of his enemy, or to stop it from defeating his will and humiliating him. Therefore, oil should be used as a weapon that will come in succession in the battle, and not as an absolute alternative weapon. As for the question: what weapon do we begin with? Well, let's begin bothers...we have not suggested the weapon of oil until we were aware that our Arab brothers are not ready to use the other weapons, and so that no one could say that we have a weapon, the use of which does not require any bloodshed, or that: we have not used the oil weapon, so lets try it, before resorting other weapons.

At any rate, any weapon that restores the rights, and is more effective, compared to another weapon, is something we wish for, and ready to try. If you want to use the weapons of our armies to be succeeded by the oil, we are with our armies, oil and people, ready to do so, along whoever is ready to so, although we prefer that we all have this honor, and only some of our countries and political systems, except if we had to, God forbid.

Brothers!

I must also say, that I have not read, or heard that the official in a nation had ever said to their enemy that they will not use their weapons against him, despite his aggression on them. Wouldn't this encourage the enemies of the nation to speed up their aggression? Or to continue it to accomplish all their goals without paying any price? They may even try to accomplish some goals that were planed at this stage, before hearing the officials of the nation say that they will not use their weapons, when they launched their aggression, or wait to see the reaction before continuing it to achieve deeper goals!

In this case, don't the Arabs have the right to use the elements of their strength to defend their lives, sovereignty, honor, and beliefs? Not using and neutralizing the elements of our strength leave our weakness breaches without protection. Therefore, neutralizing our oil, which is one of the elements of our economic strength, means that we are strengthening our enemy on ourselves and enable him to overcome us.

For these reasons, I see that:

Arabs should express their solidarity with their brothers' security and safety, and the oil exporters, including Iraq, immediately decrease the production of their oil for exportation by 50%, and directly deprive the US and Zionist entity from the other exported half, and to threaten any country or company with the same measure if they export the oil they import from Arab countries. We should thus be strongly ringing the bells of protest and solidarity, so that those who harm and kill our people can see and hear. We will thus embarrass the American Administration before its people, and make them hear the voice of Arab with a respect that is equal to their obedient or humiliating submission to the Zionist Lobby and its evil aims. This measure should be immediately effective, once agreed upon, until further notice, and until the nation's demands in solidarity with the rights of the heroic people of Palestine, without any bargaining or procrastination. The Arab should take a collective attitude, any if anyone of them deviated, God forbid, he would be described and treated by the Arab nation as if he abandoned his duties regarding his nation and its national security. This attitude should be publicly unveiled before the people of the concerned country. In this way, we would have provided the nation with whathelp it in its life and jihad, and the Palestinian people with the support by other measures as a result of the increase in the prices of oil after stopping its exportation which will compensate for the revenues one may think that the Arab exporting countries will lose by decreasing their exports, whether the compensation is total or partial.

To allocate a quota of the exported oil proportional the stand taken by the countries that express understanding or supporting stands with Arab rights. By contrast, the quota will be decreased according to the stands of the countries, which will condemn. In this respect, a special attention should be given to the members of the Security Council, especially the permanent members.

The Arab countries should work in solidarity with Islamic oil producing countries to take the same measures as Arabs as mentioned in paras. 1 and 2, above.

The Arab countries should work together, represented by oil producing countries members of OPEC, with the support of Muslum members, to have the OPEC adopt a resolution of full solidarity with this and the measures afore mentioned.

A council of a number, that will be agreed upon, of Arab ministers of Oil and Foreign Affairs, or of the minister of Oil and Foreign Affairs of oil producing countries, to follow up the details of paras. 2,3,4. The Arab Summit should be in a position that enables it to convene urgent meetings, whenever necessary, according to a number of Presidents and Kings who will be nominated by the Summit, if they are held before or after taking the measures mentioned in paras. 1,2,3,4.

The Arab nation should be prepared from every aspect to confront any reaction or aggression, in solidarity and as one nation, with the faith that the foreigner cannot force us to anything we collectively refuse, and that if the foreigner tries anything against the weakest country among us, this country will be stronger that all the force of the foreigner, when it is in bosom of its nation, under its banner and that protection of its sword, and the solidarity of its people in the inside.

Saying this, I pray to God to guide us together in implementing it, or in any other opinion you deem is a better one, if it is capable to stop the wrongdoers' aggression on our nation, in the forefront of which is the people of Palestine and to restore the usurped right of our nation, in the forefront of which is Palestine, and the our rights and the rights of the Arab countries in what the Zionist entity usurped from their territories and right.

God is Great! Alahuakbar!

Long live our glorious nation!

God is Great! Alahuakbar!

Long live Palestine from the sea to the river!

God is Great! Alahuakbar!

Let Zionism be despised along with its aggressive criminal and damned entity of occupation, and led its counterpart in evil doing: The American polices and their representatives, be despised.

Speech Of His Excellency President Saddam Hussein On The Occasion Of The Thirty-Forth Anniversary Of The July 17–30 Revolution/July 17, 2002

In the name of God Most Compassionate, Most Merciful

"Our Lord! Condemn us not if we forget or fall into error; our Lord! Lay not on us a burden like that which Thou didst lay on those before us; our Lord! lay not on us a burden greater than we have strength to bear. Blot out our sins, and grant us forgiveness. Have mercy on us. Thou art our Protector; help us to triumph over those who stand against the Faith."

God's words are True!

Our faithful and loyal people,

Courageous men of our armed forces,

People of our glorious nation,

Assalamu Alaykum Warahmatullahi Wabarakatuhu,

For thirty-four years now, and throughout these thirty-four years, the cycle of time has returned to Temmuz (July), with the grace of Allah, so that history may re-visit the present and the future in Temmuz, thus recalling the essence of its role in the history of the people of ancient Iraq, and in their beliefs; except that this time Temmuz is mobilized, and comes fully convinced, pure, loyal and healthy, to have, in its people, after relying on Allah, the glorious presence in a world which wants to have Temmuz purify the self from what might have been left in it from the past, distant or near.

Temmuz returns to us, to its nation, carrying the tools of building and construction, having acquired, from experience, wisdom and sharpness, and from its interaction with others, lessons and broadmindedness. This time, however, Temmuz also returns armed in addition to all of this, with its sward, bow, and spear, carrying its shield or gun and cannon, mounting its tank, or poised in its battle-trench which may, through caution and alertness, save life from schemes, conspiracies, and perfidy, and protect all our dear dear men, with the grace of Allah, the Powerful, the Great.

Temmuz returns to say to all evil Tyrants and oppressors of the world: You will never defeat me this time. Never! Even if you come together from all over the world, and invite all the devils as well, to stand by you, support or incite you.

Temmuz returns to us, to you, dear brothers, to meet the level of your struggle and your jihad. But its resolve, this time, is deep-rooted, with Allah's grace, to be your loyal brother or son at all times, the knight of your wishes, the father of your dreams and aspirations, and of your expectations in it on the way towards Iman, the zenith, glory and virtue.

Temmuz returns as if it were with us on every single day we have lived during our march since 17–30 July, 1968, to this day, or on the days looking forward to a bright future following this date, with the grace of

Allah, the future in which Temmuz is a partner, gracing those days with the blessing of Allah the Magnificent, or with the, spirit of Temmuz and the prayers of every noble woman, and with the inspiration derived in our heritage from the spirit of our great ancestors, towards achieving our great expectations and gaining the blessings of Allah for the people of our land, its builders, protectors and shields.

Between the time of those two glorious days of the seventeenth and thirtieth of July 1968, and this day, there are lessons and lessons, great experiences and meanings, full of glory, triumphs and achievement in the affairs of life and in the effort of prevent falsehood from prevailing over truth; thus strengthening the true believers in their expectations, action and endeavour, while repelling the disbelievers and enemies of our nation and people. So praise be to Allah in his glory, the praise of true, patient and resilient fighters, who are strong in their belief, after relying on Allah, the Glorious, with the gratitude of totally devoted and patient worshipers.

My brothers, you are the wound of my soul whenever you are wounded or hurt by a foreign power or its lackeys; you are most precious to me and to every man of honour and courage, as you ably confront injustice and aggression, refusing to allow the arrows of the tyrant and his stooges to touch your spirit, your determination, your conviction, your stand, your will and your loyalty.

My brothers, my sons, my soul; you who are true to the bond and the holy struggle in Iraq, Palestine and the larger Arab homeland, or wherever you might be in its arenas, have we are, recalling with you your revolution, celebrating the beginnings of its march and the great meanings carried by those who believed in its road, and allowing our imaginations to take us to the realms of its meanings.

Your revolution, in all its triumphs and at all levels of its sublime meanings, and in your satisfaction in it, reflects your values, and those of your strong, resilient, heroic and loyal people, the glorious people of faithful believers in Iraq. Whenever your revolution has fallen short in any aspect which you might have wished to see happen otherwise, then its excuse is the fact that it has been true to its objectives; and success comes only from Allah.

Our Arab brethren!

Valiant men and noble women of Iraq, the land of jihad, victory and virtue!

I want, on this occasion, to refer to a matter, amongst many others matters, with the details and implications of which I do not wish to burden you. In so doing, I do not wish to appear incapable of covering these details and implications, because a speech, even if it were unrestricted by time, or indeed several books, would not be sufficient; In fact, it requires volumes upon volumes and open time, without the pressure of haste. As to what ought to be said to describe, in truth the revolution, its picture and effective action, the depth of its spirit and the purity of it nature, in a speech such as this one, then this will remain a difficult task for whoever may take up this challenge, including the present speaker, who played the role that you know in planting the seeds of the revolution and caring for its growth until it blossomed, yielded fruit, delivered results and grew strong, after achieving height and stature. I would not have burdened you, my dear brothers, with what I intend to say now, had I not found it to be a moral obligation compatible with your true bond with, and love for, this march and its pioneers, as well as with the aspirations which you attach to it and which you cannot find elsewhere; aspirations befitting the sacrifices made by the people of this revolution. I wanted to assure you of the strength of your revolution through rational logical and concrete facts and achievements which the mind cannot fail to recognize. Here is one of the facts which will assure you when I remind you of it:

You know, brothers, that our most important criterion for the purity of our souls, the truth of our pledge and intention, the height of our determination and the strength of our resolve, after reliance on Allah, is the depth of our background in the examples of our nation at the advent of Islam and those who emulated them in subsequent eras, however distant from them, whether in the center of the Islamic state in the land of Syria or in Baghdad, the capital of Arabs and Muslims, or those who migrated to the land of Andalusia, and the basic example of their pledge, the falcon of Quraish.

Regardless of the level of interpretations towards the judgments of history, or the assessments of people in this or that historical cycle or symbol, we are in agreement on one established fact, which that the attachment of life to the Islamic principles of the era of the Rashideen Califs (blessed be they with Allah's grace and satisfaction), and its attachment to succeeding Califs and rulers, has changed a great deal. Whatever the differences, or points of similarity, on which we agree now, and which is most important, whether required by the new life according to the criteria of those who say so, or whether the principles become too heavy for the Califs and rulers concerned against the temptations of life, thus making them less heavy-handed in applying the princito the affairs of life and in assessing the behaviour of the Calif and the people against the behaviour of the Rashideen Califs and the companions of Prophet Mohammed the Messenger of Allah. I say that what we agree on now, regardless of interpretation in its different colours, which is the most important part of what I wanted to say in this address, is that, as time takes us away from the starting point in our march, there appears a degree of laxity in the energy, vision and activities of those in charge and in their view of the principles, as well as in their application of those principles, whether they have been tempted by the lures of life, or whether they have been prevented from attaining their desires by the difficulties of the road and the ferocity and forceful impact of counter factors.

The other matter which I do not think we shall differ on is that the growing distance, in other experiences and further examples, between the march and the time of its start, forces the requirements and circumstances of politics to take precedence over the requirements of the principles, and over the adherence to, and application of, these principles.

We started our march, dear brothers, 3.00 a.m. on the 17th of July 1968. That was a stage or a juncture which had its own mark. At any rate, none of the applications at the starting line contained a model picture of the principles of the Ba'th Party and the spirit of the revolution which we aimed to see prevail, except for what was in the hearts of the faithful revolutionaries which reflected the genuine principles we had aspired to, and which we had been resolved to apply. Indeed, what happened then, including our prescribed attainment to power in the morning of the 17th of July, was just the break needed to launch our march. Then we carried out a great operation in the structure of the revolution which was to reflect on its course and spirit. That action was taken at 3.00 p.m. on the 30th of July, thus making the opportunity for the revolution to attain to its principles and start applying them much greater than it had been during the brief interval between the 17th and 30th of July. An acceleration in the steps and measures taken increased the opportunities for both the revolution and the march to apply the principles upon which they were based and for which the true heroes of the revolution launched their revolutionary course on the 17th and 30th of July.

I do not want to burden you with more details, dear brothers. It is important, to stress, however, that we refused to become merely a regime or a government, only slightly or relatively distinguished from previous regimes in our great Arab homeland. We also refuse to measure our enthusiasm and action of principle according to what we used to be like in 1968 and 1969, or in the years that followed, so as to treat them as our ideal points of departure. Indeed, we refuse to measure the steps which we find necessary to take now by any of the steps taken during the years prior to Um-al-Ma'arik (the Mother of all Battles) and to re-adjust any step that remains incomplete according to that, as a criterion for the highest principles. Nor do we measure the steps, which we find necessary to take now, by a stance or steps taken six years ago, whether it concerns the interests of our Iraqi people at home and what ought to be done to increase the enthusiasm required for reconstruction, for social justice and for the standards of Iman, or whether it is in the field of our humane national ideology of Iman and its practical applications in relation to our commitments towards our glorious Arab nation. Nor should this apply to our positions of the faith towards the jihad or struggle of the believers in the world against imperialism, hegemony, injustice and violation of the rights of others. Rather, it is ascension, ascension and ascension, in which enthusiasm and potential which constitute, before any other step, the spring-board for other measures corresponding to renewed energy and enthusiasm, more sublime and pure in the service of the principles of our nation and people, thus ensuring continued ascension and increasing the accurateness and capability to relate the measures of action to the great principles. Our decisive criterion, when there are various alternatives and versions in front of us, is not the modest picture, but the highest and purest state; while our criterion, once an ideal example is difficult to produce from our principles, will be the examples of our great nation at the advent of Islam as well as any other great example from subsequent eras.

Is this not what you observe and can identify in the course of your great revolution, in accordance with its principles?

Is it not my duty to draw your attention to this fact, so that you will be more reassured that your march remains genuine, responsive to your interests and principles in a balanced manner, and immune against deviation; that it will not succumb to, or be shaken by, the propaganda of foreign powers; that the wind will blow away foreign rattling as the noise of an evil covetous tyrant, the enemy of Allah; and that Iraq will emerge eventually triumphant. Indeed, Iraq is already triumphant, with Allah's grace. And the people of Palestine will achieve victory;

indeed, they are already victorious through the stands taken by every Palestinian man and woman, and through their great sacrifices and their readiness to give more. The others need only to realize and learn the lesson, and know that the principles, high interests and national and pan-Arab security cannot be protected without sacrifices relative to their value and significance; sacrifices that will bring honour to our people and nation, and stand out as landmarks of honour, remembrance and historical memory. All positions taken in isolation of the principles can only be a rotten grave providing those who adopt them nothing, both in this life and in the next.

Brothers!

There is a subject which we have placed at the heart of our consideration, given it our undivided attention, and strengthened it in energy visual and concrete sense, in our heart and conscience from an early stage. We have never allowed the memory to overlook this subject or time to weaken its significance for assessment and action, from, amongst the numerous inspirations derived from our glorious faith and the lessons of our struggle and jihad. This subject is: that anything gained freely, as charity, or from a foreign source, will yield nothing but vice, and weakness before the arrogance charity and greed of the foreign source. The benefit that is gained legitimately, on the other hand, through the toil and sweat of its winners, remains good and "halal", blessed by Allah, to stay and grow through the endeavour of the people who rely on Allah. He who builds his country with his own hands will be able to defend himself and his country with his own means. But he who relies on others to think for him, or provide him with protection and appoint him as ruler of his people, will always remain valuable to the whims of his patrons who can, whenever they so desire, bring his house down over his head, and leave him in disgrace. The future is, to a large extent, part of the steps of the present. He, who ensures that his present steps are solid, careful, confident and distinguished, will ensure a bright future, God Willing, for himself as well as for the generations that seek to achieve their objectives in the same spirit and with the same resolve. He, on the other hand, who stays behind, lazy and dependent on others to make the effort for him, is sure to have a bleak and unsettled future, with no guarantees of any place for him and for all those following his example in succeeding generations.

So make the effort, people of Iraq, as you have always done, with dignity, industry, care and dedication; and increase the effort to ensure the present and the future for yourselves and for the generations succeeding you.

Fight with valour, chivalry, patience and resolve, as you have always done when forced to fight defending your accomp, your effective spirit and your faith, because these are the sources of establishing our edifice, and of the prosperity, independence, liberty, solidarity, justice and fairness to which you aspire.

Amongst the meanings which we have kept in our conscience and mind is the fact that he who compromises his principles can neither be relied on nor trusted.

He who fails to respond in kind, like a man, to the thunder of valour and lightning of chivalry, when his nation and people are subjected to injustice, remains unfit to protect, lead or defend his people and nation.

He who wants the others not to forget the virtue of magnanimity is himself expected to keep this virtue in his conscience and recall and apply it in his actions.

He who stands up against injustice, should himself refrain from causing injustice others, and should remember that speaking of justice will be meaningless if capital is allowed rule beyond its limits or influence the process of decision-making.

Political and legal justice remains meaningless without social and economic justice. The fight against the wolves and the corruptors will not succeed, if they have contacts and partners inside the corridors of government and the palaces of the Sultan.

All of this, in order to be achieved, requires the establishment and protection of justice. Authority must have its sward while power, must have its own mind, eyes and good conscience.

Brothers!

It has been thirty-four years since your glorious march began on the 17th of July 1968. During this time, and in view of all the blessings bestowed upon us by Allah, the Almighty, the Compassionate, the Merciful, the Omni-powerful, it is incumbent upon us to raise our voice of gratitude to the Almighty, praying, appealing and thanking Him for the strength and support which He bestows upon us. Hence, we say:

Oh Allah, in Heaven. You created us for a reason in your wisdom; and protected us for a reason in your wisdom. You are our God and the God of our parents, our children and our ancestors; the Lord of our descendants and of all posterity. You are the God of those who worship you, who are saved by their decision, their faith and intent. You are the destroyer of the strong-headed who allow their whims to govern their mind, conscience and soul, and who fall down the precipice of rebellion and sacrilege, destroyed by their own conduct, in this life or in the next, having abandoned their religion under the lures of their failing self. There is no God but You. Through You we repel Satan whom we abhor as we do every great sin.

Oh Allah, to You we succumb in faith and in love. To You we bow in worship, capable in victory, hailing Your Will, grateful for the blessings You bestow upon us in this instance or in others, or wherever our feet are made to bleed by the blades, spikes and edges of the road, we will not change in this and in other endeavours.

Our Allah, our Creator; and Creator of the Heavens which you lifted without pillars; Creator of the earth which You stretched and tied to the strings of Your Will. You are our God, who created the living and brought the dead back to life. We accept your decision when you make what is difficult easy and reachable, or when you delay, in your own wisdom, our victory in the field, or the fruit of our effort and struggle, thus making our feet bleed due to the difficulties and sacrifices of the road. The hearts may be affected by time to the extent, and in the manner that You choose; but our conscience will remain strong and rich in the faith. We appeal to You to keep our hearts rich with comfort and content, and preserve our Iman and worship as the healing compassion in our hearts, which are most precious, as well as in every good deed which meets with Your satisfaction.

In all this, Oh Allah, we hail Your name in praise and gratitude. You are holy and pure; and we have placed ourselves on the road of obedience to You, by free choice and in faith. If we succeed, it is through Your grace that we do. If we fail, then we believe that we have done our best in faith. If our effort meets with Your satisfaction, we praise You in your Holy state. If we are not as successful as we want, or if we go wrong, we resort to Your compassion and forgiveness; for there is no substitute to Your Will and Compassion; You Most Merciful, Most Wise and Most Capable, in whom we seek assistance.

Oh Allah, You are our God in every directions and to all extents. Creator and God of all. Praised be Your Name in Your Great Throne, and in Your Authority; help us to prevail over the forces of sacrilege, as you helped us in our endeavour and objectives, and protected us from all danger on the two days of the 17th and 30th of July 1968, and what happened between and after those two dates. In the same way as you made our will strong and firm in confronting our enemies and the enemies of our nation from that time to the present day; Oh Allah, our God and God to everything, every name and every situation which we may or may not know; which may be seen or may remain hidden. You are the Creator of everything and every situation, which may be good or may seem bad in our eyes. Increase comfort in ourselves and strengthen our hears with whatever you deem good for your true and faithful worshippers. Bring comfort, Oh God in Your Glory, and strengthen the hearts of the true faithful mujahideen in Iraq and Palestine, as well as on the other arenas of jihad in our nation.

Allah, we rely on You, seek Your support and obey Your command. Protect us against the schemes of the devil or of those to whom the devil is master. Protect us against the deviation of the self, and strengthen the meanings and status of love and loyalty towards us in our people. Strengthen, increase and deepen the sense and extent of love in our hearts, and the compassion and endearment in our souls and conscience towards our great people and glorious nation. Assist us all to attain what you desire and accept; help us in our endeavour; and destroy our enemies, the enemies Allah, of our nation and of mankind. You, who are Most Capable.

Allah, you are our God; protect us if you so desire, or give us a place amongst the martyrs. You are most powerful. Your choice is our acceptance. Our appeal is nothing but a request from the weak to the strong, from the creation to the Creator. From You, praised be Your Name, we seek help; and You are most Powerful.

Prayers be upon Prophet Mohammed, our Master, and upon his Companions. Prayers be upon all Prophets and Messengers.

Oh Allah, bestow your infinite mercy upon all good and true believers, and upon or most generous martyrs in Iraq, Palestine and all the arenas of jihad and struggle throughout our nation.

Allah, Amen, Oh Allah, God of all mankind.

Allah is great!

Allah is great!

Allah is great!

President Saddam Hussein's Address On The 14th Anniversary Of The Great Victory Day August 8, 2002

In the name of Allah, The Most Compassionate, the Most Merciful

Nay, we hurl the Truth against falsehood, and it knocks out its brain, and behold, falsehood doth perish!

Our Great People!

Our Valiant Men and Women!

Our Men of the Heroic Armed Forces!

Our Arab brethren!

Fellow Believers, Wherever you may be Peace Be Upon You!

Regardless of details, and of the nature of evolution between successive historical chapters, the human lesson derived is that the present of any nation or people cannot be isolated from its past; and that, according to this, nations and peoples have established their present, even though it might be distinguishable from their past in terms of advancement or retraction.

Of the lessons also gained from the history of mankind is the fact that greed and arrogance, when combined, lead the oppressor to do injustice not only to others, but to himself as well; once this combination of greed and arrogance has misled him into a sense of undefeatable capability and power, as he takes the road of falsehood and aggression, committing the most heinous acts and proceeding from that sick imagination, to fall down the precipice and then into hell.

One of the lessons of recent and distant history is that all empires and bearers of the coffin of evil, whenever they mobilized their evil against the Arab nation, or against the Muslim world, they were themselves buried in their own coffin, with their sick dreams and their arrogance and greed, under Arab and Islamic soil; or they returned to die on the land from which they had proceeded to perpetrate aggression. This has been the case with all empires preceeding our present time. If this is what history tells us about its judgment on all times and eras of the past without exception, can we then describe those who are trying to ignore history now except in the words which no wise or prudent person would wish to be described with?

This is the inevitable outcome awaiting all those who try to aggress against Arabs and Muslims. If anyone wants to learn from history, anyone with greed and arrogance combined in himself, he ought to remember this fact and think again. Otherwise, he will end up in the dust-bin of history, as twentieth century politicians world say.

We always stood, and continue to stand, to learn from all such lessons, whenever the horns of aggression loomed large against us. We never faced, nor will face, any aggression relying basically on our force of arms, or our muscles and the muscles of our people, but rather on the strength of our faith, in the belief that Allah always helps the faithful and their just cause to prevail over injustice.

Faith, according to this rule, is the decisive factor in linking the final outcome to the good of the people and the nation, and to self-satisfaction, with all that Allah Almighty shall extend of the means of strength provided by the faithful on the basis of His Divine instruction: "Extend to them all the strength you can provide…". We have always, along with our comrades, our people and our armed forces, asked ourselves: Can fathers and mothers discharge their parental duties towards their children when they are placed in chains under the burden of servitude? Will the children be but ungrateful apostates, if they see their fathers and mothers in chains, enduring the heavy burden of oppression, and never move to save them, break their chains, or surround them with their protective chests of faith, against all misguided evil aggressors?

Do you know, brothers in the Arab homeland, who our father and mother are, we the Iraqis, our armed forces, and the leadership of our army and people? Our mother and father are the nation and the homeland. It is on the basis of these meanings and what we recall from the lessons of history, that we took our stand in 1980 to defend our people and nation against those who sought to enslave them, put them in chains, and then leave them to decay.

Yes, this was our stand. And we recall, and never forget, that he who wants his homeland to be liberated and healthy, his nation free and unfettered, has to be loyal to them so that they will remain generous to him. Otherwise, he will remain doomed to subservience, killed by a sense of guilt, labouring under the heavy burden of contempt, of having fallen behind and failing to play his role in the position that brings pride to freedom-fighters in the eyes of their people, their nation and their homeland.

Thus, we relied on Allah, and took the position required under the circumstance, along with our people and armed forces, to confront danger, with stand aggression and defy arrogance, for eight long years which lasted from September 4th, 1980, to the date which Allah designated to be the day of final victory in August 1988.

It is also on the basis of these concepts, and the lessons derived from them, that our revolutionaries made their day in July 1968.

On these same grounds and concepts, the people of Iraq and their armed forces, led by their brave leaders against the aggression and arrogance of the United States and those who allied themselves to the Americans, or followed them under duress, or by choice, from 17 January 1991, the day of the battle of Um el-Ma'arick until today.

On this basis, the stand of loyalty taken by the faithful shall remain firm and healthy. Darkness shall be defeated, and every cloud that carries no useful rain shall be dispersed, giving way to the sun to usher in endless spring, blessed by Allah, fill with pride its people who themselves bring disgrace to the conduct of the aggressors.

The forces of evil will carry their coffins on their backs, to die in disgraceful failure, taking their schemes back with them, or to dig their own graves, after they bring death to themselves on every Arab or Muslim soil against which they perpetrate aggression, including the Iraq, the land of Jihad and the banner.

We say this to refute the grumbling and sibiliation of those bragging their power, governed by the devil, their master in every evil act and crime which they perpetrate against the land of the Arabs and Muslims, while they wade in the rivers of innocent blood they shed in the world, believing that the people of the world should become slaves to Tyranny and its threats, both declared and executed threats. But if they wanted peace and security for themselves and their people, then this is not the course to take. The right course is of respect to the security and rights of others, through dealing with others in peace and establishing the obligations required by way of equitable dialogue and on the basis of international law and international covenants.

The right way is that the Security Council should reply to the questions raised by Iraq, and should honour its obligations under its own resolutions. There is no other choice for those who use threat and aggression but to be repelled even if they were to bring harm to their targets. Allah, the omni-powerful is above all power and shall repel the schemes of the unjust.

I say this even though I had preferred to avoid referring to it, under a different circumstance, as I have generally done so far. But I say it in such clear terms so that no weakling will imagine that when we ignore responding to ill talk, then this means that we are frightened by the impudent threats which will make those who have lost all ties with God the Compassionate, and all trust in their people, tremble and shiver; and so that no greedy tyrant will be misled into an action the consequences of which are beyond their calculations.

Allah is Great!

Allah is Great!

Allah is Great!

What a pure, magnificent and melodious breeze of faith; a voice, as if recalled from the depth of our eternal heritage and history, a voice in which we find ourselves and it in us, in the same spirit raised by our forefathers in the battles of Jihad at Yarmouk against the Bizantines, and the Battles of the First Qadissiyah, in which our forefathers broke, in the Name of Allah, the ranks of the invading armies that had occupied the land of Sham (Syria) and Iraq, where they brought injustice and death, motivated by stubbornness, to remaion the side of falsehood in the face.

Allah is Great!

Allah is Great!

Allah is Great!

These our brethren the faithful and the Arabs, are the calls made by your sons and brothers in Iraq, the land of faith, as they confront the enemy who wants to harm Iraq, with total disregard to God and man, despite all the resilience and resolve with which the Iraqi people have faced this enemy who has refused to listen to any Islamic or Arab voice, and indeed rejected all the initiatives and calls for peace, which we had proposed more than once, name of the people of Iraq.

Allah is Great!

Allah is Great!

Allah is Great!

This is the call made by everyone confronting the enemies with a gun, a cannon, on a tank, in a plane, or on a naval boat, by millions of men amongst our troops, in conscription or reserve, our peoples army and our special task forces.

Allah is Great!

Allah is Great!

Allah is Great!

Attacking, defending, advancing and charging forward deep in enemy territory, chasing evil to defeat it; or forming with their dear chests the fence protecting this faithful, patient and healthy homeland; or standing, whenever Allah so wills it, behind the boarders in the same way as they did at Faw and Penjaween, in a trench here and a trench there, along a battlefront extending over one thousand and two hundred kilometers from Faw and the territory surrounding and protecting it to the south up to the head-land of Minshaf in our dear northern part of Iraq.

Allah is Great!

Allah is Great!

Allah is Great!

Our beloved call the voice of our dear Prophet, the voice of Bilal, Abi Bakr, Umar, Ali and Uthman. of Khalid, Abi Ubayda, Sa'd and Usama.

The fragrance of the Message, the voice of history, the call of the spirit carrying the body to the destination determined by Allah, to be pure, secure, aromatic, and rosy, as he is a witness to the will of Allah, or a living martyr, so destined by Allah Almighty, whose command is irrevocable, praised He be for all He wills and all He wants.

Allah is Great!

Allah is Great!

Allah is Great!

There is no God but Allah.

Allah is Great!

Allah is Great!

Allah is Great!

Praise be to Allah!

Charge on! Charge on! Charge on!

The dear chant is raised, as if the men are circumambulating around the Ka'ba, or returning to the place from which Prophet Mohammed, the Messenger of Allah, ascended to God on that Blessed Night, after they cleanse the land of Palestine from Zionist desecration.

Allah is Great! Allah is Great! Allah is Great!

With millions of gun-barrels, exchanging places on the battle-fronts, or being stationed where they ought to be from the start of the battle until Allah grants His final victory.

Thousands of artillery-guns and tanks and hundreds of aircraft, backed by millions of honourable Arabs and Iraqis and of the faithful who prayed for Iraq to be granted Allah's victory, which the Almighty graced Iraq with.

With victory, came the first expressions of gratitude to Allah, for having cleansed the hearts of the victorious faithful from all hatred, and prevented any grudge or rancour from infiltrating our souls, against the hatred and hard-headedness we had faced throughout eight years of fighting, preceded by an additional period of scheming and abuse, praying to Allah the omni-powerful, the Almighty, to spare us any such hatred or any hatred which we don't know.

Victory was born out of all this. It voice, spirit and breeze of faith were raised high, in the resounding "Communique-of-all-Communiques" on the Day-of-Days which Allah Almighty had destined to be the day of decisive victory, crowned by it on the 8th of August 1988.

Oh God! Oh God! Oh August!

How hot is year temperature, not only to ripen the date-fruit to be picked by your people, but also to break the spikes that others want to use against your people and thus defeat the unjust aggressors, in the name of Allah.

Brother to July and it link to September!

Dear month, dear day, we extend our greetings to you as we live your dear days one by one, and to every living soul and every soul that has a place in heaven, blessed by Allah, the Almighty.

Greetings similar to those we extend to our Iraqi brothers and Iraqi martyrs, to the Arabs in the forefront of whom come the heroic people of Palestine, and to every honourable Mujahid of the faithful who met his God with a pure heart.

Greeting to the people of Palestine, men and women, living and martyrs!

Greetings, Greetings to Iraq!

Greetings, Greetings to our Arab!

Nation, and to everyone of its brave heroes!

Greetings Greetings!

Allah is Great!

Allah is Great!

Allah is Great!

There is no God but Allah!

Allah is Great!

Praise be to Allah!

President Saddam Hussein Has Sent a Letter To The People Of Iraq And Through Them To All People Of The Arab Nation And All Free People In The World/September 3, 2002

In the name of God, the most merciful, The most compassionate

Once more we say: if you want to gain victory, you should start with yourself. Yes with yourself first and before any step to use the materials in the environment which you control or you think that you control it…and before you start to convince others on the possibility of victory, convince yourself and strengthen your faith in victory to the extent of absolute sureness that no wind could shake and now power could sway or eliminate it from your heart, after depending on God.

Victory is faith inside the hearts, and when it becomes a faith it become immune against confusion created by the surrounding environment including kinds of weapons and technical means that your enemy possesses, media, false news and the psychological confusion which is created by your enemy. God will bless your faith, then you will have a permanent feeling that God is near you, far from your enemy, strengthening your side and making your as a leading light that rapidly spread to shine into the hearts of others. Then the fire of your enemy will be extinguished and he will be in the dark unable to find his way to save himself from your victory upon him.

Yes, this is the beginning of victory, to add to this, you should not search for victory in the hearts of men on your side, but feel victory in yourself first and fortify it with these values. Because the men on your side (your supporters) are a lot in confrontation. Things in life and their titles are also a lot around you and are contained by your land and that of your enemy and by all that you and your enemy deal with on the level of the planet earth. People's temperaments differ being on your side or on the side of your enemy. Other states, with you or against you, have their schemes, objectives and interests which could be right or wrong. And all this, as you see, is a large perspective along with plans deriving from ideas, desires and intentions, some are logical, while the others are not according to one's opinion.

Could one triumph only with his mind? Could mind only manage to order thinks according to wishes only? While doing that needs men and their rifles in relying on a specific plan, the mind alone may be restricted to contain all that and respond to each question correctly.

Man is capable of bearing in mind things many times within seconds, and determines his capability, but he can't use his mind to know all other people's deep feelings inside or outside his country. He cannot determine all things, feelings and interests between two powers by his mind only. He also can not realize all what happens around the world. But through his faith and sureness and through getting victory within himself he would know all facts about both sides of equation whereby he would know the world too.

All that would come around him like a spotlight coming out of faith, which would lead to victory.

On this base, triumph in the glorious Qaddissyia battle and all other battles has been achieved and by faith we could win victory despite all burdens and went on away from mummified titles, spirits and their bureaucracy.

When we memorized our titles then we were thinking of them as a means to apply principles and honor of responsibility as it was inherited from our past generations. These means have come brave, trustful, sacrificing and willing to get victory in defending the faith. By this way responsibility get rid of heavy things surrounding. Then the faith makes victory. and as the ordinary soldiers and the pedigreed revolutionists sacrifice themselves for the sake of their nation when the circumstances require that, we go ahead, and according to some people's viewpoint we ventured everything: by titles, son, present, future, power or others to achieve victory after depending on God Almighty, and we totally believed that victory is surely ours regardless things, desires, plans and powers on the other side. Through this sureness and faith, after depending on God Almighty, we won victory and we will win victory at last in the battle of Um Al-Ma'arik, God Willing.

Saddam Hussein
On the 26th of Jamada Al-Akhira/1423 Hijri
September 3/2002 A.D.

President Saddam Hussein's Address on the 82nd Anniversary of the Establishment of Iraqi Army in January 6, 2003

In the Name of Allah, The Merciful, The Compassionate,

Remember thy Lord inspired the angels (with the message): "I am with you: give firmness to the Believers: I will instill terror into the hearts of the Unbelievers: smite ye above their necks and smite all their finger tips off them." This is because they contended against Allah and His Messenger: if any contend against Allah and His Messenger, Allah is strict in punishment. Thus (will it be said): "Taste ye then of the (punishment): for those who resist Allah, is the penalty of the Fire." O ye who believe! when ye meet the Unbelievers in hostile array, never turn your backs to them. If any do turn his back to them on such a day-unless it be in a stratagem of war, or to retreat to a troop (of his own)—he draws on himself the wrath of Allah, and his abode is Hell, an Evil refuge (indeed)! It is not ye who slew them; it was Allah: when thou threwest (a handful of dust), it was not thy act, but Allah's: in order that He might test the Believers by a gracious trial from Himself: for Allah is He Who hearth and knows (all things). That, and also because Allah is He Who makes feeble the Plans and stratagems of the Unbelievers. (O Unbelievers!) if ye prayed for victory and judgment, now hath the judgment come to you if ye desist (from wrong), it will be best for you: if ye return (to the attack), so shall We. Not the least good will your forces be to you even if they were multiplied: for verily Allah is with those who believe! (Allah's is the Word of Truth)

Our great people!

The valiant men of our Armed forces!

On previous occasions, we have said that our view of our history in Iraq, which is also our view of our history as a nation, is that it is tantamount to faith. This is because history, to our nation and people, is not merely a register of contextual activities. It is rather a record of sacrifices made in blood in order for the nation to preserve its qualities and maintain its role, and in order for our people as well to remain as such. What raises history and elevates it to the status of belief is the fact that the sacred blood shed in the most crucial situations for our nation to assert its traits, and its mission to augment its everlasting contribution to humanity, has been the blood of the Mujahideen who loved Allah and would therefore not hesitate to carry out, their missions as designated by Allah, the Almighty, along with the honour they had in carrying the Call of the Message of Heaven to mankind as a whole, after spreading it in their own great nation.

This is how the faithful people of our nation view history, and this is how we have read our history and believed in its meanings, and have hence stressed that our history is not merely a series of events, as in the case in the history of a lot of activities and situations in life for other nations and peoples. History is rather the reservoir in which exist, and from whose depth we derive, the laws that elevate the nation to assume its great mission for humanity, having attained the sublime status of communication with Allah, as a nation of loving, chosen believers, who are confident and obedient to the commands of the Almighty; a nation conscious of its great mission of faith both nationally and on the level of humanity, which is extended from the essence of the tenets established throughout its eternal history and the wealth of values adorning the landmarks of distinction along its mission.

After an absence from the fields, arenas and objectives of the Almighty, when He Has Willed it to be extended, your role returns again to you, Iraqi men and women of valour and sacrifice, the heroes of our valiant armed forces under all your titles...your role is regained, now that you have snatched the opportunity to re-assume it deservedly with your special traits which emanate from your great faith in all that brings satisfaction to Allah and gratification to the homeland and the nation. On the arenas of this role of yours and its eternal mission, you have presented scores of martyrs, which keeps your picture bright and unblemished, as you have evinced no reluctance whatsoever in taking the stand of faith and dignity with which you have responded to the call of history, blessed with the spirit and fragrance of Heaven.

History, which you have treated as a glorious faith, returns now carrying all the values and requirements of faith and generous sacrifice in order to strengthen its principles and the edifice of your glorious community on the basis of those principles.

History is the doctrine of the present that is linked to the spirit and values of the glorious past. Its spirit and high effect exist in you, valiant men and women. Hence our celebration of the 6th of January every year, as a historic mission of the struggle and Jihad of our heroic armed forces and faithful people, on the basis of the same values already referred to, now that you have reaffirmed these meanings through your faith and stands, through the blood shed by those martyred or wounded amongst us, and through the suffering and resilience of our prisoners of war. So this has become a day for us to recall all these meanings as we celebrate and honour the day every year. The celebration is unlike any other, because this one of honour and renewal of our pledge to the Almighty before ourselves, our people and armed forces, and our nation and humanity, as a people and army of Mujahideen, men and women who have established the foundation for this faith in the depth of our blood and suffering, and in our treatment of the spirit of history, whereby we recall history in our sacrifices and our readiness as followers of a rich and glorious Faith at present and in the future as well.

On this basis, Great people and Army of valiant Mujahideen, when we celebrate and honour the 6th of January, we take another look at, and ponder, in a spirit both pure and full of faith, unstained by treason to the principles or abandonment of the pledge we made to Allah, the nation and humanity, not only the difficulties which we have been through or which have been imposed on us, difficulties through the claws of which we have derived all that would bring dignity and pride to our nation, but also the role and stand awaiting us. This will ensure our continued adherence to the great values and mission entrusted to our nation and people on the basis of our history, rather than make our celebration of the day isolated occasion. It is indeed the basic situation. It is the road and agenda with all that is linked to it of our recent past during thirty years of glorious history and the extensions made to, or from, it. This is going to be the doctrine of faith for our coming generations, our children and grandchildren in Iraq, in the same way as it is the doctrine of the present. It is a source of pride for the Mujahideen and freedom-fighters of our nation. It is their reservoir of experience and values, together with what is derived from the struggle of our brothers in Palestine and in all other arenas and situations of honour for the people of our nation. To them, it is an example to follow and emulate, once they recall it along with the depth of the nation's history and glorious faith. It will be a torch of light linked to that ancient history of the nation, the voice of a strong lesson in the nation, scented by the blood of sacrifice, in order that our posterity will remain on the right path, son after father, regardless of the size and value of the sacrifices made, until victory is achieved over the forces of evil and injustice which mean our nation ill;infringe upon its rights and harbour greedy intentions against it.

When you, the valiant people of Iraq, renew your pledge to Allah, to yourselves, to the nation and to humanity at large, that you will continue the march of jihad, you do not only strengthen your adherence to your belief and your sacrifices for the Faith, whose meanings have been eloquently expressed, in your sacred blood, as well as in your suffering, sacrifice and perseverance, but you also ensure final victory over the enemies of Allah, your enemies. Allah loves those who rely on Him and who remain strong and honest believers. Allah does not like weaklings. If Allah blesses you with His satisfaction, for victory comes only from Him, the Almighty, Yours will be an assured triumph at the outset, and in the end when the defeat of your enemies will bring them contempt; for they have done themselves, as well as others, wrong through misjudgment and misconduct when they deviated from all honourable values on the basis of which fair-minded people come together to achieve understanding and cooperation.

But if the aggressors choose a way other than this, then, after thanking Allah, we shall all be even happier than the others. Indeed, we shall thank the Almighty if He guides the enemies to the right path, in the same way as we shall be grateful when He destroys them and brings shame to their arrogance.

Oh, Allah, pray guide the along the road of righteousness if You so decide. Otherwise, smite them with Your wrath and smash them with Your destruction blow, for they are a group of criminals

If anyone attempts to intimidate you, the people of Iraq, repel him and tell him that he is a small midget while we belong to a nation of glorious Faith, a great nation and an ancient people who have, through their civilization, taught the human race as a whole what man was yet to know.

We are the offsprings of the sword and the pen; and, in the Name of Allah, we shall fear no one in defending our right, and shall continue our march on the path drawn by Allah, in order to achieve the tasks assigned to us by the Almighty.

Our right is a clear right, as clear as is their falsehood; and we shall not be intimidated by their falsehood. Allah shall drown them in shame.

Allah is our God, and He is the Greatest. Theirs is an abject shame, while ours is an elevated status with values that will ensure Allah's content and the appreciation of free-minded humanity.

He, whose hoisted banner is adorned with the call: "Allah is the Greatest", fluttering on its post, and who keeps his pledge to Allah, to the martyrs and to the faithful, shall fear no tyrants.

Our chests are filled with the great conviction in our victory, whose fruit will be in our hands and whose banners will be all over our heads as a great people in a glorious nation, God willing.

Shame, and more shame, with defeat will go to your opponent.

And may every new year bring happiness and well-being.

We salute the Palestinian people of heroic mujahideen as well as every hero and heroine amongst the champions of self-sacrifice who confront the Zionist aggression with their lives and thus foil the wrong ideas of the American administrations which have acted in alliance with their artificial zionist creation in the crimes they perpetrate and the shame they reap.

Glorious and sublime are our martyrs in Palestine, Iraq and the nation as a whole.

Long live Palestine, free and Arab, from the sea to the river!

Long live Great Iraq and its valiant army of Mujahideen!

Long live our glorious Arab nation!

Greetings to every valiant hero and noble heroine in our nation as they repel and resist injustice!

Courageous Men and Women of our great people, and our valiant Armed forces!

We know you and trust the pledge that you have taken upon your-selves on several occasions. We are confidantes we rely on Him, the Great, Keeper of all Power, the Merciful, the Compassionate, that you will be with every new dawn for a new day, better and better until you attain the best state, with Allah Grace, to the disappointment of your desperate enemies, the friend and wicked assistants of Satan, the inhab-itants of night and the dark.

The moon, the stars and the sun will, with Allah's Grace expose all the schemes that they hide in the darkness of their minds and chests. Their arrows will go astray, while your arrows will hit them, now that Allah has deemed your struggle to be a driving force in the march of every mujahid and freedom-fighter in your nation and in the peoples of the world at large against injustice and its perpetrators spearhead by their master: Their Tyrant.

Be aware, then Brothers, that victory is yours now, in the past and on the Day of final harvesting, in spite of all the hysterical hubbub and clamour which the enemy has been making; for the enemy has many objectives behind this uproar and self-defeating pandemonium. Iraq is not the only target in this confusion, even if the noise is meant to intimidate us and to cover the aggression to be decided by the enemy whenever the devil so instructs him. The objective is rather to subject the Arab Gulf area to a full, complete and physical occupation through which to achieve many goals. These include political interference and military intervention in the countries of the region in a manner unac-customed before, with a view to securing complete control over their resources. The fragmentation of some of these countries, which has been a dream declared by the enemy since the early 1970s, and about which various enemy scenarios have been published, may have gone some way towards being achieved now, including the occupation of land, at the lowest cost possible. But the enemy will pay dearly later, on top of what it is paying at present for its reckless policies of greed and expansionism. Through its noise and rumblings, coupled with the ongoing aggression and blockade inflicted on Iraq, the enemy is providing cover for the heinous crimes perpetrated by the zionist entity against our people in Palestine.

In this respect, the enemy has achieved a lot of the objectives desired by zionism; for now public opinion is diverted completely towards the enemy's noise and mobilization against Iraq and the confusion it has created about the Gulf, leaving very little room for the zionist aggression to be attended to, condemned and confronted.

The enemy is preparing now to control entry to the Red Sea and the gate-ways to the Arab Sea, with a view to ensuring enemy interest's and security for the zionist entity, while securing transport lines for oil and military shipments there. The enemy is in full coordination with the zionist entity in this respect, and has achieved a lot of what it wanted to see achieved in order to cover the weaknesses of its agencies, as exposed before the US public opinion, vis-à-vis the events of the 11th of September 2001 and the weakness, or indeed near-collapse, of the United States economy. The enemy has been trying to divert the American people's attention from these facts, the details of which are being sought by many conscientious people there. This includes the failure of the policy of the United States towards the Palestinian question and the rights of the people of Palestine, the failure of US policies in the world in general, with anger and hatred being generated amongst peoples everywhere against those policies, as well as the failure of the US military policy in Afghanistan in the face of local resistance there. One of the objectives of the enemy's continued aggression and pressure on Iraq is to provide psychological support, in a climate of sabre-rattling, in order to intimidate the people of the Middle East and the world, and to make the inspection teams go beyond the declared objectives of the Security Council, even in the bad resolution issued in its name. So, now, instead of looking for the so-called weapons of mass destruction, in order to expose the distortion and lies propagated by those who endeavour, in vain, to deceive public opinion, the inspection teams are interested in collecting names and making lists of Iraqi scientists, addressing employees with questions that carry hidden agendas, giving special attention to military camps, to unproscribed military production, and to other matters, all or most of which constitute purely intelligence work.

The covers used to camouflage the subjects which we have mentioned, or say the largest part of them, are required for those subjects, which also need the sound of weapons and the perpetuation of crises in the Arab homeland and its periphery. In the meantime, the enemy's occupation of the Gulf and the Red Sea will have been established, which will enable the enemy whose lines of communication and transport will now have become shorter, to launch aggression and cause damage in any direction it chooses, including expanding its aggression against Iraq on the basis of strategic and tactical objectives. Nothing will therefore be more disappointing and discouraging to the enemy than for our people to be prepared, after relying on Allah, for any further confrontation expected with the enemy in addition to the aggression already perpetrated on a daily basis, while maintaining our life for the present and the future, building, building and building...with great optimism and conviction that the future is secured by firm adherence to Faith. The light of truth belongs to us, while our enemy has the darkness of the present and the darkness of distant horizons. We are fully prepared for everything and for any eventuality. Our success is in the hands of Allah, and Allah shall repel the schemes of the infidels.

In any case, we are in our country; and whoever is in his own homeland with truth on his side, and is force to face an enemy that stands on the side of falsehood and comes as an aggressor from beyond seas and oceans, will no doubt emerge triumphant, because victory always belongs to those who stand by truth in their own home while defeat certainly belongs to their enemies.

On this basis, and not under any other consideration, we conduct ourselves as we watched the hissing of the snakes and the barking dogs together with the aggression being continually inflicted on the north and south of our country. Our behavior reflects the confidence of capability which requires no hasty or perturbed behavior, but is based on the necessary calculation and consideration of which we have accumulated such experience as would make every Iraqi man and woman, everyone in our people and every soldier in our armed forces, as well as every official and community leader, well-aware of his or her task and indeed his or her position in the battle of reconstruction and the arena of confrontation, if the devil pushes those who ignite it to a precipice.

On the basis of this experience and the preparedness that rests on a solid and unshakable base of faith and conviction, it is the enemy that is confused, and it is the enemy that should seek a way out of what is regarded a mess in which the enemy has thrown itself. The enemy ought to remember the terrible end of all empires that committed aggression against our people and nation in the past.

As for the people of Iraq, their victory, with reliance on Allah, is at hand, having already existed in their chests; and it is up to the enemies to trace the echoes of their trumpets.

Allah is the Greatest!

Allah is the Greatest!

And the wretched aggressors shall be repelled.

President Saddam Hessians Address on the Twelfth Anniversary of the Grand Battle Um Al-Maarik "Mother of all Battles" in January 17, 2003.

In the Name of God, the Compassionate, the Merciful.

There are those who, on being told: 'Your enemy has mustered a great force against you and so fear them,' they grew more tenacious in their faith and replied: Allah's help is all-sufficient for us. He is the best Protector'. Thus they earned Allah's grace and bounty and no harm befell them. For they had striven to please Allah, whose, bounty is infinite. It is Satan that prompts men to fear his followers. But have no fear of them. Fear Me, if you are true believers. Do not grieve for those that quickly renounce their faith. They will not harm Allah in the least. He seeks to give them no share in the hereafter. Their punishment shall be terrible indeed. God speaks the truth.

Great people in Iraq, the land of faith, Jihad, bravery and glory!

Brave members of the gallant armed forces!

Sons of our glorious Arab nation!

Men of goodwill in the world, wherever you are!

From the bright light of dawn, from the ray of sun which has risen after a long absence, from its horizon, from the lids of the eyes which were wounded by heavy tears for people, dear for all of us, who can no more be seen, but who can become visible with the new sun, and from the horizon which God has ordained to be vast, with a new birth and life in whose skies exist green birds and a strong newborn which God has decided to be faithful to its nation, from all this your glorious Revolution and march, a new Iraq, was born. Its faith has been increased and deepened after the Grand Confrontation on the night of 16/17 1991, the grand military phase of the eternal battle of Um Al-Maarik, by the flagrance of the generous blood, suffering and commendable patience.

A new Iraq was born with firm resolution, great power of vision and a heart, which has been increased in strength by a determination for ascent and for overcoming difficulties. It was firm in its love for its nation. Its faith, which God has given it and which the situation and banner was perfumed by generous blood from its sons, has been deepened by a scarifies which God has accepted in compensation for the negligence which took over those who ruled Baghdad, and therefore the foreigners with the horny feet of their horses, found their way towards it. The radiation of its eyes over the nation and humanity has set down, after the water of Tigris was dyed with plentiful blood along with the ink of its books which were filled with science and knowledge, and which were thrown into the water in the year 1258, as a punishment for a history whose soul departed its body and for a civilization whose faith and guards disappeared. Hence, the ravens croaked in it, showing impudence to its eyes through which humanity saw its way to raise in culture after it had played its role and into enlighten those who could see that and accepted from it as a means from God to them as a reward for its faith and fear.

The new Iraq was born on such a view, and was born with it, its rifle in place of the arrow, spear and sword, to be armed so that the ravens could not be so covetous as to venture its palms and the eyes of its children.

A strong, believing and healthy Iraq was born. But the birth, as all other births which came before it in the horizon of humanity and in our nation, was not able to render ineffectual the croak of ravens, nor the hissing of snakes or the crossing of far crocodiles from the seas of their family in order to help the beasts of earth in their attack against the sun, in a desperate hope to obscure its light which radiated from Baghdad or to shed the blood of its people in a fake hope and out of an imagination that the generous blood shed on the soil of Baghdad and on the soil of Iraq could hinder the plants and trees from becoming green, from blossoming and from carrying with its fragrance pollens which might tempt the appetite of butterflies, and thus be able to carry with the news of new faith and resolution, with the dew and tears, a pollen to every tree whose branches and leaves become dry or ceased to give fruits now that the water ceased to reach its roots and was confident that no one could take care of its fruits and guard its plants, trees and growth.

With the new birth, there was Satan and his companion, the lizards of this time, who spit out their fire on the healthy body. But, as the birth of Baghdad was now healthy and proper, blessed by heaven by order of its God, and that its guard were putting their hands on their rifles during the dawn prayer on the day of birth, with great confidence in their breasts, on the night of 16/17 January 1991 and afterwards, Baghdad, in the name of Iraq, kept defending itself along with every faithful valiant and noble woman in defense of the command which God has so decided to their new birth. Their will of determination never bent.

They defeated all evil troops of more than thirty states together with those who supported them. The number of the army, which the jihadists in the Iraq army had confronted, mounted to twenty-eight. The state of Iraq stood in the face of the aggression of forty-two countries on the night of 16/17 January. The confrontation and the battle lasted for a month and a half with such momentum. Afterwards, the sanctions and aggression continued for thirteen years until the present day. Such was the defence of the Iraqis on that day and the days that followed. Others, in their turn, defended the seeds which they sowed and elevated what they had built, to the point that their fields were mixed with the spacious gardens. Plants covered the land of Iraq reminding of its past when the land of Iraq was described as the land of the black for the multitude of its plants which disappeared from Baghdad, its countryside and towns, until it appeared as if they did not exist before as one sign of its health. It had mixed with the lofty constructions, dear and visible, and was dominated by the high minarets, domes and signs of the houses of worship. And with every exaltation of "Allah is the greatest" on the battlefields, the same gratification rose high in the mosques together with the voices of worship in their places, each in accordance with his own religion and manner. A visitor could tell that he was in Baghdad even though his eyes were shut, in an attempt that a traveler could hardly recognize his feet on the map…Was there a place much better than Baghdad, where religions and racial tolerance together with constructive views being born, on the side and direction of every constructive thing of other views?

The new birth brought back once again the spirit of Baghdad, and with the birth a stand, a sword, a pen and a banner were born. The call of "Allah is the greatest" blessed the stand, the sword and the pen. The birth whose threats were knitted by the dawn and blessed by the call for prayer, was an impregnable birth to every malicious, perfidious and greedy…It could not deserve, nor could Allah and the people accept for it, but the life chosen for it by its pioneers after they asked the permission of their Lord, the Merciful. The scheming of the attackers backfired in that aggression and in the on-going aggression which they make longer to the present day. Everyone who tries to climb over its wall, be it an aggressor, an insolent, a wicked, a perfidious and an oppressor will fail in his attempt.

Is not this your description and position for the men of Iraq, the believer and loyal jihadists, and for the noble women as well? Or is there anyone who might delude himself into believing to say, after treading down his luck, that Saddam Hussein is speaking about his wishes and not about a description of a condition in which he lives and gets to know, with heart and soul, its comprehensive and detailed nature? By God, this is your description and attitude, or even a reward for your suffering, sacrifices, and patience, o brave men and women. The evil ravens and evil crocodiles, still foster wickedness and would never cease their communication with their disappointed hopes, despite the fact that their deep wounds and disgrace can not be rubbed out with the passage of time. The lizards which breathed out fire on our lord, Abraham (peace be upon him), as is often related by people, still give birth and still assign for every birth the task of breathing out fire, out of their belief that they are capable of burning away, in defiance of God's will which He chose to be cool and safe.

Hence, with the flying banner, raise high your swords and rifles, oh our dear people, and remind anyone who may still be under a delusion, so that he might not be deluded of your stand in the (Greatest March), on the day of the Grand Allegiance and in other attitudes, but if he does so, let your guns waiting in ambush for him, preceded and guided by the radiation and light of your faith necessary for safeguarding your eyes. This is because, if their ravens have a fancy and find no one to deter them, God forbid, then they would peck up the eyes and devour the hearts and brains of faith, virtue and innovation. Hold fast to your banner, the banner of (Allah is the Greatest). There is nothing but it that can help motivate the resolution to rise and give to defence its profound connotation.

Say: God is the greatest, oh brothers and sons. Remember the meanings of this great call in accordance with the profundity of your faith, so that its echo, along with your words and support, could be sounded by all towns and rural areas, by mountains and by plains. And with the help of the waters of Tigris and Euphrates and the water of the Gulf, your voice can reach not only every brave man and woman in the land of faith and Jihad, but also every loyal man and woman in the nation, every fair-minded and everyone who has an honorable stance in humanity.

When birth is associated with a stance, a determination, a pen, a sword and a banner, then birth can assume its proper role in our nation, God willing.

When we say that history is tantamount to doctrine, and is remembered by those who inherit it with contemplation, consideration and responsibility, this is because everything right is born with it and from it, and becomes a new and constant history after it gives a new birth with each glory and construction. A firm belief is its safe foundation. It becomes a doctrine carried from the past, still possesses the condition of the true birth when so remembered by its sons with the responsibility of the present, and with the due ambition for the future.

Such was the labour of the past. From its womb it begets a doctrine; new in its spirit, in dress and colour and its special path...And with the new doctrine, a strong flag-post and hand has been born bearing our pride and our guidance to faith: Allahu Akbar, to stand firm in the face of every violent wind, God willing, or evil attempt.

Yes, Allahu Akbar!

Allahu Akbar!

Brothers!

The saying that (history repeats itself) means, among other things, that aspects of the past could be repeated though they assume the colours and names of their stages...They repeat themselves should they be re-analyzed, revived and dissolved into their primary elements and ingredients as to their strength and weakness, ascent and descent, climbing and falling into abyss, good and bad, climbing to peaks and falling into abyss, pursuit of good will and virtue against pursuit of evil and vice, those who hate people and bring harm to them against those who love people and work for their welfare, the destroyers and the constructors and the like in the series of the images and their contrasts, up and down, bad and good.

Yes, it is true that history repeats itself but not on the basis of an uncontested premise of the ability to go up, as compared with the past without faith, consciousness, attitude and determination, or to give up to a descent case, as compared with the past also, except when all its items in life, man and nature are repeated to the point that it can hardly be conceived. Yet, a conscientious faith in portraying of how the role of man can be effective and ascending, of how can that faith be maintained together with its factors and causes and how can one reject any condition that may have an adverse impact on the faith, of the role of the believing and vanguard man in it and in its movement, or the denouncing of all this, is the decisive case in which history may repeat itself in the same form, here and there, whether negatively or positively.

Brother!

Baghdad in its known history, had played the role of the Arabs' and Muslims' pure eye. It was God's spear on earth, the Arabs' skull, the reservoir of their wisdom and glorious heritage, the focal point of their civilization and great radiation. That was with other supporting roles in other centres in conformity of what had happened in Baghdad or before that time. When the Mongols and Tatars reached the zenith of their strength and occupied China, India, Persia and other countries, they were unable to convert their ascent to strength by backwardness and destruction into a force capable of bringing construction, civilization and culture. The destroying force found its complex in Baghdad; the abode of civilization and peace, and made it its target for destruction which was rendered feeble because of the weakness of those who did not hold firm to the factors of ascent, its causes and results, and also of the weakness of its rulers and the betrayal of the traitors…Hulago and his troops occupied Baghdad for forty days and destroyed every live thing in it. And because the people of Baghdad, I mean the rulers in it, were not quite prepared when the Mongols and Tatars invaded the territory of China, India, Persia and the surroundings, their invasion of Baghdad was in agreement of what history had described, and which later include Syria and the parts connected to it.

But Baghdad was not in a position to defend itself properly, and therefore the eyes of Hulago's army were not gouged out on its walls nor was it extinguished in its face the venture of trespassing it, or even to deny it the chance of going ahead to others from the nation to attack them as it attacked Baghdad, till Hulago's eyes were gouged out at the hands of the Mameluke dynasty in Egypt at the famous battle of (Ain Jalut), after they were able to get prepared for it and learnt lessons from the war before them and after Hulago's intent and methods were revealed…History tells us that western peoples and circles had played, for their own reasons, a role in directing Hulago to the east, indeed to the Arab world in particular. The Jews and their supporters played a remarkably malicious role against Baghdad in the past and this conspiratorial, aggressive and wicked role is today reverting to them, to the Zionist Jews and to the Zionists who are not of Jewish origin, particularly those who are in the US administration and around who stood in opposite front of our nation and Iraq. The force in America proved itself to be incapable of educating itself. It was not able to change itself into a capability, so that its impact would be humanitarian and instructive. Zionism and prejudicial people had pushed it to search for a role through a devastating brutal instinct instead of ascending to a position of responsible ability and to its civic, cultural role which suits this age and suits the role of balanced nations and their construction role in the collective milieu and work.

Yet, Baghdad today, brothers, has its eyes pure, its mind and conscious clear of any rust or cover, and are proud of the nation and for it, in the name of God, after they have put their trust in the Owner of Potency and gets prepared to the role.

Although some eyes and minds in our nation and humanity are still incapable of seeing or perceiving the pros and cons in the nation and humanity, the people and rulers of Baghdad have resolved to compel the Mongols of this age to commit suicide on its walls and make the confrontation, in terms of meaning and sacrifice, to rise to a level which could lead other eyes and minds to be wide open of what is going around it and get elevated to its role, and make the force which it possesses after or before anyone may take this risk and is deceived by its Satan to trespass the walls of Baghdad, to be effective in the human milieu, capable of converting it into an ascent force in the milieu of constructive competition and not a brute force based on brutal devastating instinct.

Acting upon this, brothers and friends in our nation and humanity, we give our promise and make the Capable and the Great, our witness for our promise.

And acting upon this also, we have prepared our plans and muster our strength at the level of armies, people and leadership after placing our reliance on God. All success is from God.

Allah is the greatest!

Allah is the greatest!

Brothers!

The rulers of Baghdad in the past grew old. They renounced the role so commanded for them by God and deterred those who were responsible for their subjects from introducing innovations in their life affairs and defence of it when Hulago came to the walls of Baghdad in the year 1258. Thus Hulago came with the sunset and the rule passed to him with Baghdad as its capital. The Mongols succeeded and the sun set down from Baghdad at that time.

But now, despite Hulago's spirit has settled in whomsoever it has settled; in their actions, in what they did, or in what they are now doing, or in what they intend to do, of those who have been incited by the criminal Zionists in more than a place in the world, they have come to confront our nation at a time when the sons of our nation are embracing inside their souls and breasts, a great faith and a great state of consciousness of their role and of how it should be in order that they attain what it must be attained, and thus the nation could revert to its true belief, and could, with its Jihad and struggle, realize a true ascent to its great, faithful, pan-Arab and humanitarian role.

Hulago's army has now come at this age to confront Baghdad after it has born anew with the sunrise, to record, with its new youth, a level of ascent which suits it well after it has abandoned its leading role for about seven hundred years.

O Iraqis, you have indeed brought the sun back to Baghdad, and have shined in it at the time the city has been illuminated by you. But oh, how can a new Hulago destroy the city or the great Iraq, and how can the brutal, the perfidious and the greedy, after God has ordained this nation to rise again, defeat the will of determination of your brothers in Palestine as well or wherever the will of truth, steadfastness and resistance has ripened or blossomed in the breast of every believer who embraces a great confidence.

Oh people! You know that the first human civilization in history was grown, blossomed and bore fruits in Iraq. From that civilization, the air carried its seeds to reach to whomever it could reach, who, according to his own personal opinion, added colour to it to suit his own country. For this reason, it is the mother of civilization of Iraq which Hulago of this age wants to attack. So, tell him in a clear, loud voice, oh evil, halt your evil-doings against the mother of civilization, its museum and basic witness, the cradle and the birthplace of prophets and messengers. Tell him to let people, each in accordance with his human choice, to build, and to build and to build which is necessary for rising high the construction, for work, for fruitful cooperation and for the dissemination of love among people. Tell him to avoid provoking hatred and evil doings so that every one can enjoy his rights, full and complete, in such a manner that might please God and bring happiness for him in the two worlds.

Everyone in whose body the Hulago' intent and action has settled down will commit suicide at the walls of Baghdad and Iraq towns, as was the case with those who died at the walls of Jenin and Palestinian towns.

The entire nation will rise up in defence of its right to life, of its role and of anything it holds sacred. Their arrows will be on the wrong track or will recoil to their breasts, God willing.... The martyrs of the nation will turn into green birds in paradise as the Merciful has promised.

Let evil be on he who thinks evil.

Long live our glorious nation!

Long live Iraq!

Long live Iraq with its brave jihadist army!

Long live Palestine, free and Arab from the sea to the river!

Long live Palestine's freedom fighters and jihadists together with its heroic people!

Glory and heaven be for martyrs!

Glory and heaven be for the martyrs of Iraq, Palestine and the nation!

Allah is the greatest!

Allah is the greatest!

Allah is the greatest!

Saddam Hussein's Iraq

Iraq Timeline

1932 October 3—Iraq becomes an independent state.

1958 July 14—The monarchy is overthrown in a military coup led by Brig Abd-al-Karim Qassim and Col Abd-al-Salam Muhammad Arif. Iraq is declared a republic and Qasim becomes prime minister.

1959–1963—Saddam Hussein, 22-year old Ba'th Party member, flees Baghdad for Damascus and Cairo after involvement in an assassination attempt against Qasim. Cairo is then center of the Nasserite Pan-Arab ideology girding the Ba'th Party.

1963 February 8—Qasim is ousted in a coup led by the Arab Socialist Ba'th Party (ASBP). Six months of chaos follow, prompting another military coup.

1963 November 18—The Ba'th government is overthrown by Arif and a group of military officers. 5000–6000 Iraqis are executed in backlash against communism.

1964–1966 Saddam Hussein jailed as a member of the Ba'th Party.

1966 April 17—President Arif is killed in a helicopter crash on April 13 and succeeded by his elder brother, Maj-Gen Abd-al-Rahman Muhamad Arif.

Rise of Saddam Hussein

1968 July 17—A Ba'th-led coup ousts Arif and Gen Ahmad Hasan al-Bakr becomes president. Saddam Hussein, relative of Bakr, emerges as Vice President, deputy head of the Revolution Command Council (RCC), and chief interlocutor with the Kurds.

1970 March 11—RCC and Mullah Mustafa Barzani, leader of the Kurdistan Democratic Party (KDP), sign a peace agreement.

1972—Iraq nationalizes the Iraq Petroleum Company (IPC). Iran and Iraq are the region's major oil-producers and vie for dominance in the Gulf.

1973—In the wake of an attempted coup against Bakr, Saddam Hussein consolidates his control of the internal security services and management of oil resources.

1974—Iraq grants limited autonomy to the Kurds, in accord with the 1970 agreement, but the KDP rejects it. KDP rebellion fails as Iran withdraws support in exchange for possession of disputed Shatt al-Arab islet between Iraq and Iran.

1975 March—At a meeting of the Organization of Petroleum Exporting Countries (OPEC) in Algiers, Iraq and Iran sign a treaty ending their border disputes.

1979 January 16—Islamic Revolution ousts the Shah of Iran. Ayatollah Khomeini, who had lived in Iraq from 1964–1978, returns to Tehran in February.

1979 July 16—President Al-Bakr resigns and is succeeded by Vice President Saddam Hussein. Within days, Saddam executes at least 20 potential rivals, members of the Ba'th Party and military.

1979 September—Military skirmishes and propaganda war increase between Iraq and Iran.

Iran-Iraq War

1980 September 4—Iran shells Iraqi border towns. On September 17 Iraq abrogates the 1975 treaty with Iran.

1980 September 22—Iraq attacks Iranian airbases.

1980 September 23—Iran bombs Iraqi military and economic targets.

1981 June 7—Israel attacks an Iraqi nuclear research center at Tuway-thah near Baghdad.

Chemical Attacks

1986 March—UN Secretary General reports Iraq's use of mustard gas and nerve agents against Iranian soldiers, with significant usage in 1981 and 1984.

1988 February-September—Iraq military operation "Anfal" results in 50,000–100,000 deaths throughout northern Iraq. Iraq uses chemical weapons, mass executions and forced relocation to terrorize the area.

1988 March 16—Iraq attacks the Kurdish town of Halabjah with mix of poison gas and nerve agents, killing 5000 residents.

1988 August 20—The Iran-Iraq war ends in stalemate; an estimated 1 million soldiers are killed in eight years of fighting. A ceasefire comes into effect to be monitored by the UN Iran-Iraq Military Observer Group (UNIIMOG).

1989 Iraq sends military hardware to Lebanon in a proxy war with Syria.

Iraqi Invasion of Kuwait

1990 August 2—Iraq invades Kuwait and is condemned by the United Nations Security Council Resolution 660, which calls for the full withdrawal.

1990 August 6—UNSC Resolution 661 imposes economic sanctions on Iraq.

1990 August 8—Iraq appoints puppet regime in Kuwait that declares a merger with Iraq.

1990 November 29—UNSC Resolution 678 authorizes the states cooperating with Kuwait to use "all necessary means" to uphold UNSC Resolution 660; UN orders Iraqi withdrawal by January 15, 1991.

1991 January 17—The Gulf War starts with coalition forces begin aerial bombing of Iraq, "Operation Desert Storm".

1991 February 24—The start of a ground operation; liberation of Kuwait occurs February 27.

1991 March 3—Iraq accepts the terms of a ceasefire. The primary ceasefire resolution is UNSCR 687 (April 3) requiring Iraq to end its weapons of mass destruction programs, recognize Kuwait, account for missing Kuwaitis, return Kuwaiti property and end support for international terrorism. Iraq is required to end repression of its people.

1991 Mid-March/early April—Iraqi military forces suppress rebellions in the south and north of the country, creating a humanitarian disaster on the borders of Turkey and Iran.

No-Fly Zones

1991 April 8—A plan for the establishment of a UN safe-haven in northern Iraq, north of the latitude 36 degrees north, for the protection of Kurds is approved at a European Union meeting in Luxembourg. On April 10, the US orders Iraq to end all military action in this area.

1991 April—Working in cooperation with the International Atomic Energy Agency (IAEA), the UN Special Commission (UNSCOM) is established to ensure Iraq is free of weapons of mass destruction and to establish long-term monitoring program to see it remains free of prohibited weapons.

1992 August 26—A no-fly zone, which prohibits the flights of Iraqi planes, is established in southern Iraq, south of latitude 32 degrees north.

1993 June 27, US forces launch a cruise missile attack on Iraqi intelligence headquarters in Al-Mansur district, Baghdad, in response for the attempted assassination of former U.S. President George Bush in Kuwait in April.

1994 May 29 Saddam Hussein becomes prime minister and president.

1994 November 10—The Iraqi National Assembly recognizes Kuwait's borders and its independence.

1995 April 14—UNSC Resolution 986 allows the partial resumption of Iraq's oil exports to buy food and medicine. It is not accepted or implemented by Iraq until December 1996.

1996 August 31—In response to a call for aid from the KDP, Iraqi forces launch an offensive into the northern no-fly zone and capture Arbil.

1996 September 3—U.S. extends the southern no-fly zone to latitude 33 degrees north.

1996 December 12—Saddam Hussein's elder son Uday is seriously wounded in an assassination attempt.

1998 October 31—Iraq ends all forms of cooperation with the UNSCOM and expels inspectors.

1998 December 16–19—U.S. and U.K. launch a bombing campaign "Operation Desert Fox" to destroy suspected nuclear, chemical and biological weapons programs.

1999 January 4—Iraq asks the UN to replace its US and UK staff in Iraq.

1999 February 19—Grand Ayatollah Sayyid Muhammad Sadiq al-Sadr, spiritual leader of the Shi'a, is assassinated in Najaf in southern Iraq.

1999 December 17—UNSC Resolution 1284 creates the UN Monitoring, Verification and Inspection Commission (UNMOVIC) to replace UNSCOM. Iraq rejects the resolution.

2000 March 1—Hans Blix assumes the post of Executive Chairman of UNMOVIC.

2000 October—Iraq resumes domestic passenger flights, the first since the 1991 Gulf War. Commercial air links re-established with Russia, Ireland and Middle East. Regime invests more revenue in the general economy.

2000 November—Iraq rejects new weapons inspections proposals.

2000 December—Iraq temporarily halts oil exports after the UN rejects Iraq's request that buyers pay a 50-cent-a-barrel surcharge into an Iraqi bank account not controlled by the UN.

2001 Free-trade zone agreements set up with neighboring countries. Rail link with Turkey re-opened in May for the first time since 1981.

2001 February—Britain and U.S. carry out bombing raids to try and disable Iraq's air defense network.

2001 May—Saddam Hussein's son Qusay elected to the leadership of the ruling Ba'th Party, fueling speculation that he is being groomed to ensure the Takriti clan's hold on power in Iraq.

2002 February 11–15—For the first time since 1992, Iraq hosts a UN human rights expert. During the preceding years, the international community documented and reported allegations of gross human rights abuses in Iraq, including summary executions; arbitrary arrest, systematic torture 'in its most cruel forms'; coercion by means of reprisals against a family members; and mass discrimination regarding access to food supplies and health care.

2002 May—UNSC Resolution 1409 overhauls the sanctions regime goods review list to focus on military and dual-use equipment and streamline approval of civilian goods for commercial sale in Iraq.

2002 July 5—In talks with UN Secretary General, Iraq rejects weapons inspections proposals.

2002 August 2—In a letter to the UN Secretary General, Iraq invites Hans Blix to Iraq for technical discussions on remaining disarmament issues.

2002 August 19—UN Secretary General rejects Iraq's proposal as the "wrong work program" but renews offer to facilitate the return of inspectors in accordance with UNSC resolution 1284, passed in 1999. The resolution calls for UNMOVIC inspectors to spend 60 days conducting active inspections to determine what has changed since U.N. weapons inspectors were expelled in 1998 and what needs to be done for Iraq to be rid of all chemical, biological and nuclear weapons.

2002 September 12—U.S. President George Bush, addressing the UN General Assembly, challenges the UN to confront the "grave and gathering danger" of Iraq—or stand aside as the United States and like-minded nations act. The UN Security Council begins consultations on drafting a new resolution to compel Iraq to comply with previous resolutions.

2002 November 8—UN Security Council unanimously adopt Resolution 1441 outlining an enhanced inspection regime for Iraq's disarmament to be conducted by the U.N. Monitoring, Verification, and Inspection Commission (UNMOVIC) and the International Atomic Energy Agency (IAEA).

2002 November 13—Iraq accepts U.N. Security Council Resolution 1441 and informs the UN Secretary General that it will work with the resolution.

2002 December 7—Iraq provided UN weapons inspectors with 12,000 pages of information comprising a "currently accurate, full and complete declaration" of the regime's chemical, biological and nuclear weapons programs, according to requirements in UNSC resolution 1441. Iraq stated in the Declaration that there are no weapons of mass destruction in Iraq.

2002 December 19—UNMOVIC Chairman Hans Blix told UNSC members that the declaration "is essentially a reorganized version" of information Iraq provided UNSCOM in 1997, and that it "is not enough to create confidence" that Iraq has abandoned its WMD efforts.

Background Note

OFFICIAL NAME:

Republic of Iraq

Geography

Area: 437,072 sq. km.; about the size of California.

Cities: Capital—Baghdad (pop. 3.8 million 1986 est.). Other cities—Basrah, Mosul, Karkuk, As Sulaymaniyah, Irbil.

Terrain: Alluvial plains, mountains, and desert.

Climate: Mostly hot and dry.

People

Nationality: Noun and adjective—Iraqi(s).

Population (2001 est.): 23,331,985.

Annual growth rate (2001 est.): 2.84 %.

Ethnic groups: Arab 75%, Kurd 15%-20%, Turkman, Assyrian, or others less than 5%.

Religions: Shia Muslim 60%, Sunni Muslim 35%, Christian 5%, Jewish and Yezidi less than 1%.

Languages: Arabic, Kurdish, Assyrian, Armenian.

Education: Years compulsory—primary school (age 6 through grade 6). Literacy—58%.

Health: Infant mortality rate—60.05 deaths/1,000 (2001 est.). Life expectancy—66.95 yrs.

Work force (2000, 4.4 million): Agriculture—44%; industry—26%; services—31% (1989 est.).

Government

Type: Ruling Council.

Independence: 1932.

Interim constitution: 1970.

Branches: Executive—Revolutionary Command Council (RCC); President and Council of Ministers appointed by the RCC. Legislative—National Assembly of members elected in 2000. Judicial—Civil, religious, and special courts.

Administrative subdivisions: 18 provinces.

Political parties: Ba'ath Party is only legal party in regime controlled territory; Kurdistan Democratic Party and Patriotic Union of Kurdistan are opposition parties that control parts of northern Iraq.

Suffrage: Universal adult.

National holidays: Anniversaries of the 1958 and 1968 revolutions—July 14 and July 17. Flag:

Economy

GDP (2001 est.): $57 billion.

Annual growth rate (2000 est.): 15%.

GDP per capita (2000 est.): $2,500.

Inflation rate (2000 est.): 100%.

Natural resources: Oil, natural gas, phosphates, sulfur.

Agriculture (less than 6% of GNP): Products—wheat, barley, rice, cotton, dates, poultry.

Industry: (less than 13% GNP): Types—petroleum, petrochemical, textile, cement.

Trade (2000): Exports—$21.8 billion: crude oil. Major markets—Russia, France, Switzerland, China. Imports—$13.8 billion: agricultural commodities, medicine, machinery. Major suppliers—Egypt, Russia, France, Vietnam.

GEOGRAPHY

Iraq is bordered by Kuwait, Iran, Turkey, Syria, Jordan, and Saudi Arabia. The country slopes from mountains over 3,000 meters (10,000 ft.) above sea level along the border with Iran and Turkey to the remnants of sea-level, reedy marshes in the southeast. Much of the land is desert or wasteland.

The mountains in the northeast are an extension of the alpine system that runs eastward from the Balkans into southern Turkey, northern Iraq, Iran, and Afghanistan, terminating in the Himalayas.

Average temperatures range from higher than 48 degrees C (120 degrees F) in July and August to below freezing in January. Most of the rainfall occurs from December through April and averages between 10 and 18 centimeters (4–7 in.) annually. The mountainous region of northern Iraq receives appreciably more precipitation than the central or southern desert region.

PEOPLE

Almost 75% of Iraq's population live in the flat, alluvial plain stretching southeast toward Baghdad and Basrah to the Persian Gulf. The Tigris and Euphrates Rivers carry about 70 million cubic meters of silt annually to the delta. Known in ancient times as Mesopotamia, the region is the legendary locale of the Garden of Eden. The ruins of Ur, Babylon, and other ancient cities are here.

Iraq's two largest ethnic groups are Arabs and Kurds. Other distinct groups are Turkomans, Assyrians, Iranians, Lurs, and Armenians. Arabic is the most commonly spoken language. Kurdish is spoken in the north, and English is the most commonly spoken Western language.

Most Iraqi Muslims are members of the Shi'a sect, but there is a large Sunni population as well, made up of both Arabs and Kurds. Small communities of Christians, Jews, Bahais, Mandaeans, and Yezidis also exist. Most Kurds are Sunni Muslim but differ from their Arab neighbors in language, dress, and customs.

HISTORY

Once known as Mesopotamia, Iraq was the site of flourishing ancient civilizations, including the Sumerian, Babylonian, and Parthian cultures. Muslims conquered Iraq in the seventh century A.D. In the eighth century, the Abassid caliphate established its capital at Baghdad, which became a frontier outpost on the Ottoman Empire.

At the end of World War I, Iraq became a British-mandated territory. When it was declared independent in 1932, the Hashemite family, which also ruled Jordan, ruled as a constitutional monarchy. In 1945, Iraq joined the United Nations and became a founding member of the Arab League. In 1956, the Baghdad Pact allied Iraq, Turkey, Iran, Pakistan, and the United Kingdom, and established its headquarters in Baghdad.

Gen. Abdul Karim Qasim took power in July 1958 coup, during which King Faysal II and Prime Minister Nuri as-Said were killed. Qasim ended Iraq's membership in the Baghdad Pact in 1959. Qasim was assassinated in February 1963, when the Arab Socialist Renaissance Party (Ba'ath Party) took power under the leadership of Gen. Ahmad Hasan al-Bakr as prime minister and Col. Abdul Salam Arif as president.

Nine months later, Arif led a coup ousting the Ba'ath government. In April 1966, Arif was killed in a plane crash and was succeeded by his brother, Gen. Abdul Rahman Mohammad Arif. On July 17, 1968, a group of Ba'athists and military elements overthrew the Arif regime. Ahmad Hasan al-Bakr re-emerged as the President of Iraq and Chairman of the Revolutionary Command Council (RCC). In July 1979, Bakr resigned, and his chosen successor, Saddam Hussein, assumed both offices.

The Iran-Iraq war (1980–88) devastated the economy of Iraq. Iraq declared victory in 1988 but actually achieved a weary return to the status quo antebellum. The war left Iraq with the largest military establishment in the Gulf region but with huge debts and an ongoing rebellion by Kurdish elements in the northern mountains. The government suppressed the rebellion by using weapons of mass destruction on civilian targets, including a mass chemical weapons attack on the city of Halabja that killed several thousand civilians.

Iraq invaded Kuwait in August 1990, but a U.S.-led coalition acting under United Nations (UN) resolutions expelled Iraq from Kuwait in February1991. After the war, UN-mandated sanctions based on Security Council resolutions called for the regime to surrender its weapons of mass destruction and submit to UN inspections. The regime has refused to fully cooperate with the UN inspections and since 1998 has not allowed inspectors into Iraq. Iraq is allowed under the UN Oil-for-Food program to export unlimited quantities of oil with which to purchase food, medicine, and other humanitarian relief equipment and infrastructure support necessary to sustain the civilian population. The UN coalition enforces no-fly zones in southern and northern Iraq to protect Iraqi citizens from attack by the regime and a no-drive zone in southern Iraq to prevent the regime from massing forces to threaten or again invade Kuwait.

GOVERNMENT

The Ba'ath Party rules Iraq through a nine-member RCC, which enacts legislation by decree. The RCC's president (chief of state and supreme commander or the armed forces) is elected by a two-thirds majority of the RCC. A Council of Ministers (cabinet), appointed by the RCC, has administrative and some legislative responsibilities.

A 250-member National Assembly consisting of 220 elected by popular vote who serve a 4-year term, and 30 appointed by the president to represent the three northern provinces, was last elected in March 2000. Iraq is divided into 18 provinces, each headed by a governor with extensive administrative powers.

Iraq's judicial system is based on the French model introduced during Ottoman rule and has three types of lower courts—civil, religious, and special. Special courts try broadly defined national security cases. An appellate court system and the court of cassation (court of last recourse) complete the judicial structure.

Principal Government Officials

President, RCC Chairman, Prime Minister, Ba'ath Party Regional Command Secretary General—Saddam Hussein

Vice President—Taha Yasin Ramadan

Vice President—Taha Muhyi al-Din Ma'ruf

Ministers

Deputy Prime Minister—Tariq Aziz

Deputy Prime Minister—Abd Al-Tawab Mullah Huwaysh

Deputy Prime Minister—Ahmad Husayn Khudayir al-Samarrai

Minister of Budget—Husan al-Khatab

Minister of Information—Mohammed Saeed al-Sahhaf

Minister of Foreign Affairs—Naji Sabri Hadithi

Minister of Finance, Deputy Premier—Hikmat al-Azzawi

UN Perm Rep—Muhammad al-Duri

Minister of Oil—Amer Mohammed Rasheed

Minister of Trade—Mohammed Mahdi Salih

Minister of State—Arshad Mohammed al-Zibari

Undersecretary—Hamid Sa'id

Minister of Health—Omeed Midhat Mubarak

Minister of Industry and Minerals—Adnan Abd al-Majid

Minister of Justice—Shibib Lazim al-Maliki

Minister of Transport and Communications—Dr. Ahmed Murtadha Ahmed

POLITICAL CONDITIONS

The Ba'ath Party controls the government and is the only recognized political party in regime controlled territory. Recent elections allowed for only Ba'ath Party authorized candidates, resulting in the election, for example, of Uday Saddam Hussein to the National Assembly with 99.99% of the vote. The Kurdish Democratic Party led by Masoud Barzani and the Patriotic Union of Kurdistan led by Jalal Talabani are opposition parties, each of which control portions of northern Iraq. Both allow multiple political parties to operate in their areas and have held contested elections within the last year that international observers termed "generally fair". The Iraqi regime does not tolerate opposition. Opposition parties either operate illegally, as exiles from neighboring countries or in areas of northern Iraq outside regime control.

ECONOMY

Iraq's economy is characterized by a heavy dependence on oil exports and an emphasis on development through central planning. Prior to the outbreak of the war with Iran in September 1980, Iraq's economic prospects were bright. Oil production had reached a level of 3.5 million barrels per day, and oil revenues were $21 billion in 1979 and $27 billion in 1980. At the outbreak of the war, Iraq had amassed an estimated $35 billion in foreign exchange reserves.

The Iran-Iraq War depleted Iraq's foreign exchange reserves, devastated its economy, and left the country saddled with a foreign debt of more than $40 billion. After hostilities ceased, oil exports gradually increased with the construction of new pipelines and the restoration of damaged facilities.

Iraq's invasion of Kuwait in August 1990, subsequent international sanctions, and damage from military action by an international coalition beginning in January 1991 drastically reduced economic activity. Government policies of diverting income to key supporters of the regime while sustaining a large military and internal security force further impaired finances, leaving the average Iraqi citizen facing desperate hardships. Implementation of a UN oil-for-food program in December 1996 has improved conditions for the average Iraqi citizen. Since 1999, Iraq was authorized to export unlimited quantities of oil to finance humanitarian needs including food, medicine, and infrastructure repair parts. Oil exports fluctuate as the regime alternately starts and stops exports, but, in general, oil exports have now reached three-quarters of their pre-Gulf War levels. Per capita output and living standards remain well below pre-Gulf War levels.

Agriculture

Despite its abundant land and water resources, Iraq is a net food importer. Under the UN oil-for-food program, Iraq imports large quantities of grains, meat, poultry, and dairy products. The government abolished its farm collectivization program in 1981, allowing a greater role for private enterprise in agriculture. The Agricultural Cooperative Bank, capitalized at nearly $1 billion by 1984, targets its low-interest, low-collateral loans to private farmers for mechanization, poultry projects, and orchard development. Large modern cattle, dairy, and poultry farms are under construction. Obstacles to agricultural development include labor shortages, inadequate management and maintenance, salinization, urban migration, and dislocations resulting from previous land reform and collectivization programs.

Importation of foreign workers and increased entry of women into traditionally male labor roles have helped compensate for agricultural and industrial labor shortages exacerbated by the way. A disastrous attempt to drain the southern marshes and introduce irrigated farming to this region merely destroyed a natural food producing area, while concentration of salts and minerals in the soil due to the draining left the land unsuitable for agriculture.

Trade

The United Nations imposed economic sanctions on Iraq after it invaded Kuwait in 1990. The Government of Iraq's refusal to allow weapons inspectors into the country to dismantle Iraq's weapons of mass destruction program has resulted in those sanctions remaining in place. Under the oil-for-food program, Iraq is allowed to export unlimited quantities of oil in exchange for humanitarian relief supplies, including food, medicine, and infrastructure spare parts. A robust illicit trade in oil with neighboring states and through the Persian Gulf earned almost $2 billion in illegal income for the regime in 2000.

DEFENSE

The war with Iran ended with Iraq sustaining the largest military structure in the Middle East, with more than 70 divisions in its army and an air force of over 700 modern aircraft. Losses during the invasion of Kuwait and subsequent ejection of Iraqi forces from Kuwait by a UN coalition resulted in the reduction of Iraq's ground forces to 23 divisions and air force to less than 300 aircraft. Military and economic sanctions prevent Iraq from rebuilding its military power. Iraq still maintains standing military forces of over 380,000 men.

FOREIGN RELATIONS

Iraqi-Iranian relations have remained cool since the end of the Iraq-Iran War in 1988. Outstanding issues from that war, including prisoner of war exchanges and support of armed opposition parties operating in each other's territory, remain to be solved.

Iraq's relations with the Arab world have been extremely varied. Egypt broke relations with Iraq in 1977, following Iraq's criticism of President Anwar Sadat's peace initiatives with Israel. In 1978, Baghdad hosted an Arab League summit that condemned and ostracized Egypt for accepting the Camp David accords. However, Egypt's strong material and diplomatic support for Iraq in the war with Iran led to warmer relations and numerous contacts between senior officials, despite the continued absence of ambassadorial-level representation. Since 1983, Iraq has repeatedly called for restoration of Egypt's "natural role" among Arab countries. In January 1984, Iraq successfully led Arab efforts within the OIC to restore Egypt's membership. However, Iraqi-Egyptian relations were broken in 1990 after Egypt joined the UN coalition that forced Iraq out of Kuwait. Relations have steadily improved in recent years, and Egypt is now one of Iraq's main trade partners under the oil-for-food program.

Relations with Syria have been marred by traditional rivalry for pre-eminence in Arab affairs, allegations of involvement in each other's internal politics, and disputes over the waters of Euphrates River, oil transit fees, and stances toward Israel. Syria broke relations after Iraq invaded Kuwait in 1990 and joined other Arab countries in sending military forces to the coalition that forced Iraq out of Kuwait. Relations remained cool until Bashar al-Asad became President of Syria in 2000. Economic ties based on illicit oil smuggling have strengthened, but politically the relationship remains distant.

Iraq's relations with Jordan have improved significantly since 1980, when Jordan declared its support for Iraq at the outset of the Iran-Iraq war. Jordan's support for Iraq during the Gulf War resulted in a further improvement of ties. Relations have cooled since the current King of Jordan took office in 2000, but remain good.

Iraq's invasion of Kuwait in 1990 resulted in Kuwait, Saudi Arabia, and most Gulf states severing relations with Baghdad and joining the UN coalition that forced Iraqi forces out of Kuwait during the Gulf War. Iraq's refusal to implement UN Security Council Resolutions and continued threats toward Kuwait have resulted in relations remaining cool.

Iraq participated in the Arab-Israeli wars of 1948, 1967 and 1973, and traditionally has opposed all attempts to reach a peaceful settlement between Israel and the Arab States. Israel attacked Iraq's nuclear research reactor under construction near Baghdad in July 1981. During the Iran-Iraq war, Iraq moderated its anti-Israel stance considerably. In August 1982 President Hussein stated to a visiting U. S. Congressman that "a secure state is necessary for both Israel and the Palestinians." Iraq did not oppose then President Reagan's September 1, 1982 Arab-Israeli peace initiative, and it supported the moderate Arab position at the Fez summit that same month. Iraq repeatedly stated that it would support whatever settlement is found acceptable by the Palestinians. However, after the end of the Iran-Iraq war in 1988, Iraq reverted to more stridently anti-Israel statements. During the Gulf War, Iraq fired Scud missiles at Israeli civilian targets in an attempt to divide the U. S. coalition, and, since the end of the Gulf War, Iraq has embraced the most extreme Arab hardline anti-Israel position, including periodically calling for the total elimination of Israel.

Iraq belongs to the following international organizations: UN and some of its specialized agencies, including the World Bank, International Monetary Fund (IMF), International Atomic Energy Agency (IAEA); Nonaligned Movement; Organization of the Islamic Conference (OIC); Arab League; Organization of Petroleum Exporting Countries (OPEC); Organization of Arab Petroleum Exporting Countries (OAPEC); INTELSAT; Interpol; World Health Organization (WHO); G-19; G-77.

U.S.-IRAQI RELATIONS

The United States does not have diplomatic relations with Iraq; however, it does have an Interests Section in the Polish Embassy in Baghdad; address: P.O. Box 2051 Hay Babel, Baghdad; tel: [964] (1) 718-

9267; fax: [964] (1) 718-9297. Iraq has no diplomatic relations with the United States; it has an Interests Section in the Algerian Embassy in Washington, DC.

Afterword

The events of September 11, 2001 will forever be etched in the psyche of mankind. Passenger airliners hijacked and then purposefully crashed into the twin towers of the New York World Trade Center. Moments later another commandeered plane slammed into the side of the Pentagon in Washington, D.C. while yet another plane crashed into the Pennsylvania countryside when brave passengers took the plane back from its captors and diverted it from hitting other populated targets.

These attacks were surprise attacks and unprecedented in their magnitude. It was a beautiful fall day, no hint of impending tragedy, no indication that the world was suddenly about to be thrust into unparalleled turmoil. Within a few frightening seconds, symbols of economic strength and power were reduced to rubble and thousands of lives were taken. Much like the April 19, 1995 truck bombing of the Alfred P. Murrah Federal Building, in downtown Oklahoma City, citizens of America were left numb and awestruck by what was happening in their country. Then in October, terrorism in a different form reared its ugly head. This time in the form of the distribution of anthrax spores through the U.S. Postal Service. Several lost their lives through these terrorist activities and widespread disruption took place across the U.S.

Certainly, terrorism is not a new phenomenon to the global community, as many have struggled with it for decades. Terrorism is therefore by no means solely an American problem. When it strikes, terrorism involves everyone. No one goes untouched. We saw it in Tokyo when the subways were contaminated with sarin gas. We saw it over the skies of Lockerbie, Scotland and in the towns and cities of Northern Ireland and in countries throughout Central America. We have seen it

throughout the Middle East and in notable places in Europe. Terrorism touches everyone.

Bibliography

Saddam's War: the Origins of the Kuwait Crisis
and the International Response
BULLOCH, John & MORRIS, Harvey,
Faber & Faber, London and Boston, 1991

Out of the Ashes: the Resurrection of Saddam Hussein
COCKBURN, Andrew & COCKBURN, Patrick,
HarperCollins, New York, 1999
(Hardback) ISBN 0-06-019266-6

Unholy Babylon: the Secret History of Saddam's War
DARWISH, Adel & ALEXANDER, Gregory,
Victor Gollancz, London, 1991
(Paperback) ISBN 0-575-05054-3

Desert Shield to Desert Storm: the Second Gulf War
HIRO, Dilip
HarperCollins, London/Routledge, New York, 1992
HarperCollins (Hardback) ISBN: 0-246-13879-3
HarperCollins (Paperback) ISBN: 0-586-09236-6
Routledge, New York (Hardback) ISBN 0-415-90656-3
Routledge, New York (Paperback) ISBN 0-415-90657-1

Dictionary of the Middle East
HIRO, Dilip
Macmillan, London/St Martin's Press, New York, 1996
Macmillan (Hardback) ISBN 0-333-63843-3
Macmillan (Paperback) ISBN 0-333-65926-0

St Martin's (Hardback) ISBN 0-312-12554-2
St Martin's (Paperback) ISBN 0-312-17435-7

Instant Empire: Saddam Hussein's Ambition for Iraq
Simon Henderson 1991
Mercury House ISBN: 1562790072

Saddam Hussein : A Political Biography
Efraim Karsh, Inari Rautsi 1991
Free Press ISBN: 002917063X1

Saddam Speaks on the Gulf Crisis:
A Collection of Documents
Ofra Bengio 1992
Syracuse University Press ISBN: 0815670559

Saddam's World: Political Discourse in Iraq
(Studies in Middle Eastern History)
Ofra Bengio 1997
Oxford University Press ISBN 0195114396

Tyranny's Ally: America's Failure
to Defeat Saddam Hussein
David Wurmser
with a foreword by Richard Perle 1999
American Enterprise Institute Press
ISBN: 0844740748

the Outlaw State: Saddam Hussein's Quest for Power and the War in
the Gulf
Elaine Sciolino 1991
John Wiley & Sons (T) ISBN: 0471542997

Saddam Hussein
(Rourke Biographies. World Leaders)

Jane Carol Miner, Jane Carol 1993
Rourke Pub Group ISBN: 0866254773 US edition

Saddam Hussein in the Post-Gulf War:
the Phoenix of Iraq
Rosario Oxenstierna, Rebecca Carleton 1992
Gulf Centre for Strategic Studies ISBN: 1871415373

Saddam Hussein's Gulf Wars
Miron Rezun 1992
Praeger Pub Text; ISBN: 0275943240

Saddam Hussein
Paul Deegan, Bob Italia 1992
Abdo & Daughters ISBN: 1562390252

Saddam Hussein
Efaim Karsh, Inari Rautsi 1991
Warner ISBN: 0708853315

Islam and War: A Study in Comparative Ethics
John Kelsay 1993
Westminster Press ISBN: 0664253024

Rise Babylon: Sign of the End Times
Charles H. Dyer 1991
Tyndale House Publishers Inc. ISBN: 0842356185

Saddam's Mystery Babylon
Arno Froese, James Rizzuti, Wim Malgo
Olive Press ISBN: 0937422401 US edition

Mylroie, Laurie
Study of revenge: Saddam Hussein's unfinished war against America/
Laurie Mylroie
Imprint Washington, D.C.: AEI Press, 2000

Graham-Brown, Sarah
Sanctioning Saddam : the politics of intervention in Iraq/Sarah Graham-Brown
Imprint London ; New York : I.B. Tauris in association with MERIP ;
New York: Distributed in the United States and Canada by St. Martin's Press, 1999

0-595-27039-5